CREATING A CLASS

CREATING A

College Admissions and the
Education of Elites

Mitchell L. Stevens

Harvard University Press
Cambridge, Massachusetts
London, England
2007

Library of Congress Cataloging-in-Publication Data

Stevens, Mitchell L.
Creating a class : college admissions and the education of the elites /
Mitchell L. Stevens
p. cm.
Includes bibliographical references and index.
ISBN-13: 978-0-674-02673-5 (alk. paper)
ISBN-10: 0-674-02673-X (alk. paper)
1. Universities and colleges—United States—Admission.
2. Education, Higher—United States.
3. Elite (Social sciences)—United States. I. Title.
LB2351.2.S755 2007
371.1'610973—dc22 2007010897

Designed by Gwen Nefsky Frankfeldt

For the College

CONTENTS

INTRODUCTION 1

1 A SCHOOL IN A GARDEN 5

2 NUMBERS 31

3 TRAVEL 52

4 SPORTS 95

5 RACE 140

6 DECISIONS 184

7 YIELD 228

8 THE ARISTOCRACY OF MERIT 242

NOTES 267

ACKNOWLEDGMENTS 301

INDEX 307

If parents, having achieved a desirable status,
can *ipso facto* do nothing to make comparable achievement
easier for their offspring, we may have "equal opportunity."
But we will no longer have a family system—at least not
in the present understanding of the term.

Peter M. Blau and Otis Dudley Duncan,
The American Occupational Structure,
1967

INTRODUCTION

Without a tour guide to point them out, visitors to the College would have a hard time finding the classrooms. The buildings housing many of them are architecturally indistinguishable from the residence halls. One classroom is in the chapel. Several are in the library. More than a few classes take place over lunch, or in professors' homes. In nice weather they often convene outdoors.

The nation's most distinguished colleges and universities have long prided themselves on integrating formal instruction seamlessly with the rest of students' lives. Social scientists who study education, however, have long tried to pull formal schooling and the rest of life apart. They have done so with noble intentions. Aware of how consequential formal schooling is to the distribution of jobs, income, and social prestige in modern societies, they have worked hard to discern how school completion is related to other aspects of young people's biographies. Their work often gets done through statistical models that specify a numerical association between particular features of students' backgrounds (the income and education level of parents, say) and the number of school years or degrees students complete. These models often are elegant and persuasive, and they often misrepresent what they purport to explain.

Formal schooling is only part of a much larger and more complicated process called social reproduction: the transfer of knowledge, cultural perspective, and social position from one generation to the next.[1] Social reproduction takes place in classrooms, but it also happens in family rooms and on playgrounds, at parties, and in bed. It includes all the things parents do to ensure that their children will have good lives. It includes all the things that schools and congregations and summer camps do to ensure that their charges are safe and happy. Formal schooling is the infrastructure that organizes this varied process and lends it cultural legitimacy. Think of the many different kinds of things people do for kids that sound better when they are described as "educational," and you get a sense of how this legitimation process works.

In the course of doing the research for this book I became convinced that, however well intended, social scientists' statistical pictures of formal schooling inhibit our appreciation of how fundamentally schooling organizes American society. The organization of formal schooling in this country influences where people live and how they raise their children. It influences how they spend their money and go into debt. It dictates the rhythms of daily, weekly, and annual calendars. It gives people authoritative directions about how to plot their futures. It tells people what achievements their society most values. It helps people figure out who they are in relation to others. It influences when and with whom they fall in love. Social scientists are not unaware of these things—they are citizens and parents and lovers themselves, after all—but their affection for numbers often makes it difficult for them to squeeze the big picture into their research designs.[2]

In a sense this book draws an exceedingly small picture. It is about how admissions officers at a private liberal arts college make decisions. Hoping to learn about admissions officers and their work up close, I spent eighteen months as a participant observer in the office of a highly selective liberal arts college in the northeastern United States in 2000–2001. When I began, I was interested primarily in what I thought was a generic evaluation problem: how organizations make fine distinctions between people who are on paper quite comparable. At the beginning it barely occurred to me that there might be a big story to tell from that work. At the beginning I did not appreciate how that office might be a good perch from which to survey the broader landscape of formal schooling in America. I learned fairly quickly, however, that in order to understand how admissions officers made their decisions I needed to look carefully at the social machinery that delivered applications to admissions offices in the first place. I needed to figure out why people at a school with one of the most competitive admissions profiles in the country spent many weeks each year on the road, like traveling salesmen, drumming up applications. I needed to figure out why a proudly academic institution cared so much about applicants who were better at football and hockey than they were at English and math. I needed to figure out why a school with a traditionally Anglo, eastern-seaboard clientele so eagerly courted applicants who were U.S. minorities and applicants from all over the world. I needed to figure out why it seemed to matter so much that the school I studied was a physically beautiful place. In the process of figuring all of this out—and reading and talking and traveling and filing, alongside the people who did it all for a living—I became convinced that this little office offered a keyhole glimpse into the larger workings of a distinctively American stratification system.

This book is largely about privileged families and the impressive organizational machinery they have developed to pass their comfortable social positions on to their children. Studying privileged people is important, because they create the ladders others must climb to move up in the world. Nowhere is this more true than in schools, which have been official ladders of mobility and opportunity in U.S. society for a hundred years. We do a disservice to the ideal of educational opportunity, I think, if we keep the highest rungs of these ladders obscure.[3] Poking around upstairs is not without risk to those one studies, however. As will become clear in subsequent pages, admissions protocols at selective private schools are intimately entwined with institutional reputations, and the upper echelon of American higher education is a small world. As I moved through this world, I consistently made my status as a researcher explicit; I also committed to protect the privacy of people I met. I have obscured the identity of the College, its personnel and applicants, and virtually all of the other people and organizations in any way represented here.[4] Despite the fogged specifics, I have tried to make the character of settings and people vivid.

It took longer to complete this book than I had thought it would. Academics often say this, but their excuses vary. Mine is that this book appears in the wake of many recent and excellent studies about higher education by scholars across the social sciences. I wanted my work to be fully informed by the best of this scholarship, whatever its field. I am not a quantitative sociologist or an economist or a historian, but my thinking relies heavily on insights produced through these other methods and disciplinary frames. Those who track higher education scholarship in any field may wish to keep a finger in the notes, but I have written the main text for general readers. A great many people are interested in places like the College, and their interest is not misplaced. These institutions are central to the machinery of social opportunity and social distinction in America. My hope is that these pages sufficiently honor that fact and explain it clearly.

chapter one

A SCHOOL IN A GARDEN

Set at a high elevation overlooking farmland, sleepy towns, and hardwood forests, the College enjoys a geographical prominence commensurate with its stunning campus. Lovely old buildings from the early campaigns resemble pieces of a giant chess set, carefully positioned around shady quadrangles. Slate roofs and mullioned windows convey a sense of history. A few of the facades are illuminated in the evenings, making them visible for miles into the surrounding valleys. The most impressive route of arrival carries drivers through a sweeping lawn dotted with perennial beds and specimen trees. Lovingly tended, the trees are a special point of pride. Many employees can name a favorite. Each trunk gets an annual skirting of fresh mulch. The sycamores near the chapel receive special medications.

The campus is an important constant in the College's history. Like many private schools throughout the northeastern United States, this one was built by Protestant churchmen at what was once a cutting edge of American frontier. Hilltops were school builders' preferred sites for hygienic as well as symbolic reasons. Higher elevations were presumed to enjoy cleaner air, a notable advantage in a coal-burning industrial society, and also encouraged flattering allusions to Athens and Zion. The virtues of this particular hill have long been touted by College boosters. An information pamphlet for prospective students published in 1917 promises tidy walks crisscrossing under "fine old trees, which form the backdrop for the brown-grey buildings." "In a situation so beautiful and naturally healthful," explains another passage, "the College is further safeguarded by a modern sanitation system and its own water supply from spring fed reservoirs." Later literature describes the physical plant in other terms but continues to praise its beauty. A 1973 viewbook quotes a student's enthusiastic description: "This is a beautiful campus. In the fall especially, it's the most gorgeous place I ever hope to see. The air is clean and you are just totally removed from all the things that are making it so hard to live in cities these days."[1] Technological advances in color photography and the luminous capacities of computer screens would give subsequent advocates ever more vivid tools for disseminating their news. Surveys of admitted students throughout the College's history would confirm the campus as a prominent factor in many matriculation decisions.

Schools like this one—private, lush, residential, and with selective undergraduate admissions—constitute only a tiny fraction of the colleges and universities in the United States, yet they enjoy historical and cultural influence in great disproportion to their number. They are among the nation's most enduring and most emulated organizations. Early Americans built schools to train religious leaders of many different faiths, to gain an edge over neighboring towns and denominations, and to put particular towns and cities on the map. A school on a hill could be a light in the darkness, a glimmer of intellectual sophistication, a sign that a community was going places, making progress, looking up. As the frontier moved westward, the older institutions became models for school founders in every corner of the country. Colleges in the northeastern United States became benchmarks of excellence in virtually all things: curriculum, faculty, athletics, admissions, aesthetics. Even today, with the thousands of U.S. colleges and universities, degrees conferred by a relative handful of private, highly selective, affluent colleges and universities "back East" bear a subtle but unmistakable cachet.[2]

For eighteen months in 2000 and 2001, I lived and worked at one of these schools as a researcher. I resided in an apartment on its campus, ate often in its cafeterias, borrowed books from its library, and took my exercise on its wooded trails. I spent most of my working hours in the College's Office of Admissions and Financial Aid, where I tried to get as close as I could to the people who made decisions.

I was not alone in my interest. Selective admissions policies have been the object of increasing public fascination and debate in recent years. Courts, legislatures, and college presidents argue over the appropriate criteria selective schools should use when figuring out who they will admit. Magazines rank "the best" institutions by how many applicants they turn away. Growing numbers of private consultants make their livings off of the anxieties of people facing the elite college search.[3]

Despite all of the attention being paid to selective admissions, however, we know remarkably little about how admissions officers go about making decisions about real applicants in real time. I wanted to know how the decisions got made, and with what consequence for those who hoped to someday attend schools like the College. There are many excellent historical studies, and quite a few workplace memoirs by admissions officers themselves, but almost no reports based on critical scholarly observation.[4] Also remarkable is that, despite all the hype about selective college access, apparently no scholar in any field has taken a stab at explaining the hype itself. Many parents, especially those of the affluent upper middle class, worry ever more and ever earlier about their children's fate in the selective college admissions game, but it is not clear why. Why, in a society where a decent college education has become almost as accessible as a good cup of coffee, when virtually every state in the union underwrites at least one good research university, has admission to a handful of very expensive, often geographically remote private schools grown ever more competitive in recent years? What, if anything, has changed that makes attendance at particular institutions, and not just any college, seem so important to so many? I suggest an answer to these questions by looking out on the landscape of contemporary America through the front door of a highly selective private college.

I went to this place with a long-standing interest in two features of our national culture that are as influential as they are contradictory. On the one hand, Americans place very high value on the appraisal of people as individuals. Whether in schools, workplaces, or department stores, we believe that individualized consideration is better than standardized care. We like personalized attention, first names, and custom made. On the other hand, we put great faith in the fairness of universal standards. In our schools, workplaces, and courts of law, we tend to believe that everyone should be evaluated on the same terms. We tend to be suspicious when institutions make exceptions to their officially universal rules, using terms like *special preferences* and *discrimination* to call foul on the deviations. We might in theory settle the contradiction between universalism and individualism by making a clear choice between them when we build our institutions, creating systems for the management of human beings in which either the rules apply to absolutely everyone, or in which there are no hard-and-fast rules at all. But we don't choose. Instead, and despite the contradictions, we tend to create institutions that mix the two ideals together.

Nowhere is the commingling of individualism and universalism more apparent than in schools. On the one hand, we tend to view personalized instruction as the sine qua non of educational excellence. We sing the praises of small classrooms and "individualized education programs." We are understanding when people demand choices about where their children will go to school. Many parents and teachers alike cry to the heavens when school officials ask that standard curricula be taught in standardized ways. On the other hand Americans are zealous educational universalists. On the political left, progressive reformers have long and quite successfully championed a dream of universal schooling—initially to the point of literacy, next to the completion of high school and, in recent years, to college degrees. The 1954 *Brown v. Board of Education* U.S. Supreme Court decision, considered by many to be a sacred event in our national history, preaches a gospel of educational universalism, making explicit the notion that public schooling should be apportioned equally to all citizens. On the political right, reformers have recently, and also quite successfully, pressed for universal measures of students' academic accomplishment and school performance. The centerpiece of the Bush administration's No Child Left Behind Act, for example, is the obligation that schools receiving federal funding demonstrate the progress of their students through standardized tests. It is difficult to imagine a more universal measure of individual performance than machine-graded, multiple-choice exams backed by the authority of the national government. Rather than making a choice between individualism and universalism in our schools, then, we pursue the virtues of both ideals at the same time.

Highly selective liberal arts schools like the College also embody the commingling of individualism and universalism. On the one hand, their signature organizational characteristics are their intimate size and their mission of service to students as whole persons. On the other hand, the competition for admission means that these schools also are beholden to powerful cultural expectations that they evaluate every applicant according to universal standards of merit.

At their admissions front doors, elite liberal arts schools are expected to be individualistic and universalistic simultaneously. This is why it seemed to me that an admissions office would be a good site for examining what happens when these two ideals are brought together routinely, with what advantages and costs to applicants and schools.

An additional thing that had long intrigued me about liberal arts colleges is that they are quintessentially American institutions. The liberal arts organizational ideal—of a small, residential campus, geared primarily, if not exclusively, to highly individualized undergraduate instruction—was invented and nurtured in the United States, and in stark contrast to our model of research universities, it has not traveled beyond national borders. One looks almost in vain for schools built on the liberal arts model anywhere else in the world. I began my inquiry suspecting that the national peculiarity of the liberal arts form might hold some larger lessons about culture, schooling, and social class in America. This book is my effort to work out those lessons. In the following pages I briefly sketch the scholarly traditions that inform my effort, as well as the overarching themes of this book. I also provide a tour of the office that was the setting for my fieldwork.

College and Class

College educations are now crucial components of our national class structure. Most people presume that a college degree is a prerequisite for a financially comfortable adulthood, and a large corpus of sociological research on the relationship between educational attainment and life chances largely confirms the conventional wisdom.[5] Attainment of the relatively secure, well-compensated jobs held by the affluent upper middle class virtually requires a college education. Those without college degrees increasingly are relegated to less lucrative and less stable work. But even though there is wide agreement about the economic importance of college, there has been enduring controversy on the question of why educational attainment has come to play its now-pivotal role in the American class system.

One answer, often called the *reproduction* thesis, holds that variation in educational attainment essentially is a coating for preexisting class inequalities. The reproduction thesis was built from Karl Marx's insights about how powerful groups inevitably create social and cultural systems that legitimate their own class advantage. From this perspective college degrees, and the classroom time and schoolwork they represent, provide palatable justification for the tendency of privileged families to hand privilege down to their children. Adherents of the reproduction thesis support their argument by pointing out the obdurate correlation between parents' socioeconomic status and their offspring's school completion in general.[6] And of the Horatio Algers who do not fit this general pattern—the high academic achievers who graduate from prestigious colleges and go on to positions of wealth and influence, despite the odds—reproduction theorists explain that the exceptions are important in giving the education system its veneer of class neutrality. It is important for public acceptance of the whole enterprise that at least some of the less advantaged can make schooling work for them.

A second answer, which we might call the *transformation* thesis, makes different sense of the very same correlation between family privilege and educational attainment. This thesis argues that the replacement of traditional social hierarchies with educational ones is a definitive chapter in every society's progress toward modernity. German sociologist Max Weber, the first proponent of the transformation thesis, famously argued that as societies modernized, inequalities of family, caste, and tribe gradually give way to hierarchies predicated on individual achievement. In modern times individuals accumulate status and power as they move through the elaborate bureaucracies that characterize all industrial societies: large corporations, centralized governments, highly bureaucratized religious organizations, and schools. These forms of organization tend to distribute rewards on the basis of demonstrated individual accomplishment, not inherited privilege.[7] The transformation thesis would have us see that the ultimate value of college degrees lies in their capacity to confer advantages independently of their recipients' social backgrounds. If the correlation between parents' privilege and children's educational attainment were exact—if accomplishment in school neatly paralleled class origins—then schooling would not be so coveted by people from humble backgrounds. As it is, education is broadly perceived by people from all social classes as an effective mechanism of social mobility, because it *is* capable of moving people up, and down, the class hierarchy.

During the 1960s and 1970s, social scientists became adept at assessing these ideas empirically, using statistical techniques to model the relationships between family background, educational attainment, and individual prosperity over the life course. Exploiting a growing cache of numerical data sets and ongoing advances in computer technology, researchers such as Peter Blau, Otis Dudley Duncan, and Christopher Jencks developed a rich tradition of empirical scholarship about the role of schooling in mediating social inequality. Although work in this tradition is vast and diverse, two of its findings have been remarkably consistent: formal schooling does indeed have independent effects on individual life chances, and, at the same time, parents tend to use formal education as a primary means of handing privilege down to their children. Educational transformation and educational reproduction, in other words, go hand in hand.[8]

In a series of influential writings in the 1970s, sociologist Randall Collins deftly integrated the two theses, creating a term so pithy and evocative that it has shaped public and scholarly conversations about college ever since. Collins argued that the reproduction theorists were correct: the terms of social privilege are deeply contested in every modern society, and the haves perennially seek to translate their advantages into forms that render them legitimate in the eyes of have-nots. But he added that the transformation thesis also is true: privileged groups create educational institutions that have considerable independence from the people who pay for them. Schools function as quasi-autonomous third parties between haves who support them and have-nots. The academically accomplished kids who attend Harvard or Stanford on full scholarships, and the tuition-paying rich kids who flunk out of the same schools, are living embodiments of this institutional autonomy. Collins described this system of educational legitimation as *credentialism,* and the educationally stratified world it engendered *the credential society.*[9]

During the same decades that social scientists were developing this line of inquiry, the U.S. federal and state governments were actively building the largest higher education infrastructure in world history. Part of the justification for this expansion had to do with the more optimistic of social scientists' findings on education and individual life outcomes. If people's employment and earnings prospects were measurably improved through postsecondary schooling, the policy reasoning went, then a virtuous government would be right to expand opportunities for college attendance. In the decades following World War II, the U.S. state and federal governments did precisely that. Between 1945 and 1980 they dramatically grew the size and mission of public research universities, provided many millions of dollars in student grant and loan programs, and elaborately subsidized a whole tier of institutions—community colleges—to provide truly mass higher education opportunity.[10]

The United States was so successful at increasing the ranks of college graduates that as early as the mid-1970s social scientists were talking about "credential inflation"—the diminution of the value of college degrees in a labor market that was being flooded with them. As with credentialing before it, the credential inflation idea caught on quickly with the general public. It helped people articulate their sense that a mere college degree might not be sufficient for the attainment of upper-middle-class comforts. Many came to presume that the optimal educational choices were to earn additional credentials in graduate school or to seek especially prestigious and supposedly more valuable undergraduate degrees.[11] This is the most prominent explanation for the recent growth of demand for seats at colleges with nationally recognized names.

Worries about credential inflation notwithstanding, policy makers and the general public have conceived of college so optimistically for so long that pointing out the very limited extent to which expanded college access has changed the distribution of privilege in this country remains an unpopular thing to do. Nevertheless it is true: higher education has not been the great American equalizer. To be sure, there are proportionally more college graduates in this country than in any previous era, but, with only a few exceptions, the overall distribution of educational attainment remains stubbornly correlated with socioeconomic background.[12]

This does not mean, however, that the expansion of higher education has been without consequence for the character of the national class system. My research suggests that one profound result of higher education's expansion has been the entrenchment of a complicated, publicly palatable, and elaborately costly machinery through which wealthy parents hand privilege down to their children. My intention in this book is to reveal this machinery and explain how it organizes American society more generally.

The pursuit of college credentials is the widest and most dependable path to the good life that American society currently provides, and the terms of college admission have become the instructions families use when figuring out how to ensure their own children's future prosperity. The rise of the credential society has been accompanied by a value system in which the terms of college admission are also the goals of ideal child rearing and the standards of youthful accomplishment in American popular culture. These goals and standards are most explicitly depicted in the attributes elite colleges say they are looking for in applicants: measurable academic and athletic ability, demonstrated artistic accomplishment, and formally recognized philanthropic service.

Affluent families have a big advantage in meeting these goals and standards because they have relatively more resources to invest in doing so. Keenly aware of the terms of elite college admission, privileged parents do everything in their power to make their children into ideal applicants. They pay for academically excellent high schools. They shower their children with books and field trips and lots of adult attention. They nurture athletic talent through myriad youth sports programs. They encourage and fund early glimmers of artistic interest. They channel kids with empathic hearts toward exotic and traceable forms of humanitarian service. In the process of doing all of this, affluent families fashion an entire way of life organized around the production of measurable virtue in children.

On this line of thinking, the ever more frenzied activity surrounding selective admissions in the nation's most comfortable neighborhoods and school districts is essentially ceremonial. By the time upper-middle-class seventeen-year-olds sit down to write their applications, most of the race to top colleges has already been run and they already enjoy comfortable leads. For these kids the big question is not whether they will be admitted to an elite institution, but which particular schools will offer them spots. Nevertheless the intense final lap of the admissions race has profound importance as a ritual of just deserts. The simple fact that precise outcomes remain uncertain for everyone up to the very end serves to assure us that admission prizes are never won without persistence, steady wits, and hard work.

Status Counts and Status Rivals

How do all of the families with children in this race know just which colleges carry the most prestige? This is the puzzle to which much of my own inquiry attends, in large measure because the scholarly literature is virtually bereft of solutions. Rather than try to figure out what makes some schools more prestigious than others, social scientists typically rely on demand as prestige's proxy: the more people who apply to go there despite very low odds of admission, the more elite a school must be.[13] But remarkably, just where extraordinary desirability comes from is almost never directly considered.[14] Instead social scientists have relied on a tautology: the more people want to be admitted to a place, the more elite its diploma.

I will show that there is wisdom in this tautology, as long as we perceive of admissions statistics not as proxies of status but as status itself. In the absence of any definitive authority to decree which colleges and universities in America were to be the best, educators themselves worked out, over the course of the twentieth century, two systems of calibrating their status relative to one another. One system is admissions statistics. The measure of an institution's prestige has come to be defined, in part, by the proportion of each year's applicants it turns away. I take up this argument in detail in Chapters 2 and 3. Perhaps because status by numbers seemed too coldly calculative, perhaps because Americans have always been a little skeptical about academics and their ivory towers, educators also worked out a second system to mark institutional status: intercollegiate athletics. This system works much like the pecking orders that develop in school lunchrooms and playgrounds, in which children's popularity is marked by the company they keep. As I will explain in more detail in Chapter 4, in U.S. higher education the prestige of any one school is determined in part by the prestige of the other schools it meets on its playing fields.

The importance of undergraduate admissions selectivity and intercollegiate athletics to institutional status goes far in explaining why colleges and universities care so much about these aspects of organizational life. Admissions and sports are not mere adjuncts to the main business of U.S. higher education. They are integral parts of the whole enterprise.

Physical Education

One of the many revealing documents in the College's archive is a survey report from the late 1930s titled "A Study of the Reasons Given by 145 Members of the Freshman Class for Their Coming to the College." It is impossible to know the degree of rigor with which this survey was carried out, but its figures tell an evocative story. The survey appears to have given respondents a choice of some sixty factors that may have influenced their decision to attend the school. The list ranges widely, from "Academic reputation" to "Fraternity connections" and "Infirmary care." The single most frequently cited reason for attending is an item under the category "Physical Aspects": *Attraction of the campus* garners 67 mentions, a virtual tie with *General advantages of small college* and *Academic reputation*. Little wonder, then, that a document titled "Tentative Publicity Program," filed alongside the survey results, includes *Beauty of the campus* high on its list of recommended emphases.

This beauty is an asset that the College carefully maintains and actively promotes. Many of the facilities put up in recent years pay homage to the structures surrounding the oldest central quadrangles. As if in defiance of cost, stone facades and slate roofs adorn even some of the newest and largest buildings. Tidy footpaths, immunized to mud by an intricate terra cotta drainage system, lace through terraced gardens so beguiling that they are favored sites for wedding photographers. Otherwise quiet summer afternoons rumble with the din of motorized maintenance as physical plant workers aerate, mow, and fertilize many acres of lawns. In a custom shared by many of its similarly spectacular peer institutions, the College annually produces a full-color calendar of the most favored campus views and distributes it free to the institution's many alumni and friends.

Yet despite the great care and pride with which colleges attend to their physical appearance, sociologists of education have almost entirely ignored campus aesthetics. It is as if we have presumed that the job of conferring credentials is the most, or even the only, important work elite schools do. This blindness to aesthetics is part of a larger myopia in the sociology of education, and in the scholarly literature on stratification more broadly, about the sensual aspects of class. While we have become ever more sophisticated in our appreciation of how educational credentialing works, we have given ever less attention to the myriad ways in which schools produce a whole range of social values: intellectual, physical, aesthetic, and emotional.

Insights of the French sociologist Pierre Bourdieu provide a useful corrective to American sociologists' narrow focus on credentials as the primary produce of schools. Bourdieu argued that social class is about much more than where people fall in a society's distribution of wealth. It also entails particular patterns of aesthetic production, consumption, and sensual experience. What a society calls beautiful, for example, and what it makes beautiful in turn, are every bit as important to marking class distinctions as wealth and credentials are. On this line of thinking, it is no accident that in the schools to which they send their children, as much as in the neighborhoods they live in and the museums they patronize, the upper classes in every society go to great lengths to define what is beautiful and then surround themselves with the material embodiments of those definitions.[15]

On this line of thinking about class distinction, the physical appearance of human bodies matters as much as that of the physical worlds those bodies inhabit. Aspects of our corporeal bodies—how we carry them through space and attend to their shape, adornment, and longevity—also are important ways through which we mark class differences. Because bodies are such visible and consequential embodiments of class, parents go to great lengths to maintain and improve their children's physical health and appearance: through clothing, diet, and personal hygiene, and, significantly for purposes here, through sport and exercise. This, I will argue, is how the institutional status interests supporting college athletics and the class interests of families come together. The rigors of team athletics serve to maintain inter-organizational status clubs and, at the same time, to develop physically impressive men and women.

Hard Choices

Because social scientists have so long been interested in the role of schooling in social stratification, they have developed a large body of knowledge about those factors that, in the aggregate, predict admission to and graduation from elite schools. We know that admission to elite schools is highly correlated with parents' socioeconomic standing—in large measure because affluent parents translate their privilege into educational opportunities, which in turn produce the academic achievement rewarded by selective colleges. We know also that wealthy parents invest heavily in the extracurricular enrichments through which extraordinary athletic and artistic talents are developed. Considerable evidence makes it clear that athletic talent, especially, is systematically rewarded by selective college admissions offices. We know that elite schools systematically favor applicants who are children of their own alumni—presumably because these so-called "legacy" admissions will curry favor with alumni and make them more generous donors to their alma mater. And we know that since the 1970s, selective colleges have given systematic preference to members of certain minority groups—presumably in response to public demands for the racial integration of elite higher education in the wake of the civil rights movement.[16] Yet for all of the quantitative evidence social scientists have amassed about who in general is admitted to elite schools, we know very little about how admissions officers go about the business of making decisions.[17] Even though we know that selective colleges favor the academically and athletically accomplished, the children of alumni, and members of particular racial groups, we have relied almost entirely on inference to explain how *particular* decisions are made. To wit: we have not looked carefully at how admissions officers know what they do about applicants, how they organize and make sense of that information and assess its validity, and how they adjudicate between what might be regarded as competing attributes of applications. We know almost nothing about how officers balance incentives to reward high academic accomplishment, athletic skill, legacy or minority status, and the ability to pay full tuition. We have not looked carefully at the many exigencies faced by real admissions officers in their day-to-day work, or at the strategies officers have devised to manage these exigencies.

Sociologists have learned a lot about how decisions are made in complex organizations generally, however. We know that for any consequential choice, evaluative authority tends to be dispersed among multiple parties. We know about the difficulties inherent in getting all of the relevant parties to a decision onto the same page or even into the same room at the same time. We know that the amount and kind of information available to decision makers is crucial to what decisions ultimately get made.[18] I here put these insights into the service of understanding elite college access in particular, and the organization of elite schooling in America more broadly.

Oft-repeated wisdom in admissions circles is that officers do not evaluate applicants; they evaluate applications. The distinction is important. Officers may never meet the people represented in the files. Instead they assess what they call the "admissibility" of applicants on the basis of the information at their disposal: test scores and grade point averages; the academic profile of the sending high school; the content and detail of recommendation letters; assessments of athletic talent logged by college coaches; standardized assessments of financial need. Assembling a strong application file is a crucial step in any bid for admission to an elite college, because decisions often are made exclusively on the basis of the information inside the file.

However, as I will explain in detail, the ability to assemble a strong application is not evenly distributed across the population. Those without an inkling of how decisions are made by admissions officers are at a distinct disadvantage. Those who do have such inklings develop them at various points in their or their children's academic careers. If one gets wise to the system only when the student in question is a junior in high school, it is too late to remake choices that could have been made to better advantage years before. Even if parents are wise to the system on the day their children are born, their knowledge is of little consequence if it is not matched by the resources required to put it into practice: the means to live in a community with excellent schools, expert college guidance, and a student culture with a forward orientation toward college; the time and cash to invest in after-school sports leagues, summer music camps, private tutors, and horizon-expanding travel.

The fact that elite colleges make admissions decisions primarily on the basis of applicants' documented accomplishments is a triumph of meritocracy. The days when old-school connections were enough to get through the doors of top schools, and when dark skin or a Jewish surname were enough to be excluded, are over. In their place has arisen an information-based evaluative regime that nevertheless systematically favors the wealthy, well educated, and well connected. The mechanisms of preference have changed. Measurable accomplishment is the baseline criterion selective colleges now use to sort applications. But in general, only the relatively wealthy are able to afford the infrastructure necessary to produce that accomplishment in their children. Upper-middle-class Americans have responded to the triumph of educational meritocracy by creating a whole new way of life organized around the production of measurably talented children and the delivery of news about kids to the right places at the right times. This system is expensive and time-consuming. Consequently, the distribution of elite college acceptance letters is as skewed by class as it has always been.

That admissions statistics and athletic competitions are primary mechanisms of status differentiation in our national higher education system; that elite colleges are sensual and emotional organizations as much as academic ones; and that the machinery producing the talent and information now demanded by elite colleges is elemental to the class structure of American society—all are rather large arguments for a small book about a small school. My goal in making them is to suggest new solutions to enduring puzzles about schooling and inequality in the United States. The importance of those puzzles makes them worth a reach.

The Study and Its Setting

I studied this particular school in part because I believed that the College's position in the firmament of U.S. higher education would make lessons learned there especially revealing. The College is not the most elite school of its kind. It is highly selective—far less than half of its applicants are offered admission each year. However, the College admits a larger proportion of applicants than the most prestigious private institutions in the country. The College's position near, but not at, the top of the institutional status hierarchy probably makes it even more sensitive to the pecking order than schools at the very top. As the member of any club well knows, provisional members are especially attentive to terms of admission. I suspected that the College was a good place to study selective admissions because, unlike its most prestigious peers, it does not have the luxury of making or breaking the rules.[19]

It was my great good fortune to find an admissions office whose people were willing to welcome a long-term visitor with a long list of questions. Their generosity introduced me to a whole world of the academy about which, despite many years as a student and professor, I knew virtually nothing. In a busy office I tried to make myself useful, figuring I would get in the way less often if I kept moving and that I would learn more about the work by actually doing some of it. I tried to say yes whenever I was offered a task: making coffee, helping out during parent receptions, interviewing applicants, proofreading drafts of admissions literature, shoveling snow. As I developed a track record on smaller jobs, people gradually offered me larger ones. In time I was monitoring part of the College's Web presence, conducting information sessions for visiting families, drafting promotional literature, reading applications, and, eventually, going off-campus on my own to recruit for the College. I did my best to record in written fieldnotes all of what I saw and heard and did. My hundreds of pages of typewritten notes are the evidentiary spine of this book.

To fill out my research I interviewed athletics coaches and human resources personnel at the College, as well as guidance counselors, admissions officers, and admissions consultants elsewhere. I also assembled a large archive of memos, forms, statistical reports, and promotional literature generated by the College's various offices. Finally, I made multiple visits to the College's own archive, housed in its library, in an effort to place my contemporary findings in the context of the school's history.

My status as a researcher was always explicit. I made it a habit to tell people I encountered at the College, and on the road, about my two hats: that I was working for the admissions office but that I also was a sociologist and a college professor—a professional student of the admissions process. I was pleasantly surprised to encounter virtually no skepticism about my dual role. If anything, I was humbled that most high school guidance counselors, parents, and prospective students seemed not to much care much about my status as an academic and tended to get on with their own business pretty quickly. Of course I was not a "real" admissions officer, and because of that I consistently was careful to refrain from contributing to final admissions decisions. This was fairly easy to do. My own opinion about particular applicants was only occasionally, and usually ceremonially, solicited. I suspect this was one of the ways that officers reminded themselves that, however routine my presence may have become, I ultimately was a guest on their terrain.

I have concealed the identities of the people of the institution I studied and given pseudonyms to all of the people and most of the organizations that appear in this book. Especially telling details about the school where I did my fieldwork, such as its size, the number of faculty, and the most telling admissions statistics are either not reported or slightly altered to protect institutional anonymity. I have blurred identities in this way for two reasons. First, the College exists in an exquisitely competitive organizational world in which institutional identity and status are gauged largely by numbers, and in which admissions offices routinely vie with their peers for the affections of the very same applicants. It has not been my intention to write an exposé on the practices of one particular college, and I am eager to protect the well-earned integrity of the school I studied. Second, I believe this study reasonably represents patterns of practice throughout the whole little world of elite private higher education in the United States. In other words, this book's object is a single school, but its subject is selective private colleges and universities generally.[20]

The Office and Its People

The College's Office of Admissions and Financial Aid was located in an old house, a rambling colonial near the main entrance to campus. The building was tidily maintained. Groundskeepers planted flowers each spring along the walkway leading up to the main entrance. In December there were evergreen wreaths on the front doors. Inside, the public front rooms were tastefully appointed with subtle wallpaper and slightly worn furniture in a period style. Hardwood floors creaked benignly beneath sturdy carpets. Heavy curtains were left open to frame tranquil, tree-shaded views. It was the sort of place to which one might imagine going home for an idyllic Thanksgiving holiday—if "home" were in one of the well-heeled suburbs of New York's Westchester County, up Chicago's North Shore, or out Philadelphia's Main Line, the sorts of places where many of the College's students and alumni resided.

The office was open to visitors during regular working hours Monday through Friday and for half days on Saturdays. Just off the entry foyer arriving guests found a receptionist's desk, often a hub of activity. Here was where each new visiting party was greeted, where volleys about the character of the weather and the length of drives just completed were exchanged. Here was where campus interviews were scheduled and confirmed, and directions were given to an adjacent waiting room, a large and comfortable space that sprawled back along the entire length of the building.

A usually closed door at the back of the main entry hall afforded passage to a markedly different realm, the clerical office, where overhead fluorescent lights and a modular partition system signaled administrative territory. This was where each year's thousands of application files were carefully tended by three full-time employees. Open shelves covered one long wall where active files were kept in alphabetical order. A fourth full-time staff member with a desk here devoted most of her workdays to managing the office's relentless current of outgoing mail. By custom any walk through this long narrow room was a pleasant gauntlet of mutual hellos. Behind this room was a functional kitchen often put into the service of official entertaining and the less formal staff parties that lightened moods each season. The popsicles and bottled water that student tour guides offered free to visitors in the summertime were kept cold there. Back farther still were two large rooms where bushels of literature—viewbooks, calendars, forms and mailers and inserts of all kinds—were stored. Also in these rooms was a bank of weary old cabinets housing the files officers dutifully maintained on all of the high schools with which their office had had any connection.

A flight of stairs adjacent to the kitchen led up to Financial Aid, a department whose work had some autonomy from Admissions even while it was functionally and architecturally subordinate to it. Financial Aid had its own receptionist and its own long shelves of applicant folders. All applicants who requested consideration for financial aid from the College were "packaged" by this department and had separate files kept on them there. Two financial aid officers did the packaging, a task in which aid applications were assessed according to two sets of criteria, one backed by the U.S. Department of Education and the other by the large and vastly influential non-profit corporation, the College Board. Another full-time staff person administered the multiple government loan programs that were part of many students' aid packages. Still another employee oversaw the disbursement of government grants and endowed scholarships.

A corridor running the entire length of the second floor connected the financial aid offices at the back of the building to the upper landing of the front stairs. Most of the rooms off of the hall were devoted to office space for admissions officers. Even the most junior officer (the entry-level title was "assistant dean") had her own physical space, with windows and a door that closed—real estate indicative of a higher status than all of the clerical staff. In addition, because they represented the school in public and had ultimate authority over the fate of applications, admissions officers' positions had more glamour than officer-level posts in Financial Aid. Primarily because I had come to study admissions decisions—but doubtless too because I fell for the local status game—I spent most of my time with admissions officers and came to know them best.

The junior officers all had several things in common. All of them were in their twenties and thirties. All of them were good conversationalists, capable of easy smiles and clever turns of phrase. None of them anticipated careers in corporate America. None of them were hard to look at. With the exception of two officers who had graduated from large public universities, all had completed their college educations at schools very close in character and prestige to the College. There were no Ivy League degrees among them, but there were no low-status credentials either.

Conventional wisdom in the admissions world holds that junior positions in admissions are great first jobs: that they hone interpersonal and organizational skills; that a short stint in the profession is no detriment to a résumé; and that many parts of the work are fun. But seasoned officers also confessed that the job had a significant burnout factor, that the work could become repetitive and the extensive travel a chore. There also is limited room at the top of the field. In admissions the status of a job is tied directly to the selectivity of the employer, and because fewer than a hundred colleges and universities in the country are selective, the number of senior-level administrative positions in the occupational hierarchy is very limited.[21] In this sense the College, with its three full-time senior officers, had a fat top tier.

Val Marin, senior associate dean, had come to town when her husband took a job at a prominent regional arts institution. She had been the director of college guidance at a private day school before moving to the small hamlet in which the College is located. Val had responsibility for recruiting applicants at many of the most fashionable private schools along the Atlantic seaboard. She also directed the office's recruitment of international students, a job she clearly loved: traveling literally all over the world and cultivating relationships with families wealthy enough to send their children to a costly American private school. Val was an expert in the blood sport of cocktail conversation, and she was an enthusiastic hostess. When officers wanted to hold work-related social events in an intimate setting, they often were granted access to Val's home. Favorite recipes could be requested for the menus. Wine glasses were never empty.

Susan Latterly, director of admissions, was the administrative head of all the admissions personnel. Because her formal responsibilities included office management, she served as an important bridge between the admissions officers upstairs and the clerical staff down below. She was a consummate diplomat. People respected Susan's intelligence, her unflagging work ethic, and her two decades of experience in the orbit of the College. You had the sense that anything on Susan's desk would get done well and on time.

Liam Rizer, dean of admissions and financial aid, had been recruited in the mid-1990s with a specific mandate to improve the College's admissions selectivity. He was wooed away from a position comparable to Susan Latterly's at an elite private research university. Liam often said that what he liked about the College was that you "can really put your arms around it." And he did. On a small but often contentious campus, Liam was widely held in high esteem. He was a gifted communicator. He knew how to convey good news humbly and bad news strategically—so that people found themselves admiring his candor even when they did not like what he was saying. Liam was genuinely charitable, too. When I made my first inquiry about the possibility of doing this research, he did not respond with suspicion. Instead he invited me to a meeting with his senior officers and asked us all to think about how my presence might be an asset to the work of the office.

In his generally affirmative occupational outlook Liam was not alone. Wherever I went in that rambling old house, I found people who seemed favorably disposed toward their work and toward the College. This was true even after I had been on the premises for months, long after the instinct to make nice before a stranger would have eroded. It was almost as if people's employment contracts had stipulated good moods, as if some baseline optimism had been ordered by decree. This is not to say that the office was free of unhappiness. It was clear that limitations of the place, the job, and the colleagues often got under people's skins. The low pay, the long winters, and the often-heavy workloads were talked about, but the conversations rarely ended on notes of sheer complaint and they invariably took place at some remove from the public front rooms. Although I imagine I was excluded from airings of the dirtiest laundry, I do not think that impressions were managed just for me. In fact I quickly learned that this management was expected of me also. I found myself maintaining a cheery demeanor during my hours at the office, especially in front of guests.

The official good mood in Admissions did not always sit well with faculty, many of whom were quite vocally grumpy about the College and its various purported sins: that it was too conservative, too provincial; that it cared too much about varsity sports and too little about diversity; that it genuflected too shamelessly to trustees and wealthy alumni. Perhaps because they believed they were wiser to the College's problems, faculty sometimes derided admissions officers for the remarkable consistency with which they saw sunshine behind rain. In time I came to understand that faculty grumpiness was a luxury of their insulation from the school's most crucial resource flows. With very few exceptions, professors dealt with prospective students and their families only after they already had fallen in love with the College, already had sent first checks to the bursar and signed on to four years at the place. For the most part trustees and big donors were, to the faculty, abstractions—caricatures to be gossiped and speculated about when puzzling decisions got made upstairs. Given their comfortable positions at the core of the organization, faculty could choose to ignore how important outsiders' impressions of the College could be.

As a group the faculty enjoyed much cushier jobs than those who were hired to mind the front door. There was no tenure in Admissions. With the exception of Liam Rizer, Admissions personnel had no consequential role in college governance. Salaries for junior officers were something over half those of assistant professors. Yet it was the people in Admissions who most viscerally embodied the school for the outside world. As one of the junior officers, Danesha Adams, put it, "I've come to think of Admissions as the mouth of the College. . . . We represent it. That's our job." Liam Rizer once said to me that the receptionist who answered the phones in Admissions was one of the most important people on campus. Another time he talked about the people who mowed the lawns.

chapter two

NUMBERS

In many ways the College is the students it admits. Professors assess the quality of their classes on the basis of the students who sit in them. The football and tennis and lacrosse teams, the choral ensemble and debate club, are only as good as their student players and members. The campus is virtually without a culture, intellectual and otherwise, when the students are away. Because tuition is the College's primary source of revenue, students are vital to cash flow. Until the day they die, students remain members of what the Development Office calls the College "family," its web of alumni whose collective fortunes, material and otherwise, contribute crucially to the stature of their alma mater.

Another way in which the College is its students has to do with the statistical character of each year's admitted class. Measures of each cohort's academic accomplishments, such as their average SAT scores or the percentage of admitted students graduating in the top 10 percent of their high school classes, are prominent indexes of the College's academic prestige. The proportion of nonwhite U.S. citizens is a widely cited measure of that amorphous institutional value, "diversity," while the geographical dispersion of students' hometowns (how many U.S. states are represented? how many foreign countries?) marks the extent of the College's cosmopolitanism. Most prominently, the College's overall academic stature is gauged by the proportion of each year's applicant pool that is offered admission. This number—"selectivity"—is a metric of institutional prestige as commonplace as it is ironic. The quality of the College is gauged by the proportion of each year's applicants who are not allowed to enroll.

The use of numbers to assess institutional quality is so deeply embedded in our higher education system that we tend to take it for granted. We take for granted that schools with tiny acceptance rates are excellent, that high aggregate test scores measure a campus's intellectual intensity, and that a student body hailing from all fifty states is in itself a good thing. Figuring out why such numbers have become so important in the U.S. academic world takes us right to the heart of the main business of higher education: status.[1]

Status by Numbers

Status is the amount and kind of prestige that organizations, groups, or individuals enjoy in comparison to others. The mechanisms people develop to accrue and maintain status tend to be crucial to the overall machinery of modern societies. Max Weber was the first sociologist to explain this in detail. One of Weber's primary arguments with Karl Marx was that societies were shaped by struggles, not only for political and economic supremacy, but also for what Weber called "status honor." Put most simply, Weber's contention was that people care not only about how much money and influence they have but also about how they are regarded by others. People who have wealth and clout want others to believe that they have it deservedly—that their having has been earned or conferred according to rules that govern both haves and have-nots. Weber understood that raw power, without status to render it legitimate, is inherently unstable. Economic and political conflict would be inevitable unless the haves enjoyed a high degree of positive social regard. For Weber, status went far in explaining the durability of modern capitalist societies despite the huge inequalities they created. Those who held on to their power over time and across generations were able to do so because they had figured out how to maintain status honor for themselves and their offspring.[2]

An obdurate fact about status for anyone wishing to have it is that *someone else* has to confer it. Parties seeking to bestow honor on themselves are invariably regarded as self-serving, their efforts a sham. Imagine any competition whose organizer is both judge and contestant, and you understand the basic problem. People cannot award the prize of status to themselves. To get around this problem, status-seekers need mechanisms for conferring status that function more or less independently of the parties who want it. University of Iowa sociologist Michael Sauder calls these mechanisms *status systems*—rules for the distribution of status that obtain within some community of persons, groups, or organizations, and that have some autonomy (though not necessarily complete independence) from all of the parties seeking prizes in that particular status game.[3]

Schools like the College became prominent players in American society only when they coalesced into a status system for the Anglo-Protestant upper classes by the early decades of the twentieth century. During these years, attendance at a handful of private East Coast institutions came to be regarded as an important rite of passage for young men (and to a lesser extent, women) destined for positions of social prominence. Partly because native WASP elites were growing ever more nervous about passing their privilege on to their children in a rapidly diversifying United States, partly because ambitious educational leaders managed to convince parents that sending their children to academically rigorous residential schools was one good way to do this, the College and its peer institutions assumed new importance in the organization of American society. They became meeting grounds for the children of prominent families from geographically distant cities, training grounds for the inculcation of gentlemanly and womanly virtues, and proving grounds for the demonstration of cultural literacy, critical intellect, and leadership capacity. Schools like the College gradually assumed what historian Harold Wechsler calls a *selective function,* sorting young contenders for social prominence and then grooming them for influential futures.[4]

Not every school, however, could assume the job of producing legitimate elites. In a free and decidedly entrepreneurial America, many hundreds of colleges had been built by 1900. The nation's legacy of religious pluralism meant that numerous denominations had founded numerous schools to train their leaders. Civic boosters nationwide had supported hometown schools to enhance the cultural stature of many towns and cities. Utopian impulses to create ideal, total communities had led to the founding of still more institutions. The organizational universe of U.S. higher education thus had capacity for far more students than even a rapidly growing national upper class could fill with its sons and daughters. Because elites are, by definition, a small minority of any population, the purview of elite production could not be shared equally among all of the nation's schools. As is true in any crowded organizational sector, the collegiate field of early twentieth-century America was rife with competition for tuition dollars, elite patronage, and institutional prestige.[5] If elite higher education were to sort a relative few among many who were especially and deservedly elite, the colleges would have to have *their own* status systems—rules for determining which few institutions among many were the most elite, which diplomas carried the most prestige.

Throughout the nineteenth century, educational status systems had been local affairs. Colleges competed with other schools in their own cities and regions for the patronage of prominent local families; the degree to which any one school was able to corner the market on local patronage defined the limits of its institutional prestige. So the University of Pennsylvania, Princeton University, and the Quaker Swarthmore and Haverford colleges vied with one another for the sons of Philadelphia society. In New York, Columbia competed not only with nearby Princeton and Yale but also, and with greater success, New York University and City College for the children of the local WASP establishment. Harvard's elaborate and carefully woven ties with Boston's Brahmin families proved to be one of the tightest educational status systems in turn-of-the-century America. Boston's famously cohesive upper class and Harvard University's wealth and institutional prestige are enduring legacies of the association.[6] But as the population of the United States grew larger, its geographic reach greater, and its business organizations more extensive, the capacities of these local status systems were pushed to their limits. If schools were to confer portable status advantages for an increasingly mobile and heterogeneous society, they would need to develop systems of institutional recognition that transcended local boundaries. As the twentieth century progressed, a truly national inter-organizational status system took shape that we might call status by numbers: the use of admissions statistics as indicators of organizational prestige.[7]

Social theorists and historians have long understood that numbers have great utility for facilitating cooperation and control in complex societies. Parties who otherwise know little about each other can coordinate their behavior as long as they share some numerical version of reality. Numerical currency systems make economic exchanges possible between people who know nothing about each other except the price at which they are willing to buy or sell. Numerical time and navigational systems facilitate nautical, rail, and air travel across far-flung geographies, regardless of the languages spoken by the parties behind the wheels. Censuses, "vital statistics," and profit-and-loss statements enable leaders of political and economic empires to capably rule their provinces from a distance, as long as the relevant stakeholders agree on the validity of the numbers on which big decisions are being made.[8]

Numbers simplify comparison. Sociologist Wendy Espeland has shown in detail, for example, how U.S. government officials developed new numerical tools for making exceedingly complex comparisons in the post–World War II era. The task of bringing water to the arid Southwest in the mid-twentieth century challenged government decision makers to develop means of assessing trade-offs between wildly disparate values: the sanctity of Native American lands that might be deluged by new dams and reservoirs; the importance of maintaining endangered riparian habitats; the goal of economic development; the dream of making a desert bloom. Their solution was cost-benefit analysis, an evaluation process that attempted to transform all the varied dimensions of decisions into numbers that could be easily assessed.[9] Of course, the utility of numbers for making comparisons is not limited to massive public works projects. Everyday choices are made much simpler through standardized pricing and ranking schemes. Anyone who has compared prices per ounce of comparable laundry detergents, or settled an uncertainty about where to go to dinner by consulting the figures in a *Zagat* restaurant guide, understands this.

Finally, numbers facilitate decisive competition—the determination of winners and losers. Sports provide myriad examples. A big reason why young children's playground games so commonly generate conflict is that their rules of measurement are elastic. Absent authoritative parties to enforce just how points are to be accrued, players squabble among themselves about who has earned what.[10] Such conflicts are serious business when grown-ups invest heavily in their own games. The evaluation of Olympic figure skating underwent dramatic reorganization when competitors cited traceable national biases in the scoring practices of official judges. Consequently a new and more rigid scoring system was devised by Olympic authorities. Skaters now must earn points by completing clearly specified moves at particular moments in their routines and suffer clearly specified deductions for particular errors and omissions in their programs.[11] Numbers facilitate competition the same way that they facilitate cooperation—namely, by obliging all competitors to be assessed with the same measures.

Given the many organizational advantages of numbers, it is perhaps little surprise that higher education leaders developed metrics for determining the relative status of U.S. colleges and universities over the course of the last century. Unlike France and many other countries with state-centered higher education systems, the United States never had a definitive state authority to decree which institutions of higher learning were to be regarded as the best. And unlike England, the United States had no one or two ancient universities that held an undisputed cartel on the grooming of elites. Instead U.S. schools pursued their ambitions in what was, beyond the level of particular cities and regions, a status anarchy. People might easily name what were generally regarded as the most prominent schools in particular locales, but there were no nationally definitive indexes of institutional quality. This state of affairs was manageable in an era when most schools cast nets for students largely within their own local communities. But as the country became more tightly integrated by rail and telecommunication, as the population became more mobile and diverse, and as eastern colleges and their traditional patrons developed more national aspirations, the demand for truly national organizational status systems became more pressing. And of course there were the organizational *arrivistes,* out in the hinterlands, the University of Chicagos and Stanfords, each with their own local patrons and boosters, who were eager to have their institutions assessed on a par with the more established eastern schools. Hinterland upstarts stood to gain from status systems that were portable and transparent enough that they could accommodate new players on shared terms.[12] In this context of national growth and integration, higher education leaders gradually came to use admissions statistics as indicators of institutional prestige over the course of the twentieth century. Simultaneously, the practice of courting students from every state in the union as a mark of institutional cosmopolitanism also diffused to every college and university vying for a national stature.

The College's archives contain annual reports of admissions activity for most of the years between 1941 and 1995. The most prominent entries on each report describe the proportion of admitted students relative to the number of received applications. The 1941 report lists, at the very top (section 1.1), the number of applicants and the percentage of applicants admitted for the classes of 1943, 1944, and 1945. Each year the acceptance rate was near 60 percent. Section 1.5 of the report is titled "Disposition of [Class of] 1945 Non-Matriculants." It sorts the numbers of those who did not accept the College's offer of admission into the categories *entered the colleges of their first choice* (28), *entered other colleges because of financial reasons* (10), *entered other colleges because of larger scholarships* (4), *entered other colleges because we offered no scholarships* (2), *plans to reapply for the Class of 1946* (1), and *planned to transfer remained where he was* (1).

Section 2.2., titled "Geographic Distribution," breaks down the percentages of the entering classes of 1942–1945 into those whose hometowns were in the College's county (23.9 percent for the class of 1942), the College's state (76.2 percent for 1942), four neighboring states (10.5 percent), and "All Other States and Foreign" (13.3 percent).

Section 2.5 is titled "Secondary School Quartile Standings," a measure of where matriculants fell in the rankings of their high school classes. Of the members of the class of 1942, 59.1 percent fell in the first quartile, 24 percent in the second, 12.3 percent in the third, and 4.6 percent in the fourth. An additional line of data, titled "Above Median," specified the figure 83.1 percent.

Section 3, "Comments," makes note of "a 5% drop" in the College's overall number of applicants between the classes of 1943 and 1945. This decline evidently was a problem, because the author wrote:

> It is impossible to show definite causes . . . but the following factors seem to bear upon the situation:
>
> 3.11 *School Visitations:* Whereas last year 93 [high] schools were visited only 75 were called upon this year. Probably this effected [*sic*] the number of applications although such an effect might have been offset by the additional time spent in the office developing other parts of our recruiting program. . . .
>
> 3.12 *Competition Intensified:* It is generally known that most colleges this year have taken the largest freshmen classes in their histories. For example, Yale, Harvard, and Dartmouth set out to increase the size of their freshmen classes by 150. [Names of other liberal arts colleges] each hoped for fifty more freshmen, and Princeton sought an additional 75. Since the number of men entering college was no greater than in the past (indeed if study were made, it would probably show a decrease because of defense jobs), some colleges had to suffer. . . .
>
> 3.13 *[The College] in New Competitive Group:* It seems apparent from the papers of our applicants who applied to other colleges . . . that we are competing more and more with colleges like [names of several other liberal arts schools], Dartmouth. . . . Although we may have received fewer applications because of this, it is healthy competition. It means, however, that we must improve our recruiting and

must also step up our entire program if we are to increase our number of applications. . . .

3.14 *The National and International Situation:* The national and international situation unquestionably diverted some of our potential applicants to . . . defense jobs.

This short document speaks volumes about the context in which the College was doing its work in 1941. Not only the number of students admitted, but also the proportion of admitted students to applicants, was reported. Despite the fact that for every year covered in the report, the College had many more applicants than it needed to fill its classes, even a small drop in application numbers was met with detailed explanation. Additionally, the geographic distance students were willing to travel to attend the College mattered to admissions reporters in the early 1940s. Prose commentary made clear what the numbers implied: that the College existed in a highly competitive organizational field, and that its current status in that competition was to be gauged by admissions selectivity.

Subsequent reports take the same general format of the 1941 document, even while they include varying amounts and kinds of information. The 1947 and 1948 reports distinguish "Veteran" from "Civilian" applicants. "Scholarship" applicants were distinguished from "Non Scholarship" ones in the 1950s. The first report in the archives to give any information about applicants' "College Board Scores" is dated 1959. A new data category, "Minority Group Applications," appears in 1973; a category for gender was added in the 1970s as well. From 1982 onward each report carries considerably more numerical detail—no doubt partly because developments in computer technology made it ever easier to carve up and print out quantitative information, but probably also because, as we will see in subsequent pages, competitive pressures on selective college admissions offices grew ever more intense as the twentieth century progressed.

Despite the changes, a few features of the reports remained constant. First, overall admissions selectivity, as defined by the proportion of all applicants offered admission each year, invariably gets top billing as the initial piece of information conveyed to readers. It appears invariably as a sort of master statistic, the summary data point. Second, the geographic dispersion of admitted students' hometowns retains prominence up through the most recent documents in the archive. Third, the reality of inter-organizational competition is evident in all of the reports, with textual emphasis given to lateral and upward comparisons with other schools in the status hierarchy. Fewer than a dozen of the greater Northeast's most prominent colleges and universities are consistently mentioned, while lesser known, less selective schools a stone's throw from the College receive less attention.

Facts and Figures

College boosters have long used numbers to paint flattering pictures of their institution to outsiders. The earliest viewbook held in the school's archive, published in 1923, carries a page of "Interesting Facts about The College." The list includes:

> Number of buildings, excluding faculty residences and
> fraternity houses
> Acres of property
> Acres of campus
> Value of college buildings and property
> Productive endowment funds
> Productive endowment per student

Expenses of college course per student paid by the College from endowment

Average cost per student of room and board

Total annual income of funds for fellowships and scholarships

Courses given

Volumes in the Library

Pamphlets in the Library

Periodicals received in the Library

Rhodes scholarships at Oxford awarded to College men

Periodicals published in the College

Number of graduates

Total number ever in attendance at the College

Number of College men who served in the Great War

A 1937 viewbook has a similar page of "Interesting Facts." Both lists represent the College as a place rich in physical resources (buildings, library volumes) and financial ones (endowment size, endowment per student). Academic quality is represented by counts of specific, extraordinary accomplishments (numbers of Rhodes Scholars and periodicals published). Notably absent, at least in the eyes of a contemporary reader, are numerical measures of what are now often called student demographics. The lists contain no statistical descriptions of the young people who were attending the College: nothing about race or the proportion receiving financial aid, for example. Nor do the lists present any information about what economists might call human capital: students' SAT scores and the educational accomplishments of faculty, for example.

The penchant for publicizing numbers proved enduring, even while the preferred facts and figures changed in kind. Authors of the 1994 viewbook declare that "96% of the faculty members hold the most advanced degree in their fields" and brag about a "10-to-1 stu-

dent-to-faculty ratio." The fact that "typically 35% of the junior
class studies with the College's [study-abroad] programs" is presented as good news, as is the statement that "life at the College
could not be more vibrant or varied, with 98% of all students living
on campus, 80 student-run clubs and organizations, and a never-
ending array of events and activities to attend." There is mention of
the size of the student government's annual budget ($140,000), and
of the field hockey team's "sixteen consecutive winning seasons."

A subsequent viewbook produced in the late 1990s has an even
more elaborate deployment of quantitative good tidings. Five full
pages near the beginning of the 47-page publication are a shower of
numbers. A large, colorful font announces, "More than 1/3 of science students have a one-on-one research opportunity with a faculty
member and 170 have co-authored journal articles with professors
in the past five years." Pie graphs show that 30 percent of College
classes have 10 students or less, that 51 percent of surveyed seniors are "hectic but happy," and that 33 percent report having
had lunch, dinner, or coffee with a professor during their time at
the College. Quantitative descriptions of the student body also are
prominently displayed. Under the heading "A diverse community,"
very large type declares "42 states, 31 countries," and "14% multicultural." At the end of the century, as at the beginning, boosters
used numbers to sing the College's praises. What changes are the
kinds of counts that are emphasized. Viewbooks produced at the
end of the century give relatively less play to the College's physical
and financial resources and relatively more to its human endow-
ments: the credentials of the faculty, the demographic character and
reported satisfaction of the students, the nature of relationships between students and professors.

Although it is impossible to ascertain, on the basis of this very
limited evidence, just why the authors of later viewbooks opted to
represent the institution with rather different facts and figures, I sus-

pect it is no accident that the newer forms of numerical representation became attractive during the years when *U.S. News & World Report (USN)* was enjoying ever greater celebrity for its college-ranking scheme. The popular magazine feature that began in 1983 as an informal survey of college presidents had, by 1994, become an elaborate statistical undertaking and a major force in U.S. higher education. The innovation of the *USN* rankings lay not in their use of numbers to stratify and compare institutional prestige. Colleges and universities had been doing that for years. The magazine's revolutionary invention, rather, was a universal ranking scheme that purported to encompass the whole of higher education in America. *USN*'s evaluative reach was unabashedly comprehensive. The magazine claimed that its rankings could distill, into a single number, the overall quality of each institution it considered, and it used that number to place each school into a precise statistical relationship with all of its peers nationwide.[13]

So, for example, for each of the 229 schools evaluated in its 1994 rankings of the "Best National Universities," *USN* compiled statistical data on such things as admissions selectivity, enrolling freshmen's average SAT/ACT scores, the proportion of enrolling freshmen in the top 10 percent of their high school class, percentage of faculty holding doctoral degrees, alumni giving rates, and the student/faculty ratio, as well as each school's score on a reputational survey. All of these numbers were integrated into a single score according to an equation developed by *USN*. Each school's score subsequently was compared with the others to determine rankings within a single hierarchy. In 1994, Harvard, Yale, and Princeton were ranked 1st, 2nd, and 3rd, respectively. Notre Dame University was ranked 19th, and the University of California at Berkeley 23rd. By statistical alchemy, all of the myriad differences between Eastern Ivy, the Fighting Irish, and the birthplace of the counterculture were distilled into handful of easily comparable facts and figures.

By the mid-1990s, *USN* was annually offering numerically ranked lists of not only "The Best National Universities" but also "The Best National Liberal Arts Colleges." In 1994, 164 schools including the College were ranked in this category.[14] As we will see in subsequent chapters, "the rankings" (as many officers called them, without need of further specification) have proved to be highly influential in how the nation's elite institutions go about making admissions decisions. They also have extended the long tradition in U.S. higher education of conceiving of quality numerically.

Measuring Up

The many powers of numbers make them tempting instruments for deceit. Financial scandals large and small demonstrate that people can lie with accounts as well as with words. But the same things that make numbers powerful—their comparability and clarity—also enable third parties to assess any particular number's accuracy. Anything that can be measured can at least in principle be measured again, which means that all measures are susceptible to scrutiny. This is why, when law or custom obliges people to report them in standardized ways, numbers are used less often for outright lies than for technically plausible fudges and fibs.[15]

U.S. colleges and universities constantly are called upon to offer standardized numerical representations of themselves. College guides and ranking schemes, government credentialing and philanthropic agencies, not to mention high school guidance counselors and prospective applicants, routinely ask schools to describe who they are with a long list of numbers: total enrollments; counts of majors and faculty members and sports teams and clubs; admission, retention, and graduation rates; student/teacher ratios and average class sizes. The numbers are consequential because they implicate particular schools in inter-organizational pecking orders. This is why admissions officers take their numbers so seriously, and why the most savvy officers figure out how to make the numbers as flattering as they legitimately can be.

The first big job I was given in the office was to carry out the College's participation in an Internet college fair. The event mimicked fairs that happen live in countless high school gyms across the country each year. The fairs are rather like trade shows, but for college, with seventeen-year-old clients. Admissions officers from many different institutions convene at them to distribute literature and talk up their schools to potential applicants. The College had paid several thousand dollars in fees to participate in this Web version. I had been given the job of administering the fair because it was scheduled during the busy fall season and officers' plates were full.

Part of the job entailed submitting descriptive material about the College for the fair's database; information would subsequently be accessible to the prospective students who logged on to the site. I wanted to be sure to get the data right, so I scheduled a meeting with Susan Latterly to go over the information before I submitted it online. Just as Susan and I were getting to our business in the conference room, Liam Rizer opened the door and sat down to join us.

I began by making my way through a worksheet provided by the fair's organizers to assist people like me in assembling the information requested by the database. I posed each item as a question to Susan and Liam, who replied to each one in turn.

Number of students. Liam knew this one off the top of his head.

Number of part-time students. We agreed that the answer was "none," even though I knew that in fact there were part-time students at the College, among them a number of College employees who participated in a special program for adult learners. Liam and Susan knew this program well. It was administered in tandem with their office.

Percentage of minority students. Liam said, "Campus-wide it's 10 percent, but for the entering class it's 14 percent. The numbers keep going up a bit every year, but still the campus-wide number is about 10 percent." "Of course that doesn't sound as good," he added with a grin. "Let's use 14 percent for that."

I said, wryly, "So the job is to use the most flattering accurate numbers possible."

"Right," Liam said. "The most flattering accurate defensible numbers possible."

Percentage of students from out of state. Again, Liam gave me a number off the top of his head, 60 percent. A subsequent comparison of this figure to a spreadsheet of enrollment data from recent years revealed that Liam's assessment was generous. In fact, 55 percent of the class of 2004 were from out of state, as were 58 percent of the class of 2003 and 57 percent of the class of 2002. Liam apparently had rounded these numbers upward, suggesting, in the process, that the College was just a tad more cosmopolitan than it actually was.

Percentage of students who are international. There was some discussion about this. The most recent incoming class was 6 percent international, but for the entire student body the figure was a bit lower because previous classes had fewer students from abroad. "Say 5 percent for that," Liam advised.

Questions on tuition and board fees could, I was told, be answered by checking one of the admissions brochures.

Percentage of students receiving financial aid. There was discussion. Susan suggested that the answer was about half the student body. Liam said, "Well if you include people who receive federally sponsored Stafford loans that number is higher. Say 60 percent for that one."

Average class size. Liam said, "I think it's twenty-four. That average kind of hurts us."

Susan agreed. "We don't usually use average class size, we use [the] percentage of classes with 20 students or less."

Liam said, "The thing is, we have lots of classes with four or five students, but we have a few really big ones, so that hurts the average." I agreed that 24 was not the most flattering number, while I wrote it down and moved on.

Student/faculty ratio. I was pretty sure I knew this one, and said, "10 to 1, right?" I was.

Percentage of faculty with terminal degree. Liam said, "I think that's 98 percent," Liam said. I wrote it down.

Number of full-time faculty. I said, "I think it's 175."

Liam said, "I think actually it's 186."

"Hmm. I thought it was a bit lower than that . . . but you would likely know better than me," I deferred.

Susan settled the matter. "As long as it matches up with total number of students and the student/teacher ratio."

I was learning. "Right," I said, with a slim grin that was echoed by my companions. I did a quick glance at the other two relevant numbers and said, "Well [in that case] it would have to be higher than 175 I guess." No one suggested that I check with the dean of faculty, or with Personnel.

Percentage of students admitted. Someone—by the time I wrote up my fieldnotes I could not remember just who—said 33 percent, a figure that struck me as a little low. Admission rates for the three prior entering classes all were notably higher, and therefore less flattering. But because the data requested by the form specified "Entering Class Information," the most impressive number was in this case also the correct one.

We weren't finished, though. Liam said, "Actually . . . I just got the final numbers for the entering class from [name of the College's institutional research officer]. She said that at the very end the percentage of students accepted was 33.54 percent. Which we would need to round to 34 percent."

"Oh!" Susan's face expressed surprise, then dismay. "Geez. And we've been saying 33 percent everywhere."

Perhaps there was another way. Liam worked it out. "What happened was, with our kids [on two special scholarship programs], a requirement of admission is that they successfully complete [a summer school program]. Well, two of them didn't finish the program. So technically they weren't admitted, they certainly didn't join the entering class. So, if we take them out, the percentage accepted drops to 33.48 percent, or 33."

We all smiled. "Mitchell, please be kind to us in your book," Liam said jovially. He had told me early on that he enjoyed the numbers his work entailed. His evident pleasure that morning in the conference room was proving the point.

He went on. "Another thing that happened with [institutional research] was about the percentage of students in the entering class in the top 10 percent of their [high school] class." This was a very important figure, because *U.S. News & World Report* uses it as part of its institutional ranking scheme. "When [one of our staff] calculated this figure, she calculated it from 90 percent. But [institutional research] uses 89.5 percent. Which they say we can do because that's how the estimate works. If we use 90 percent, the percentage of students in the top 10 percent of their classes is 53; if we use 89.5 percent, that number changes to 55."

I was impressed. Simply by using the lowest possible number that could legitimately be rounded to 90, the College nudged a consequential figure a little further in the right direction.

Perhaps I should have been dismayed by Liam's tightrope walk on the line of verity, but even after multiple assessments of this meeting I was never quite sure how to call it. It was certainly the case that Liam worked hard to represent the College in the best possible statistical light, but he also was careful to stay within the technical confines of truth. Then too, I had seen quantitative social science up close long enough in my own line of work to know that public representations of most numbers had at least some measure of artfulness to them. Liam's savvy quantification struck me as analogous.

In subsequent months I also would hear accounts—never verified by authoritative third parties, but plausible enough to at least potentially be true—of techniques competitor schools used to froth up their own numbers. Val Marin told me about a colleague elsewhere who bragged to her about his school's exceptionally large numbers of applications from international students. The kids from abroad apparently were encouraged to apply online, for free. "And then you reject 'em all. But you have their applications," Val explained, veering into inference. I continued by asking her about something I'd heard about from a former admissions officer at an elite southern university, a practice in which the school counted as "applicants" everyone who submitted any material at all, regardless of the completeness of the files.

"Oh, you mean counting expressions of interest, or short versions of the application, or incomplete applications, as applications?" Val asked. "Yeah. Common. We don't do that. In fact I think we're quite conservative in what we count. So if you think about it, our numbers are very, very good considering that we report them pretty straight," she said.

Making the numbers make the school look as good as possible was part of the job. Doing it well could earn one accolades from colleagues. One evening over dinner, Susan Latterly told me of her admiration for Liam Rizer in this regard. "I've learned a lot from him, I really have." This from a woman who had spent an entire career in the same field as Liam. "I mean, he came in and really tightened things up, especially on our numerical reporting. Like, for example, if a figure was 14.5 percent and a higher figure was desirable, he'd report it at 15. Which is not inappropriate, you're rounding the figure appropriately. But we hadn't thought that way. And, taken together, a lot of those little things are where a lot of our improvement [in selectivity] came from."

That Liam was good at the numbers, and enjoyed them, suited him ideally for the job of head dean. By contrast, Susan Latterly made clear to me that the pressures accompanying the numbers left her in no hurry to assume her boss's job:

> [It would be] kind of exciting to be in with the [senior College officers] and making decisions and all of that. But at the same time it's a job where how you are doing is really clear. People can look at the numbers, the admissions statistics from year to year, and know how you're doing. I don't think it's like that with the Dean of Students, say, where it's going to be harder for someone to figure out if you're not doing your job right. So, it's a lot of responsibility and a lot of pressure. And at this point in my life, with my daughter at home, I don't need that.

The fact of the matter was that the College constantly was being evaluated by consequential outsiders on the basis of its admissions statistics. This meant that head deans like Liam Rizer constantly were evaluated by their own superiors on the basis of the same numbers.[16]

However else he may have felt, Liam seemed to keep his sense of humor about it. I sat in on several meetings with College trustees regarding admissions and financial aid, meetings that invariably included a presentation from Admissions on the most recent office statistics. One time Liam began his presentation by saying, "All the numbers that should be going up are going up, and all the ones that should be going down are going down." He said it boldly, with a twinkle in his eye, then he paused, very briefly, before getting on with the report, but nobody laughed.

chapter three

TRAVEL

There are three reasons why I clearly remember that chilly October morning. One: I was dressed and ready to go considerably earlier than my professor's self would have started his workday. Two: I was waiting for Susan Latterly, the administrative director of the admissions office, the person directly below Liam Rizer in authority, the serious, intelligent, extremely organized woman who betrayed her seasoning in this business in little ways every day. I had grown impressed by her ability to work very long hours, track a hundred details, banter easily with student interns and office staff, and command the deference of the junior officers. I would be spending the entire day with Susan, accompanying her on visits to several public high schools in a nearby metropolitan area. The trip would involve hours in the car, just the two of us, a bubble of privacy in which conversation is more or less expected, bliss for the ethnographer. I was eager with anticipation, and a little bit nervous. Three: It was Halloween.

It was the height of what admissions officers call "travel season," the autumn weeks between the start of the school year and the Thanksgiving holiday, when officers fan out from campus to spread word of the institution and maintain relationships with guidance counselors—the people "on the other side of the desk," as officers often describe them—who help high school students navigate the college entrance process. Like many other schools, the College carves up this work geographically. Officers are assigned particular "territories" of the nation, or the globe, in which to travel, and they also conduct the primary evaluation of applications from these same geographic areas. The idea is for officers to accrue familiarity with a region, nurture thick ties with particular guidance counselors, and follow particular students from the beginning of their interest to yield season in the spring. Partly because she had so many administrative responsibilities in the office, partly because her own hometown was in the region (always considered a plus in territory assignment), and partly because she had children at home, Susan assumed much of the ground within easy driving distance of the College.

Her car rolled into my driveway a few minutes shy of the prearranged 7:50 arrival time. A smile through her windshield was my 'good morning.' As soon as I opened the passenger door, Susan, all business, said, "I've got to stop at the office. There is a student from Sparta-North who interviewed [with us] but whose name I can't remember. I've been thinking about it all night and it hasn't come to me, so I want to check her file before we go." Susan knew that a student interested enough to drive out for an interview would probably be at the information session we would offer at Sparta-North High School later that morning. It is was a small thing, the ability to use a first name on first sight of an applicant or a guidance counselor as if you had not had to think about it at all, but for admissions officers it is the sort of thing that matters, the sort of thing you know can tilt an opinion of your school in a favorable direction.

The travel is important. The College's reputation and the quality of its applicant pool are dependent upon its connections with high schools nationwide. Of course the College courts students from its own region; Susan and I were headed no farther than a hundred miles from campus that morning. But even on its own turf the College competes for top students with schools all over the country. The reasons for this are, as I outline below, complex, but the bottom line is that these days any top school's audience must be national and even international in scope. If the College is to be competitive with the best institutions in the country, its name must be on the lips of guidance counselors in Houston, Minneapolis, and San Francisco. Its freshman seats must be coveted prizes in affluent suburbs from coast to coast. Though some of the task of maintaining a national presence falls to other parts of the College's division of labor (faculty are supposed to develop national reputations in their academic disciplines; the development office cultivates alumni relations all over the place), the lion's share of the job falls on Admissions. This is why officers travel.

We saw in Chapter 2 that officers care a lot about the numbers representing each year's entering class because those numbers are primary metrics through which institutional status is now assessed. But the numbers are not the only basis on which people make college choices. Even though quantitative representations place schools within fairly clearly delineated prestige hierarchies, they go only so far in generating preferences for any particular institution over all others. It is hard to fall in love with a ranking. Admissions officers understand that the college choice is an emotional, aesthetic, and interpersonal matter, not just a technical one. What the school physically looks like, the personalities conveyed by its tour guides, and the manner in which receptionists answer their phones all contribute bits of data to a full picture of a place. Admissions offices are the primary circuitry through which these bits flow, which is why officers spend considerable time engineering the wires so that the stuff getting through to outsiders sums to a flattering image. Travel season is a big part of this engineering.

Going on the road with admissions officers taught me important lessons about generating good impressions, about how hard it can be to achieve genuine human contact at the borders of complex organizations, and more broadly about the distribution of college opportunity in America. I learned that for highly selective schools like the College, student recruitment is inseparable from the maintenance of interpersonal relationships. Officers travel to connect with potential applicants, build professional ties with guidance counselors, and in general distribute their attention in ways that officers hope will have enduring benefits for the College. Enduring relationships develop most often with high schools that have the resources to reciprocate on the College's gifts of attention and thereby make admissions officers' work much easier. The travel also taught me that elite schools like the College exist in a peculiar organizational landscape, in which applicant pools are determined less by physical geography than by the socioeconomic stratification of secondary education, on the one hand, and by the competition for students among top colleges and universities, on the other. In this peculiar terrain, the appraisal of applicants as individuals is a deeply contingent, very costly, and largely self-interested affair.

Why We Were Traveling

Susan was quickly back at the car with the prospective student's name, Lorena, lodged securely in her memory. We were on the freeway in a matter of minutes, a bucolic autumn countryside blurring past at interstate speed. After some chatty exchanges about the day's beauty and itinerary, I asked Susan if she might tell me how she got into admissions, twenty years ago, and about how the work had changed over that time.

"When I first started in this business, in the late 1970s, the whole process of admissions, at least at places like the College, was very different than it is today," she said bluntly. "Back then it seemed that there were more or less plenty of good students for everybody, plenty to go around, and so admissions was more about presenting what kind of institution you were, and then helping people make the right decisions."

"Kind of managing the flow," I suggested.

"Right. We were not doing the kind of active recruiting that we do now, and thinking about new ways to attract good students."

"What changed?"

"Well a lot of things changed. First of all, there were simply changes in the numbers of people going to college. When I first started in this business, we were still looking at the tail end of the baby boom, there were a lot more college-aged kids. The numbers declined there for awhile. . . . And another thing that happened was the increase in college tuition. It used to be that . . . we would admit the class we wanted in Admissions and then pass the class over to Financial Aid and they would package them, and we didn't really think about the financial aid budget, there was always enough to cover the kids that we had selected. But that started to change. College costs went up and we had more and more people who needed financial aid, so we had to start thinking, more conscientiously, about how we were using that financial aid. And then finally there were the changing demographics of the country, that we really need to be thinking nationally now about where students who fit [our] profile are. There are now many more of them in the South and the West."

Susan's off-the-cuff account touched highlights of the complex recent history of selective higher education. The huge surge in births between 1946 and 1964 called the baby boom, the demographic tidal wave that transformed every institutional system in its wake, is a crucial part of the story. As has been amply documented elsewhere, the 1960s and 1970s were expansionist years for American colleges and universities. After World War II, the U.S. government embarked on the most ambitious effort to expand higher education that the world has ever known. The research tiers at the top of the system grew under the cold-war mandate to outproduce the Soviets in scientific progress; at the bottom, the founding of hundreds of new community colleges made a postsecondary degree a realizable goal for millions. In between these two tiers, private schools like the College also enjoyed rich government largesse: in the tuition grants and subsidized loans many students received, and in direct financial support for the construction of new academic facilities and dorms. Throughout the 1950s and 1960s, institutions new and old, public and private, large and small enjoyed prosperous years and anticipated bright futures.[1]

Times had changed by the late 1970s. Members of the high crest of the baby boom had moved through their prime college years by then, and the flow of college applicants began to level off. Many schools had invested heavily in expanding their facilities, only to experience slackening enrollments just as new infrastructure came on line. And although government investment in higher education was hardly over, the long recession of the 1970s, coupled with the energy crisis and the property tax revolts of the era, dried up much of the public funding available for higher education.[2]

Schools that had entered the post–World War II era with solid reputations, long-established student flows, and a measure of endowment wealth were better prepared for the changing circumstances, but they were not immune to them. As Liam Rizer once explained to me, talking retrospectively about his own career in selective college admissions:

> [In] the late 1970s we were just coming off the big numbers [of applicants], the big expansion, and that was leveling off, and people were making predictions about the future, about declining numbers. And you saw it. And that's when a lot of changes started happening. That's when you started thinking differently about recruiting. And

with development too, that's when many schools started working at raising money on a whole different scale, and in different ways. You had to. You had to find new ways to do business, that's just all there was to it.

Technological changes further changed how colleges and students found one another. As Harvard economist Caroline Hoxby has deftly explained, dramatic net reductions in the prices consumers paid for airfare and long-distance telephone calls collapsed distances between schools and students. As the twentieth century progressed, it grew ever easier for academically accomplished Californians to consider attending a New England college, for New Yorkers to imagine four years at Stanford or UCLA, and for ambitious "regional" institutions that enjoyed proximity to major airports (Atlanta's Emory University; Houston's Rice; Minnesota's Carleton, Macalester, and St. Olaf colleges) to lure students nationally.[3]

To be sure, the vast majority of those going to college still attend an institution within commuting distance of their homes; but for the cream of each year's applicant pool the college search is a truly national endeavor. High school students with top grades and test scores and exceptional extracurricular accomplishments look literally everywhere for schools that best "fit" them, while in turn the schools, eager to claim stellar test-takers and athletes and valedictorians as their own, go after the strongest applicants regardless of zip code. The most coveted applicants, "the students everyone wants," as the College's president once candidly described them in a speech to faculty, are those who have the magic combination of tiptop academic accomplishment and parents wealthy enough to pay full tuition. There are only so many of these prizes in each year's cohort of graduating high school seniors, and they live all over the place.

In the wake of these changes it is perhaps not surprising that the way officers talked about their work changed as well. "It's interesting to watch the change in language," Susan said as we approached our first destination, "It used to be that we didn't talk about marketing at all, at least not publicly. That word was taboo. You weren't supposed to be marketing, this was academia and that is not what we were doing. But that's gone now. Now we talk about marketing all the time." Within the space of Susan's own career, the work of assembling entering classes to the nation's elite private schools had been transformed. What was once a largely regional process of courting and shepherding students became a hot competition among schools all over the country for the choicest applicants everywhere. Admissions officers did everything they could to maintain the College's profile alongside all of the other schools vying for the top performers in each year's cohort of high school seniors. Officers could not take it for granted that the most accomplished kids in their own backyard would even be considering the College. This is why we were traveling.

Keeping in Touch

We pulled into the parking lot of Handeville High School, our first of three scheduled stops that day, a few minutes before the designated hour. Our appointment was scheduled for 9 A.M., and by my watch it was 8:48. Susan noted the time. "We're early," she said.

"That's always the way to be!" I responded cheerily. But Susan popped right back, "We can wait a few minutes in the car. The last thing you want to do is show up fifteen minutes early for a school appointment." It was my first indication of several that day that guidance counselors were very busy people. Seasoned officers knew they could not be too courteous with counselors' time.

Handeville's home was a low brick structure at the edge of an asphalt ocean, its own parking lot. Comparable to thousands of other schools built in growing suburbs during the baby-boom years, its most remarkable characteristic was its humble height; the building appeared to be all one level, the advantage of no stairs likely coming at the cost of horrifying heating bills. Landscaping was sparse, almost nonexistent. We entered the building with the boisterous last waves of arriving kids.

Just as we came inside, Susan spotted a tall, dark-haired man, perhaps fifty years of age, in shirtsleeves and a modest necktie. He walked over and greeted Susan warmly, they knew each other professionally. Susan introduced me as "a sociology professor who is traveling with me this year," and the counselor, Frank Melucci, led us into the counseling office. It was a large facility—I could discern at least four generously sized rooms—and its purpose evidently included considerably more than college guidance. One room had the appearance of a job-placement office; along one wall was a row of plastic boxes labeled "Career Clusters," with each box containing literature for a particular field of work. I noticed a fat book on one table titled *Occu-Facts*. In a second room were many posters advertising particular colleges. I would see hundreds of these posters during my travels, because virtually every college and university in the country produces one for mailing to guidance offices like this one. I noted that most of the posters here at Handeville were from institutions with humbler reputations than the College's.

I knew from having been on the road a bit already, and from talking with several officers, that the ideal high school visit went something like this: You arrived on time and the counselor, with whom you already had at least some acquaintance, took a few minutes to chat with you. Ideally he or she had handpicked a few students who were in the ballpark of the College's academic profile and who already had some inkling of interest in the school. The physical setting in which you met with the students was relatively quiet and removed from visual distractions. You were given a good twenty minutes or so of uninterrupted time to talk to these kids about the

College and about the details of the application process. Even if they didn't know a thing about your particular school, ideally the kids knew something about academically selective schools in general and about liberal arts colleges in particular. They had at least some sense, in other words, of how the game of competitive admissions is played, and of the different prizes for which they might compete.[4]

Officers only rarely experienced this ideal when they were on the road in real life, and in general the likelihood of experiencing it diminished the farther away one moved, in socioeconomic distance, from guidance offices in wealthy communities. During our first few minutes at Handeville High, Susan Latterly and I were doing pretty well. We had arrived on time. We had seen the counselor and had been granted some time for a friendly exchange. After that, though, our luck quickly gave out.

There were no students to see us. Mr. Melucci offered what I would soon learn was a standard apology—*I'm so sorry we don't have any students to meet with you today*—but he did have a nonstandard explanation. We had come at homeroom hour, during which a Halloween costume contest was being broadcast on the school's closed-circuit television station. I imagined it might be hard for any college rep to compete with that. Mr. Melucci invited us to stay for the broadcast, and the three of us sat, uncomfortably at first, then gradually more at ease, as the fifteen-minute program ran its course. We swapped quips about the hilarity of the costumes. I was particularly amused to learn that beneath the fiction of a chain-smoking rock-and-roll star lurked the school psychologist.

While she watched, Susan culled through the folder in which Handeville kept information and promotional material about the College. It is common practice for guidance offices to keep such files, and a common courtesy to invite visiting reps to update the contents. Susan plucked out the old brochures. "These are going home to the archives," she said wryly, replacing the dated items with glossy new ones whose design had been hired out to a fashionable marketing agency. I thought of the countless times Susan's little task had been carried out by other admissions officers, all those file folders resting quietly in the guidance offices of thousands of high schools, their contents perennially creeping out of date. Their maintenance was just one of the many administrative costs inherent in a higher education system structured as a competitive market. Officers take for granted that if students and their families are going to choose a school, they must have information about it, and that any printed or electronic information has a limited shelf life. It always has to be updated. The whole system makes for a lot of clerical work.

Once the television was turned off our conversation shifted into a kind of trade-show mode. Susan asked about the profile of Handeville's senior class. How many students went on to four-year colleges directly after graduating? About 48 percent, Melucci said, just under half. And where did they go? The largest numbers attended several regional campuses of the state's public university system, he said; significant numbers also attended flagship public universities in the region.

"How about the kids who would meet the College's profile," Susan asked directly, "kids in the top 10 percent of the class?"

A few looked at the region's Ivy League institution each year, Melucci said. He didn't specify any other schools. He added that he would love to send kids the College's way if any showed an interest. "I'd love to hear about anything new that you have going on there," he added. Susan took the opportunity to talk a bit about the College's recent curriculum changes and some new programs specifically designed for first- and second-year students. "Sounds interesting," he responded, only cordially. He had no further questions.

It was quickly becoming evident to everyone that the visit should be drawing to a close. After a few more pleasantries and an answered question about driving directions, we were on our way. "It was nice that we were able to see him," Susan said after we had left. "If he hadn't seen us coming in, in the hall, we might not have seen him at all. But since he saw us and then there were no students I think he probably felt obligated to talk with us." There was no hint of complaint or sarcasm in Susan's voice.

Back at the car in the chilly sunshine, she volunteered, "A friend of mine just took a job in the counseling office of [another local high school]. She used to be an admissions officer and now she's on the other side of it, and we've joked with her, 'OK, now that you're a guidance counselor you have to be sure and be nice to the AO's!' Because she's seen our side of it. But her caseload [at the high school] is so big that they just don't have the time. She told me that she figured out that she would not have the time to meet with every one of her students for twenty minutes, and get through all of them, in one academic year. Not even twenty minutes each, let alone getting to know them or really helping them with a problem or with college advising. So you're busy all of the time."

I found this particularly sobering, because the high school where Susan's friend worked was widely regarded as one of the best in the region. If counselors were overworked even at a good public high school in a solidly middle-class community, I could only imagine how thin counselor coverage might be as one moved down the socioeconomic ladder. I said, "Overworked all the time, it sounds like."

"Yep. That's right. And the last thing you want is an admissions officer from some college knocking on your door in the middle of the day. . . . If you have kids who are facing real problems, you know, the kids who might be dropping out of school or who are discipline problems, the bottom of your list is going to be . . . the good kid with the high grades who is choosing among four-year colleges."

I thought for a moment about the daily triage of someone in Mr.

Melucci's shoes. The kids who were heading to schools in the College's league were perhaps the least of a counselor's troubles, were perhaps no trouble at all and so might receive less attention than the "problem" kids, the squeaky wheels. Be that as it may, schools like the College are interested only in a typical public high school's relative stars: the kids in the top 10 percent academically, the ones with high test scores, the extraordinary athletes. This fundamental difference between the objectives of college reps and the workplace exigencies of many guidance counselors is what makes school visiting a hit-or-miss operation for admissions officers and interactively awkward for people on both sides of the desk.

Our next appointment was at Sparta-North High School, some twenty minutes away. Susan anticipated seeing there the owner of this morning's forgotten name. We became a bit lost en route, which I found surprising; Susan had lived in this region virtually all of her life and knew this city well. Nevertheless the intricacies of the suburban streetscape can be confusing, especially when one is in a hurry. We did arrive on time, though, pulling into the school's parking lot right near the dot of our 10:25 A.M. appointment. Susan and I exchanged remarks about the appearance of the school, which was easily a notch or two below Handeville in architectural charm. Its cinder-block form abutted a treeless hillside with the hard geometry of a factory or a prison. It looked foreboding even under the ideal conditions of a sunny autumn day.

We made our way through a warren of stairwells and corridors. All of the interior spaces looked the same to us, but we knew we had found the counseling office when we spotted a woman who was honoring Halloween by wearing a sandwich-board résumé. She was one of the guidance counselors, and like her costume she was all business, greeting us briskly (my fieldnotes record no friendly banter, no exchange of names), directing us to one of many tables in the office's converted classroom and then leaving us be. Susan earlier had said that Sparta-North organized all of its rep visits into a "college table" format, in which several reps come simultaneously and are obliged to sit at tables for a full hour regardless of whether any students show up.

We did not have to wait long before we got our one and only inquiry. That checked name came in handy—Lorena did show up to see us just as Susan had suspected she would. Casual and talkative, Lorena seemed more than pleased to talk with us for a full hour. We covered a range of topics: sports (she particularly liked basketball and soccer); other schools she was considering (two of the College's direct competitors); Sparta-North High and her current classes there (especially English and one called "Health"—required but, Lorena thought, very silly); and the sciences, which Lorena liked especially. Susan encouraged Lorena to return to the College for an overnight visit. Admissions would be happy to arrange it, Lorena had simply to call in advance.

The ringing of a class bell ended our conversation, pleasantries were extended all around, and Susan and I were on our way. Would Lorena likely be admitted? I asked in the car. Susan wasn't sure. Lorena's academic record was good but not excellent, she did not have any particularly strong extracurricular accomplishment, and she likely would be costly in terms of financial aid. In the argot of the office, Lorena *didn't bring us much.* She was not an academic star. She was white, female, and local. She would cost the College some money.

Susan had expressed no particular sentiment for either of the first two schools we had visited that morning, but she seemed to hold our third stop, Paul Robeson High School, in particular esteem. "It's got a real interesting mix of students," she said. I knew that "interesting mix" was not merely a cover term for *minority kids.* Traversing the halls at our previous stop had revealed a large minority enrollment at Sparta-North too, but Susan had no special praise for that school. Robeson's curb appeal further piqued my interest. Perched at the top of a hill and surrounded by mature trees, the lines of its aging modernist architecture still retained their dignity. At least on the evidence of outward appearances, this was a school people cared about.

Our appointment was for 12:30. We arrived during the bustling few minutes between class periods, but Susan knew her way to the counseling office so we quickly found our destination despite the rivers of young people streaming through the halls. Just as we reached the office she spotted a middle-aged man and greeted him with a smile. The guidance counselor returned the welcome; he and Susan evidently had some prior familiarity. He appeared to be in a hurry. He said he would "try to make the meeting if he could," then quickly dissolved into the activity around him. We did not see him again.

On the upside, a number of Robeson students showed up to see us. Susan began by asking people where they were in their college search—were they looking for big schools or small ones, liberal arts colleges or research universities? No one had a ready answer. Some said they didn't know. At that instant it was clear that these the kids were not on track for selective college admission. It was October 31. Early Decision deadlines at the most competitive schools were either twenty-four hours away (November 1) or two weeks away (November 15). If seniors did not even know what kind of school they might be interested in by now, it was virtually too late for them to commence the search and application gamut leading to a highly selective college. I watched as Susan shifted her posture, changed her tape. "The College is a liberal arts school," she began. "That means the education that we offer you is not intended for any particular occupation or career." Instead, she explained, the idea behind the liberal arts is to provide students with skills that they can take into any field in their adult lives. She went on to talk about other ways that liberal arts colleges, which tend to be small and intimate, differ from large research universities, many of which are great schools in cosmopolitan communities but where it is harder to receive individualized instruction. It was the sort of information that counselors at competitive private high schools might have given their students a year and a half earlier.

Like she had back at Handeville High, as we were leaving Susan said about the Robeson counselor: "I'm glad we bumped into him, or we might not have seen him." By the standards I would absorb from the officers in time, our trip that day had been a modest success. "We want to make sure that these schools keep us in mind, remind them that we would be happy to see applicants from them," is how Susan had put it in the car. "We want to keep the channel open."

Keeping the channel open is considerably easier at schools serving children from affluent families, the costly private and well-funded public schools where college guidance is the top priority of richly resourced guidance offices. Beth Cole, one of the junior officers, had said as much to me the previous summer while she was planning her own fall travel. She explained why it was much easier to make visits to private high schools:

> So many times at the public schools, you show up and there is no one to talk with you. There are no students, either the visit wasn't announced or it was announced but the counselor didn't, you know, go out and find the kids who might be interested in you. So maybe they put a sign up or something, but it's a crap shoot whether anyone will come. Or you may not even see the counselor. So it can be frustrating. Not all of the public schools are like that. Some of them have very elaborate college counseling programs, and they're easier for us to work with. A lot of the suburban schools are like that. And you know at these schools and the private schools, you go [and] you will

see the counselor, the counselor will have arranged for the students to get out of class to talk with you. They're set up to work with us. So it's more efficient for us.

This is how the work exigencies of admissions officers interact with a stratified system of secondary education. High schools serving affluent families have the means to create favorable conditions for admissions officers to do their work. The conditions include guidance counselors with caseloads small enough to know individual kids particularly well, counselors whose primary job is to get students into selective colleges, counselors with enough time and knowledge to prescreen potential applicants for particular schools. It is not just, as others have argued, that privileged applicants enjoy counselors who are able to pull strings with admissions officers.[5] It is also, and more fundamentally, that generous counseling dramatically lowers the search costs inherent in finding solid applicants for particular schools. The fact that both prospective students *and* college personnel benefit from good guidance counseling suggests how fundamental this service is to the structure of the entire admissions enterprise.

Earlier that fall I had gotten a glimpse of what first-class guidance counseling looks like when I accompanied Alan Albinoni, another junior officer, on several days of travel in the orbit of two large eastern cities. Our itinerary was almost exclusively filled with private high schools. The one exception, and the first stop on a tightly scheduled morning, was a public high school serving an affluent suburb. The school's tidy, generously sized building was ringed by tennis courts and several manicured playing fields. Its parking lot, where Alan and I stood and chatted for a few minutes upon our early arrival, was tastefully set back from the tree-lined boulevards intersecting near the main entrance. I said a word about the top-drawer impression the school exuded upon arrival. Alan concurred.

Alan used his tiny window of time in the parking lot to do a quick check of the file for this high school. The College keeps files on hundreds of schools across the country, and around the globe, with which it has had contact. They are vital tools in the maintenance of good relationships with high schools. The files include statistical profiles and promotional literature generated by the high schools specifically for college admissions personnel; notes written by officers on prior visits, with information as varied as driving directions, ad hoc impressions of guidance officers and the student body; and information about applications received from the high school in recent years. The files enable officers to quickly discern "how we've done here lately," as Alan put it, with the number, relative quality, and yield rate of applications from a particular school. A well-maintained file enables even rookie officers to know the sort of place they are entering and to predict the kind of reception they will encounter inside.

Officers often try to customize each visit a bit. While planning the trip back on campus, Alan noted that a student from this particular school had enrolled at the College last year. Alan e-mailed the student and said that he would be visiting the student's alma mater, how was everything going, might Alan bring greetings to the kid's guidance counselor back home? Alan had printed out the affirmative e-mail response as a reminder to deploy the tidbit of cultivated news with the counselor when the time came. *Kid X says hello, I just heard from him, he's doing great this year.*

The high school's spotless interior belied its daily service to eleven hundred students, nearly 90 percent of whom would go straight to college upon graduation. Facilitating their transition was a large guidance office staffed with multiple officers and located in a spacious facility that apparently had been freshly renovated. In the comfortable waiting area, the furniture felt and smelled new. The library of school catalogs included one of the College's. A television and VCR were dedicated to the viewing of college information videos, which were shelved nearby. There was a receptionist, who responded to Alan's inquiry with "Oh, yes, the College, you're in here," while directing us to a conference room equipped with a large table and perhaps a dozen nicely upholstered swivel chairs.

We had a brief and friendly exchange with one of the guidance counselors, whom Alan seemed to know. Alan offered the gift of the greeting from the former student, and the officer responded with what sounded like a largely professional enthusiasm: "Great, great." Meanwhile about nine students filed in. Over the course of our half-hour visit it became clear that several kids already had the College on their radar screens. Campus visits had been scheduled, friends now in attendance consulted, Early Decision considered. Students had specific questions. A young woman inquired if an SAT score of 1150 would be sufficient for admission. Answer: "No single score will get you in or keep you out of the College," Alan said. A young man wanted to know if it was better to get relatively lower grades in harder classes, such as AP and honors courses, or relatively higher grades on a weaker curriculum. Answer: Equivocation. "We certainly would like to see people taking the most challenging courses they can, relative to the opportunities in their schools. But we also want high grades." After thank-yous and keep-in-touches all around, we were off to our next stop.

Alan drove while I navigated. He said several times during our trip how much easier it was to move between destinations with a second person in the car. With me along, he didn't have to worry about the clock, the next visit, the directions, and the road all on his own. If we kept up the good teamwork "we might even get lunch," he said cheerily. The midday meal could easily get sacrificed to the contingencies of the schedule, because as a rule officers tried to fit in as many visits as possible between the beginning and ending of a typical school day, roughly 8:30 A.M. to 3 P.M. Students could not be expected to arrive at school early for a college rep, and afterschool hours were usually booked with sports, music practice, and other commitments. Even so, it could be difficult to see many of the strongest kids during school hours. Serious students were sometimes reluctant to miss class.

However, the most important purpose of the visits was not the students but the counselors, at least as Alan explained it to me. My fieldnotes from this trip read:

> Alan says that the real role of traveling is to maintain relations with the school counselors, not the kids. Why? Because the AO's [admissions officers] have ongoing relationships with the counselors, not one-shot ones, and because the counselors serve as brokers for kids over the long term. Favors get exchanged over multiple years, e.g., [the College gets] several strong candidates from a single school over a couple of years, then maybe [it returns] the favor down the line by admitting a weaker candidate that the counselor really wants as an admit. Ideally, it seems, quids pro quo develop over time between the counselors and the AO's. Thus actually seeing the counselors serves to maintain those relationships, and also gives counselors the opportunity to talk with AO's about bad calls. . . . As Alan says, "You want to give the counselors the opportunity to talk to us about bad judgments we might have made, or to clear up miscommunication." [I ask] "Because you have an ongoing relationship with these folks, right?" "Right, exactly" [he responds].

Here is why Susan Latterly counted our Halloween visits successful despite their apparently lackluster returns. No students had showed up at Handeville High, but Susan got a good half hour of face time with the counselor. At Robeson High she had at least made human contact. She had recognized the counselor in the hallway, greeted him warmly, shaken his hand. She had kept the channel open.

The roads were becoming more curvy, the foliage more leafy. A realtor would have said we were headed upmarket. The rest of the day would be filled with visits to private schools. Our next stop, Ina

Tokel School for Girls, hugged a ravine on what looked like the grounds of a former estate. The guidance office was not nearly as elaborate as the one at our last stop, but given that Ina Tokel enrolls seven hundred students in grades K–12 (average class size: 15), a single person in one airy office was probably sufficient for top-notch college counseling. I suspected that Cara Hathaway, the polished, extremely articulate, thirty-something woman who greeted us upon arrival, would not have it any other way.

Ms. Hathaway had arranged for three girls to talk with us that morning. They arrived, as if on cue, just minutes after Alan and I had settled in. The subsequent exchange was subtly managed. Cara sat at a desk only slightly removed from our conversation. She gave off the appearance of working, there was a pen in her hand and paper beneath it, but it was evident from her eyes that she was tracking every word of the exchange taking place alongside her. Occasionally she would prompt one of the girls to ask a particular question or talk about a particular interest or accomplishment. Her interventions were friendly but firm, as if she were a beloved nanny assigned the task of ushering her charges into college. It was impossible to say if the girls complied with Cara's wishes out of desire or obligation or some mix of the two. What was clear was that the girls knew their roles in this little scene, that Cara knew her actors well, and that no one besides Cara was directing the show. "I bet you'd want someone like Cara Hathaway doing college guidance for your kid, right?" Alan said when we were back in the car.

The residential enclave we were now traversing was famous for its large number of costly private schools. It did not take long for us to arrive at Corbett Academy, another girls' school—older, larger, and more famous than Ina Tokel. Once again we pulled into the parking lot with a few minutes to spare. Once again Alan checked the file, scanned the data. The College had received a few applications from Corbett girls in recent years and had even accepted one or two, but there had been little luck with yield. Alan looked at the academic numbers of the Corbett students who had applied. He shared the page with me and said with a grin, "We're not getting Corbett's finest."

In the world of selective admissions, we had gone upmarket. Corbett consistently sent its top performers to places like Berkeley and Stanford and the top of the Ivy League. For the most part, schools in the College's own peer group only had a shot at girls nearer the middle of Corbett's class. Or below the middle. Still, by most standards this excellent school's modest achievers were very good admissions prospects, which was why we were visiting. Even Corbett's less fine would enter college well prepared academically, and their generally affluent families could absorb the College's full tuition and board costs with little, if any, financial aid.

Sure enough, the two students who showed up to talk with us were not the most impressive high school seniors I had ever met. Alan would concur with my assessment afterward in the car. The College's recent track record with Corbett would probably not be reversed this year. However, the girls' guidance counselor, a cheery woman perhaps in her fifties, made a much stronger impression. She greeted us with a wide smile, she was so very glad we had come. She had little to say about the students we had just met but was eager to engage in conversation about what she saw as the hype developing around Early Decision in her field, how as far as she was concerned it was just getting way out of hand, with even modestly selective schools admitting up to half of their entering classes early. It was changing the whole system, she thought, and not for the better, what with all the anxiety it was producing among students and parents. Alan nodded his head and added a few of his own points. This was shoptalk, of the official variety. It was different in content from the conversation Susan Latterly had with Joe Melucci on Halloween, but it communicated exactly the same thing. It said: *We are colleagues. We inhabit the same world.*

Our next stop, Owens Hill School, was only a few blocks away from Corbett. I was beginning to appreciate how distinctive statistically similar schools could be. Corbett and Owens Hill served more or less the same affluent demographic, but the feel of the two schools was instantly palpable. Corbett had been walnut paneling, uniforms, towering trees, the patina of age and old money. Owens Hill felt lighter and cheerier somehow, still proper and preppy but in a more relaxed way. Its freshly painted hallways and stairwells bubbled with young people's energy. Then again, my rosy impression likely was biased by the warmest reception Alan and I had enjoyed all morning. The two counselors who met us, attractive women old enough to have children in college themselves, talked with Alan as if the three of them went way back.

In a sense they did. There were several strands in the tie between the College and this school. First, Alan had been traveling in this region for some time and had cultivated ongoing exchanges with many of the counselors on this circuit. Second, Owens Hill had allowed the College to use its facilities during a regional "interview night," an event in which admissions officers assemble local alumni to interview prospective students in their home cities. Such sharing of real estate was a clear indication that the high school and the College occupied comparable status niches in their respective organizational communities. On neither side would reputations be tainted by such an association. Finally, the ace in the hole: one of Owens Hill's guidance counselors had sent her own child to the College.

In the vernacular of selective admissions, the College and Owens Hill *had a thing going*. "We've got a little bit of a thing going with Owens Hill," Alan had said in the car. At the time I thought it was merely Alan's provocative turn of phrase, but hearing it several times from several people in subsequent months encouraged me to see it as a more general term. Having a thing going means that exchanges between the College and a sending high school have developed some consistency. The College, for its part, has enjoyed a consistent stream of solid applicants from the high school with which the thing is going, and consistently has seen some of these kids matriculate. The high school has developed a reputation for *sending us good kids,* another locution common among the officers. The high school in turn enjoys the positive disposition of admissions officers toward applicants sent their way.

Getting a thing going requires tender courtship, because these affairs are propelled by the same engine that often derails them, namely, status competition. On the one hand, officers seek the very best kids they can get from any particular high school. The College does not want a reputation among blue-chip guidance counselors as a port of last resort, a safety school. On the other hand, guidance counselors at competitive high schools face strong incentives to get their students admitted to the most selective colleges possible. At the very best high schools in the nation, admission to selective colleges and universities is the *raison d'être*. Competitive admissions are a big part of why families pay such steep prices (in property taxes, or tuition) for excellent high schools in the first place. Realistic parents and guidance counselors understand that not every senior will be admitted to Harvard or Stanford; even so, the goal is *always* to get kids admitted to better schools.[6]

In other words, the status concerns of admissions officers and guidance counselors are in fundamental conflict: counselors want admission offers from the most competitive colleges possible, so in general they push even their weaker applicants as high up the selectivity pecking order as they can go. Admissions officers want the most accomplished kids possible, so in general they seek the best applicants they can get from any particular school. This conflict of interest creates circumstances in which it is easy for both parties to send mixed signals. Gestures of diplomacy can easily be misinterpreted. Tentative efforts at cooperation can easily go awry. Getting a thing going means finding a sweet spot whereupon cooperation between admissions officers and guidance counselors can be mutually beneficial. The benefits of such relationships, and their precariousness, are what make them so prized. Wise officers and counselors attend to established things with care.[7]

This is the dynamic that warmed up the greeting Alan Albinoni and I received at Owens Hill. It is probably why, throughout our visit, we were kept in the presence of one genuflecting senior who, the counselors happily confided, was considering applying to the College under Early Decision. It is perhaps why the student was genuflecting, perhaps why he took the time (or was given it) to take me on a tour of campus while Alan and the counselors talked business. It is almost surely why there was business to talk about. Gifts of attention were being offered and received under presumptions of mutual goodwill. A thing was going.

Critical readers might see all of the above as evidence of bias, even discrimination, on the part of admissions officers who systematically favor schools serving affluent families. What about all those other high schools, in lower-income rural areas and at the cores of our faded industrial cities, where, doubtless, dedicated teachers and guidance counselors work with strivers who dream of seats at schools like the College? Why don't officers spend more time looking for them? The answer is that recruitment to selective schools is a deceptively complex information problem, one that is virtually impossible for admissions officers to solve without the cooperation of people on the other side of the desk.[8]

Consider that the College already pays many of the search costs inherent in finding qualified students for their institutions. Good money is spent on viewbooks and catalogs and sophisticated Web sites intended to spread word of the school far and wide. Mass mailings are hardly free. The College spends tens of thousands of dollars annually to cover officers' travel expenses, not to mention the wages that compensate officers for the hundreds of hours they spend on the road. Because resources always are limited, officers tend to invest where they are likely to see some return. Alan and I could have spent our travel days visiting urban public high schools, but in all likelihood the fruit of our labors would have been comparable to what Susan Latterly and I accomplished on Halloween. Returns, both to the College specifically and to the ideal of college access generally, probably would have been small.

Quite simply, visiting officers cannot connect with guidance counselors and high school students all by themselves. The best-laid travel plans can get an officer only as far as a high school's front door. After that, officers are entirely dependent on other people's schedules and other people's knowledge about what a school visit means. Officers cannot by themselves rearrange the workplace priorities of guidance counselors. They cannot by themselves schedule a block of uninterrupted time to talk with students or figure out which kids they should see. They cannot do the advance counseling students need to really profit from time spent with a visiting officer. Officers cannot, in other words, pay all of the costs of reaching qualified applicants on their own. Instead they try to do the best they can in light of their always limited resources.[9]

Not surprisingly, officers' first tendency is to visit high schools at which they already have invested in solutions to their chronic information problem, places where the College's reputation already has been developed, where guidance counselors already are known on a first-name basis, where trickles of solid applications already have begun to flow. When there is room in the itinerary to add a school or two, it is hardly surprising that officers seek out venues with the guidance services that make connecting with kids possible. What *is* surprising, in light of their chronic information problem, is that officers so consistently visited schools serving less-privileged, less-well-counseled students. To be sure, my day with Alan Albinoni was

filled entirely with visits to affluent schools with upmarket guidance
offices. But the Halloween travel with Susan Latterly was a different
matter. That day was an effort to keep the channel open at schools
where the College had a much harder time getting its signal across.

I learned firsthand about how the chronic information problem
shapes student recruitment when I traveled on my own during the
second autumn of my research, a seven-day tour of duty that included schools in the Portland (Oregon), Seattle, and Vancouver areas. During the year of my fieldwork, the officer responsible for this
territory had moved abroad. I had dropped unsubtle hints to the senior deans that I would "love to be able to recruit out there," my
hometown was in the territory, it would be fun to give recruitment
travel a fuller try. Perhaps because they needed coverage of the region anyway, perhaps because the College drew few students from
the territory and so had little to lose, I was given the job.

I here confess to a considerable bit of arrogance going in. I
had come to think of the Pacific Northwest as an untapped opportunity for the College. The region was growing, and its cities had
many prosperous upper-middle-class families. Unlike back East, it
had only a handful of selective private colleges. Compared with California's highly competitive public research institutions, entrance
requirements at the flagship Universities of Oregon and Washington
were relatively modest. I suspected it would be easy for schools
like the College to take some of the cream from this region's high
schools. All we had to do was get out there and skim it.

The first step was to decide on which high schools to visit. The
seasoned officers instructed me to "go to the school files"—the carefully maintained manila folders like the ones Alan Albinoni had
consulted in the car—and to look at the itineraries of officers who
had covered the same territory in recent years. In general I was
encouraged to visit schools from which we had seen interest in
the past. Where had we gotten applicants? Good ones? Matriculations? Aha, I thought, here was systematic bias: the College favored

schools that had sent it business before. How on earth, I thought to myself, could it cultivate a larger or more diverse applicant pool if it kept recruiting at the same schools year after year? I also was encouraged to visit particular schools: Richardson, where we had an especially close tie with a guidance counselor; Holy Father Academy, from whence a current College student had come; and Ida B. Wells High School, one of those special public schools with strong academic track records that officers fondly described with words like *urban, diverse,* and *interesting.* Val Marin mentioned to me several times that Ida Wells was "a really interesting school" with a lot of "real interesting students." I also added a few schools in my hometown, public high schools serving the upper-middle-class families that, I was growing ever more certain, selective colleges coveted most.

Travel planning is not simple. Officers are obliged by the permissions and timetables of guidance counselors. One cannot show up unanticipated or at a time of one's own choosing. Itineraries must be plotted with sufficient travel time between schools, no small feat in unfamiliar cities. Visits can be made only during normal school hours, and there is a strong incentive to schedule as many visits in each travel day as possible, to make good use of invested time and expenses. Coordinating the schedules of multiple schools while plotting a manageable journey through time and space can be quite a puzzle. A single change can unravel a whole sequence of carefully arranged appointments. I had a sense of accomplishment and relief when the planning was done.

I had been particularly eager to visit three high schools in my own hometown, schools I had known rather intimately as a teenager, in neighborhoods whose demographics neatly matched those of the College's typical student. I prepared carefully for these visits. I contacted guidance offices in advance. Per office routine, I made sure that our office's secretarial staff sent out informational posters and confirmed my appointments. I showed up on time.

I had little success. My writings on forms titled "High School Visit Report," the completion of which is another part of officers' standard procedure, betray the lackluster returns. Of School One I wrote:

> Lots of work to do here—most grads [attend] 4 year schools but majority go to regional state universities. That said, this is an <u>affluent, growing</u> community & is probably worth a bit more effort. I suggest 1) a visit next year and then one every 2–3; 2) that we do [a regional] college fair (counselor recommends); that we invite counselor on a motorcoach tour. FYI, though, [name of school] seems not to be pushing kids to look East; consider counselor caseload of 400/1.

Given his hundreds of students it is perhaps remarkable that I got any time at all with a counselor at School One. Of School Two I wrote:

> Total washout—no one signed up for my visit, so no students. Didn't speak with guidance counselor, rather [with] the secretary. I remain confident that [names of schools] are worth the effort, but we need to do more for name recognition here.

Of School Three:

> A disappointment. . . . [It is] largely white, upper-middle class, suburban. 75% attend college (2 or 4 year) & about half of these go out of state—"mostly Oregon, Washington, California," says the secretary . . .—the only adult I got to see. Just one kid—a real slacker, probably cutting class, didn't even fill out [an information] card. We have a girl from [this school], Ella Joseph '02. . . . Demographics make it worth a periodic visit—these are <u>our</u> kids & if they're thinking East they should think of us.

Note the underlined <u>our.</u> Note the exasperation it conveys. This entry was written on the second of my two days in this city, my hometown, the one where I was best equipped with the local knowledge that I arrogantly had thought would help me skim cream. Schools

One, Two, and Three were ones that I had made sure to include on my schedule, on the naive assumption that a visit would automatically be met with student interest and counselor time.

I had better luck at a couple of the private schools in town. My time at the Richardson School, for example, was fruitful:

> A great visit—met with [name of counselor], who is friends with [someone at the College]. She has been to the College several times, but not on the motorcoach tour—& would like to come. Terrific school—"elite" . . . but very laid back culturally. Met w/ 1 very interested kid . . . from whom we probably will get an app. Found us because of our environmental studies program; I will be eager to follow up. Currently we have a Richardson student, [name], '02. Richardson should be our beachhead in [this] area, given the connections. Let's go every year.

Note the underlined us. Note how it conveys surprise and pleasure at meeting a student who had sought out the College, rather than the other way around. Note the "connections" I identify between the College and Richardson, and how they serve as evidence for a claim that the College should start any larger recruitment initiatives there, rather than at Schools One, Two, or Three.

I also met with positive returns at Tall Pines Academy, a school that enjoyed a reputation on a par with Richardson:

> Great counselor who has been on the motorcoach tour recently. Says we have a Tall Pines student currently at the College. Must look up name (class of '05). 3 students: Darren Everson, who plays lacrosse; Roger Chang, Korean I believe, interested in business. Most interest from Le Po, a Vietnamese national. . . . Tall Pines could be a beachhead in [this city]. [Counselor] knows us well & seems to like us, too. Every year.

Note the underlined every year, the emphatic advice I give to the next officer traveling in this region. Note how I advise that priority be given in the future to schools that had sent the College students in the past, to counselors who had handpicked particular kids for me to meet, to counselors who 'knew the College well and seemed to like [it].' Lessons of experience were beginning to kick in.

I also had success at some of the public schools I visited, such as Palisades Heights High, located in an affluent suburb of a different city:

> An excellent public w/ a well-organized guidance office, & a strong College interest—every year. Spoke w/ 3 students, 2 only briefly, b/c of [sports] practices. Tina Moore, w/ whom I talked further, is strong on first impression so let's see the numbers. Let's also try to get [these counselors] on the motorcoach tour. . . . <u>LOTS</u> of potential here— let's do it.

At Palisades Heights I had enjoyed a reception comparable to those I had received at costly private schools. Note my emphasized <u>LOTS</u> of potential.

Then there was Ida B. Wells High, the "interesting" public school Val Marin had specifically encouraged me to visit. Ida Wells was housed in an imposing turn-of-the century structure near the heart of one of the region's most cosmopolitan cities. The sleek skyscrapers of a vital downtown were a stone's throw from Wells's address in a neighborhood that had seen better days. The school itself was very impressive. Its hallways were boisterous with young life but also orderly. Its student body was multicolored. On the one hand, I imagined sending my own child there. On the other hand, there was the guidance office, of which I wrote:

> An interesting case. Ida Wells is a respected magnet school—very heterogeneous racially/culturally. Many kids apply to privates [colleges]. Dara Carroll is <u>very</u> new to college counseling, e.g., couldn't pronounce [name of elite eastern school] and didn't seem to realize that [College X and College Y] are in the same league. But she's nice, smart, & educable. Seems merely to be directing traffic currently—

one guidance counselor for the entire school (plus interns). Expresses interest in the motorcoach tour, will hook her up for that. This could be a good source school for <u>interesting,</u> multicultural kids. Met w/ one girl, a serious junior [athlete]. Will keep in touch. . . . Annual visits might help with Carroll—she's an opportunity that <u>some</u> college should take.

Ida Wells had everything the College could want from any high school—strong academic performers with their sights on private schools, multicultural kids, and a good reputation in a city with lots of cream to skim. The only thing it lacked was the counseling that would link its students with the selective schools coveting them.

My experience suggests that the relatively weak student flows from less-advantaged high schools to selective colleges are not a function of race or class discrimination per se. They are, rather, the consequence of variation in the organizational infrastructure linking students to selective schools. Selective colleges and universities rely heavily on high school guidance counseling to prep students for the college search, and also to help particular admissions officers locate particularly suitable applicants. The recruitment choices officers make may easily be misinterpreted by critics because the amount and quality of guidance counseling varies directly with the socioeconomic privilege of the people being served. But the mechanism through which this privilege is rendered an admissions advantage is not discrimination. It is information.

Flying home, I found it easy to recall every student I had met. There was Brian Scott, the earnest kid at Richardson who was particularly interested in the College's environmental studies program; Le Po, the foreign national at Tall Pines with only pretty good grades and test scores, shy but determined; Hal Cohen, who, at the tender age of fifteen, had started his own philanthropy, now legally incorporated and thriving, the kid who would be a shoo-in for one of the College's generous merit scholarships; Tina Moore at Palisades Heights, whose solid grades, modest financial need, and exotic zip code made her the sort of applicant the College would be happy to see in its Early Decision pool; Debra Abramson, who had offered me a copy of her A-laden high school transcript, a résumé detailing her many extracurricular activities, and flattering words about the beauty of the College's campus, which she already had been out East to visit. If any of these young people ended up applying to the College, they would be more than a sheet of statistics when I sat down to review their applications. They would be *people,* with faces and physical demeanors and personalities, people in whom I had invested time and effort in meeting, and who had similarly invested in meeting me.

I also recalled the guidance counselors. There was the dismissive man at Holy Father Academy who, in the thirty seconds he took to brush me off, asked me to "say hello to Liam Rizer for me"—a little signal that if Holy Father needed to, it could talk directly to my boss. There were the two counselors who hovered over me like a visiting grandson when I visited Riverwood Country Day School, alma mater of storied electronics entrepreneurs. There was Dara Carroll at Ida Wells—well meaning, poorly informed, and almost surely overworked. It was too bad, I thought, because I knew that officers back East would kill for better access to her students. There was Linda Romanelli at Palisades Heights, who had e-mailed in advance with regrets that she would be unable to meet me but who, in the parking lot on the way to her car, upon seeing me and merely suspecting the nature of my errand, had walked up to me and said, "You must be the gentleman from the College. So nice to meet you." It was easy to recall how that recognition had made me feel: welcome, respected, on the radar screen.

Flying home, it did not occur to me to think about the hundreds of high schools it had never occurred to me to visit—in the rural districts that saw most of their graduates go straight into the workforce or to community colleges, in the urban neighborhoods without the luxury of an Ida B. Wells, neighborhoods where few, if any, kids imagined attending expensive private colleges on the other side of the country. It did not occur to me that I had traversed remarkably narrow demographic slivers of the cities I had visited: affluent suburbs, wealthy urban enclaves, and one or two celebrated pockets of academic excellence in downmarket neighborhoods. The entire journey had been an elite exercise.

Red Carpets

Many institutions send admissions officers to high schools, but they also move people in the other direction, bringing guidance counselors to the institutions' own turf. For many years the College had cooperated with other selective private schools in its immediate region, arranging sequential half-day visits to multiple campuses for literal busloads of guidance counselors from around the country. Twice yearly, a comfortable rented motorcoach carried some forty counselors on the three-day journey. Recruitment travel in reverse, the motorcoach tours enabled the College's officers to convey good impressions of the school to a highly consequential audience. Officers hoped that these visitors would collect rosy pictures of the College, keep them stored in their mental data banks, and call them up when advising potential students and their parents.

The motorcoach tours are important parts of the College's recruitment effort for several reasons. First, they enable officers to connect efficiently with very large numbers of potential applicants. A guidance counselor's perception of a school is potentially available to that counselor's entire student caseload each year. The relatively small investment in underwriting counselor travel can accrue returns over many years as the visitors use their firsthand impressions to steer potential applicants toward particular schools. Second, the motorcoach tours provide good opportunities for a college to disseminate its news. The new dormitory, performing arts center, or study-abroad program can be presented with fanfare to captive and influential audiences. Third, the tours provide yet more opportunities for admissions officers to sustain face-to-face relationships. Over beers at the happy hour or wine at dinner (there is never a shortage of alcohol), officers can thicken ties with guidance counselors that might somehow be of use down the road.

In the first season of my fieldwork Val Marin asked me to help with arrangements for an upcoming motorcoach tour. I was flattered and a little bit nervous, but of course I agreed. To my relief I quickly learned that this wheel had been invented so long ago and had rolled through campus so many times that it was virtually on autopilot. The basic format and schedule of the visits were the same from year to year, which made it easier for staff at all of the cooperating institutions to put on their shows. My job was essentially to fill in some local blanks. As usual there would be the faculty panel directly after the campus tour; I was to hone the topic and choose the talking heads. As usual there would a happy hour in a local pub; I was to cajole the manager into letting us offer other, better wines than were usually on the menu. As usual there would be a buffet dinner; I was to negotiate with the caterer.

The mood for motorcoach tours was officially cheery, upbeat. E-mail communications with staff at other schools on the tour were liberally sprinkled with smiley faces and exclamation points. There seemed to be an official consensus that the motorcoach tours were "fun." They also were serious business. No details were left to chance. Val conferred with Liam Rizer about the precise route the bus would take from the interstate to the College's campus, so that the local landscape would be viewed from its most attractive angles. She conferred with Susan Latterly about what sort of gift should

be offered to the counselors—T-shirts? coffee mugs? college pen-
nants?—and to me confessed dismay that the gift baseline was a
moving target. "Each year it seems we're upping the ante a little
bit," she said bemusedly. She kept notes from year to year about
small things that would improve subsequent tours. One note titled
"Motorcoach Tour Reminders" had multiple cues for the caterers:
"Make sure that they understand to prepare the caesar salad . . .
Keep penne and roast beef. [Seafood] Newburg not good. Appe-
tizers—good, especially the artichoke dip. [Serve] tiramisu in gob-
lets." Another note advised future organizers on the sufficient number of salt and pepper shakers. This fastidiousness was not a tick
of Val's personality. Quite the contrary. She had a reputation in the
office for being a big-picture sort of person. But when it came to
managing impressions for guidance counselors, no one topped Val
Marin.

During a final check of the room setups, soon before the motorcoach arrived, Val continued to fluff the pillows. We were in a vesti-
bule through which the counselors would be passing several times
while on campus. I glanced at a stand holding an old edition of the
student newspaper and saw that there was a more recent edition,
still tied in its bundle, resting nearby. I moved to replace the old edition with the new one, saying casually that we probably should have
the most recent copies available for the counselors.

"Hmm, isn't that the one where the students are trashing the
new [alcohol] policy?" Val asked wryly, "The one that has the editorial that says 'If you want to have a good time, transfer'?" I pulled a
copy out of the bundle and leafed through the pages. Indeed there
was a page-long editorial expressing the general opinion Val had
paraphrased. Val and I also noted that a humor column included
the word *prophylactic,* prominently printed and very evidently mis-
spelled. She threw me one of her trademark vaudeville scowls and
said, "I don't think so, no."

I took the bundle of newspapers and put it on the floor next to the stand carrying the old editions. Val took it a step further, pushing the bundle back with her foot so that the incriminating new editions were virtually behind the newsstand. "I don't want to make it unavailable," she explained campily, "but I do want to make it a little harder to find." Sure enough, when the arriving counselors piled off the bus and waited in the lobby for their student tour guides, many of them grabbed copies of the older edition of the paper.

Because the motorcoach tours were bit of a junket (the free meals and accommodations, the free-flowing booze, the special treatment, the chance to get out of the office), they were a good way for officers to initiate new relationships with guidance counselors. This is why I had suggested, in my notes on high schools in the Pacific Northwest, that several of the counselors I had met be invited on a tour. It was an offer of hospitality that could help officers get new things going, and it was the kind of experience counselors tended to remember. I subsequently met several counselors during my fieldwork who would make a point of telling me that, yes, they knew the College, they had been on the motorcoach tour, they had had such a good time.

Grand Tours

Val Marin was hardly the only officer to mind the details. A staff meeting I attended in the spring of 2001 included a long conversation about the design of a single piece of outdoor furniture. It was to be positioned at the main entrance to the admissions building and hold maps and other literature about the College for any visitors who might show up when the office was closed. Susan Latterly had put the issue on the meeting agenda, explaining that she would be having workers from the physical plant come over to spec out a replacement for the painted hutch currently in use. What should the new item be like, she asked, commencing a rather large exchange about a rather small cabinet. Should it be mounted on the wall, or on a pedestal? What color should it be? Should it perhaps have Plexiglas doors? Slots for different kinds of brochures? Such issues were the object of more than a few minutes of focused discussion. At one point Alan Albinoni turned to me and quipped, "Chapters 11 and 12, right Mitchell?" It was a joke, about both the topic under consideration and about the notes I was making of it for this book. Alan shared the quip with Liam Rizer, who was sitting between us. One of them looked at me (the notes fail on precisely who) and added a sarcastic "Aren't you glad you're getting all of this?"

The fact of the matter was that I was not only getting it, I was feeling it too. But I said nothing, only grinned. I knew it would not have been my place to mention the many times I had walked through the front door myself and thought, *that hutch doesn't look very good.* It would not have been my place to add an opinion on a related issue, namely, that the potted geraniums at the entrance needed to be looked after more carefully. In the space of nine months, I had come to look at the College's physical campus as an officer might. I was thinking a lot about first impressions and how they could be improved.

By the spring of 2001 I was beginning to appreciate just why the impressions conveyed to the ten thousand visitors received by the College each year were so carefully managed. I had learned that the kids who visited were more likely to be serious about actually attending the College than were those who never made it to campus during their college search. I had learned that prospective students often named their first-choice school on the basis of impressions gleaned during campus visits. I had come to realize that the parents of these visiting students were, in the aggregate, a notably well-heeled lot. They disproportionately lived in the upmarket neighborhoods and sent their children to the tonier high schools in which prevailing opinion could make or break the prestige ambitions of a selective college.

It is conventional wisdom in the world of elite schooling that colleges that may seem comparable on paper can be quite different from one another in real life. Guidance counselors and private admissions consultants consistently encourage their clients to make their final college choices only after they have seen their options firsthand. This advice is intended to correct a chronic information problem confronted by applicants and their families during the college search: the searchers face a choice that they believe is consequential, but they often know little about the choices. This is why there is such a voracious market for college guidebooks and private admissions consultants, and why ranking schemes such as the ones produced by *U.S. News & World Report* garner so much attention. It is why, as when they select a new physician or purchase a home in a new city, people engaged in the college search tend to gather advice from any friends, coworkers, and distant relatives who might have special insight about the available options.[10]

Among those who face the problem of selecting among selective schools, the campus visit is regarded as the ideal and even necessary basis for making informed decisions. The reason is simple. Visits convey a lot of information, in the form of feelings and aesthetics as well as facts. In much the same way that a conversation over coffee tells a love-seeker considerably more about a potential mate than any profile on an Internet database, seeing a campus firsthand enables prospective students to make finer distinctions than are possible on the basis of viewbooks and college guides. This is why selective schools so carefully attend to appearances. Every new campus visitor is another first date.

Guidance counselors and admissions consultants also advise their clients to make campus visits for purely strategic reasons. Visits convey information in both directions. They are an important marker of what admissions officers call "interest," by which they mean something rather specific. Officers regard interest as a tangible quantity, something applicants are presumed to possess more or less of for particular schools. Because so many young people headed toward selective colleges apply to multiple schools and enjoy multiple admission offers, gauging applicants' interest in a particular institution is one way officers try to hedge their bets for the spring yield season. Savvy applicants know to make gestures of interest because they signal to officers that an application is a serious one, that an offer of admission may very well be accepted, that the institution in question is not in the dreaded category of "safety school," a port of last resort.

Officers regarded any contact with the College or its personnel as a marker of interest, and they invested considerable energy in keeping records of these contacts. Students attending information sessions at their high schools were asked to fill out cards with their names and addresses, which subsequently were entered into an office database. E-mail correspondence of any kind was printed in hard copy and added to application files. The application form itself specifically asked students to mark whether they had attended one of the College's information sessions, visited campus, stayed on campus overnight, or had an interview. Among these various expressions of interest, the campus visit was sometimes regarded as a litmus test. Not visiting could cast a shadow over an application, especially if the applicant lived within easy driving distance of the College.

Individual campus visitors often scheduled stops at two or three schools in a single day. Admissions staff took for granted that theirs was but one stop on what often was a very long circuit of visits, a journey sometimes jokingly described as the "grand tour." The phrase is resonant. In the nineteenth and early twentieth centuries, America's upper-class families commonly sent their children on "grand tours" of Europe, an experience intended to polish manners and confer worldly sophistication. That practice faded in tandem with the rise of a different system of overseas study. Since World War II, affluent parents increasingly have relied on elite colleges to arrange their children's "study abroad" in the form of academic terms spent in exotic locations all over the globe. Transnational itineraries are now largely left up to academic professionals. At the same time, ever more family energy is devoted to the stateside college search, which may itself take weeks of parental vacation time and cost no little money.

A typical campus visit lasts a couple of hours. It includes a walking tour, conducted by a paid student worker; an information session akin to those offered at local high schools; and an optional interview with an admissions officer or a paid student intern. Interviews are usually about thirty minutes in duration, after which interviewers "write up" the exchange on a standard form that is subsequently added to the application file. The character and function of these interviews is noteworthy. In the world of paid employment, obtaining an interview is an accomplishment; one "lands" a job interview and celebrates that earlier cuts have been made. In the work world, interviews also tend to be an important part of an employer's evaluation machinery. One can "bomb" an interview and thereby lose a job.

By contrast, interviews at the College were only occasionally influential in determining final admissions decisions.[11] Nevertheless officers believed that the act of having interviews was important, both for applicants and for the College. Having an interview was itself a way of expressing interest. Not having one could suggest an applicant's ambivalence about the school. At the same time the interview provided an opportunity for the College to perform an official commitment to evaluating applicants as individuals. The office invested considerable organizational resources conducting over three thousand interviews each year—as much to affirm the College's commitment to personalized evaluation as to learn more about applicants. Officers hoped that those thousands of interviews sent a message to applicants that, yes indeed, the College appraised them as whole persons.

That the interviews were heavily symbolic explains why officers did not worry about having student interns complete large numbers of them. Who conducted the interviews mattered less than that they happened at all. Nor did level of interviewer skill seem to matter much. College alumni completed hundreds of off-site interviews for the College each year with little or no training. That the interviews were largely symbolic would explain why Liam Rizer had me start conducting them without any instruction whatsoever. Sometime during the first weeks of my fieldwork he handed me a form, pointed me toward an office, and told me to go to it.

There are several reasons why I clearly remember one of my very first interviews. One: It was a beautiful evening in late summer, with fading sunlight fluttering through the main quadrangle's lovely old specimen trees. Two: I was still new to all of this, eager to display my eagerness to pitch in, to take instruction, to learn quickly. Three: My interviewee was somewhat exceptional, a dark-skinned African American girl from an industrial city in the Midwest. She and her parents had pulled into the office's parking lot at the very end of the day, after most of the staff had already gone home. Liam and I had lingered over a meandering conversation. Because I was on hand and available, I took the interview while Liam took care of other business.

I recall that the girl was shy. She sat near the edge of her chair and took me in with her head turned sideways for our entire, somewhat awkward exchange. It seemed we were both unsure of ourselves, if for different reasons. She told me she had learned of the College from the *U.S. News & World Report* rankings. She and her parents had driven out to see the place for themselves.

After the interview Liam and I chatted briefly with the family before thanking them for coming and encouraging their continued interest. We watched as they returned to their car and pulled out of the lot. Would they reconnoiter the campus? Would they come back the next day for a guided tour? Would we see an application? At that moment it was impossible to say, but Liam did know this: "Boy, you don't see that very often. A black family, from out of the region, coming all this way for a campus visit. You don't see that every day."

White families were much more common—well-heeled ones, who arrived with remarkable frequency in Volvo and Mercedes station wagons and luxury SUVs. They often would be fresh from visiting a competitor school, or mindful of the clock for their next appointment down the road. We would offer them coffee and a seat in the office's comfortable parlor while they waited for an information session or a walking tour or an interview to begin. In time I began to pick up on expressions of kinship among people in that waiting room. Their children attended the same high schools back home in Charlotte or Boston or on the Upper East Side. It was uncanny, their summer houses looked out on the same beaches. They were members of the same country clubs. They sent their kids to the same sleep-away camps. Perhaps they had gotten caught in the same blizzard on the way down from that other school, had first crossed paths on the campus tour at Dartmouth a week ago and, what do you know, here they were again. They tended to be happy exchanges, little reminders about the shared inhabitancy of a small world.

chapter four

SPORTS

If you approach the College from a certain angle, its picturesque central campus appears to float, like a stone ship, in a sea of green. You see it first through the golf course, with its lackluster greens, often compared unfavorably with those at rival schools. Then there is the field where the soccer, rugby, and field hockey teams practice, its weedless expanse artfully cross-mowed with a diamond pattern in summer, its evergreen border a backdrop for many viewbook photos of students at serious play. Beyond it are the artificial-green tennis courts, and the football field, its classic open bleachers and old-fashioned press box betraying only a distant relation to the elaborate facilities provided for NCAA Division I programs. And out behind the field house (with its indoor track, hockey rink, squash and basketball courts, natatorium, and state-of-the-art fitness center) is an all-season green on the edge of a hardwood preserve, where lacrosse matches compete annually with the emerald riot of northeastern spring.

Prospective students visiting from a typical suburban high school might be impressed by these amenities, but only if they had not already taken campus tours at several other institutions the College calls peers. As with virtually everything else in U.S. higher education, support for intercollegiate athletics is stratified. Gary Wilcox, the former swimming coach and director of athletics at the College, painted the comparative picture for me during a long interview. We were sitting in his tidy office, just off a vaulted lobby where trophies of recent victories were displayed in tastefully illuminated cabinets. Through an office window I glimpsed the summer color of a leafy quadrangle. The athletics facilities blend seamlessly with the academic buildings of the central campus.

Though well into his forties, Wilcox had the youthful appearance of someone who had spent a lifetime attending to physical fitness, including his own. His guy-next-door good looks were enhanced by a warm smile and welcoming demeanor that likely put prospective students and their parents at ease.

Gary told me that the College's most recent annual athletics budget was just over $2 million. This sum was in addition to the costs of maintaining the athletics physical plant, which fell under different budget lines and remained unknown to me. About 50 percent of the $2 million went to salaries, and much of the rest covered transportation, meals, and lodging for teams traveling off-campus for competitions. Gary assured me that this budget was modest, that in fact it was the second lowest in the league of premier northeastern schools of which the College is a member. The only school with a lower budget was one "with no football team, which is a big expense," he said. "So [our budget is] really not a lot of money." He added that annual per-school sports expenditures in the league topped out at around $4 million.

Gary said he did not want his budget to match those of the biggest spenders, but that he did want the College to at least be in the middle of its pack. "Not at the top, not at the bottom, but in the middle. And this is something that we continually need to talk about [around here]. What do we want from our athletic program?" He continued, without prompting, on a topic that clearly was of importance to him:

[Tony Evers, the College's president] and I talk about this all the time. If he were sitting here today he would say something like, "We want competitive performance in all areas." Well, OK then, how do we support that goal? . . . My thinking is, an excellent athletic program would enhance everything else we do here. Because you know what? Many, many good students are also good athletes. And we lose them to [names of more academically selective schools]. Because those schools have the academics and they have the winning [sports] programs, and they have the facilities.

Even for NCAA Division III schools like the College, intercollegiate sports is a highly competitive game.

That game has been increasingly scrutinized in recent years by academic policy makers, education scholars, and angry faculty members, who have written extensively and often critically about the scale of institutional commitments to sports.[1] Even the most cautious of these critics worry that athletics programs' varied costs—financial, social, and academic—are cause for concern. For William Bowen and his colleagues, for example, current investments in sports are especially problematic at schools such as the College—small, highly selective institutions whose primary focus on undergraduate academics makes them the conscience of American higher education. In two highly celebrated books, Bowen, James Shulman, and Sarah Levin document just how far schools like the College now go to field competitive programs: expanding coaching staffs to accommodate greater numbers of teams and to better nurture the ever-improving skill levels of high school athletes; competing with rival schools for primacy in as many sports as possible; and, most troubling to the authors and very pertinent for purposes here, lowering otherwise lofty academic standards in order to admit talented athletes.[2]

Despite such concerns, there is general consensus that college sports are here to stay. Even the critics argue that they generate important benefits for students: lessons in teamwork, discipline, and commitment; school spirit; and the sheer pleasure of engaging in skilled physical activity in concert with others. Yet few have recognized just how deeply sports are woven into the fabric of American higher education, and into upper-middle-class American life more generally. Athletics are not mere adjuncts to the main business of the nation's elite colleges and universities. They are part of the main business. Indeed, college sports have done much to structure the field of American higher education as we know it today.

During my fieldwork I learned that developing a full understanding of college admissions required me to understand college athletics. These two domains of institutional activity are so deeply intertwined that in some respects each is an extension of the other. The deep relationship between these two parts of the institution mirrors a broader commingling of athletic and academic stature that is elemental to the organizational field of U.S. higher education. I demonstrate this here by placing the relationship between sports and admissions at the College in its larger historical and inter-organizational context.

Borrowing insights from historians, I argue that athletics programs are an important prestige system for all of American higher education. A single school's status is determined partly by the status of the other schools it faces on the playing field. This is why even the most academically rigorous institutions care about who their athletic opponents are, and about faring at least decently in sporting contests with their league partners and status rivals. Because maintaining even passable teams requires skilled athletic leadership, elite schools hire ambitious coaches, whose career prospects are closely tied to their teams' win records. At their home institutions, these coaches constitute formidable on-campus interest groups with vested interests in getting talented athletes through the admissions door. Additionally, football coaches often enjoy additional political support from school trustees, who tend to view the stature of a football team as emblematic of the general reputation of a school and of their own memories of alma mater.

Many researchers have noted how athletic talent competes with academic accomplishment in the admissions process at selective schools, but few have appreciated how athletic and academic excellence also are complementary components of the student recruitment process. Students choose schools for multiple reasons, and the ability to participate in a particular sport at a competitive level of play is often an important one. Because so many talented students also are serious athletes, colleges eager to admit students with top academic credentials are obliged to maintain at least passable teams and to support them with competitive facilities. Admissions officers and other institutional officials understand that for every academically excellent school with a pretty good sports program, there is a rival institution that pegs higher on both dimensions. This is why few schools can afford to sit out the fiercely competitive game of intercollegiate athletics.

Finally, a close look at the place of sports in the nation's most prestigious colleges and universities raises new questions about the relationship between elite education, class, and the social production of human bodies. Just as poverty is carried by its subjects in the form of chronic medical ailments and bodies whose appearance is often far from normative ideals,[3] so too is affluence embodied in the often beautiful physiques of students at the College and its peer institutions. Along with good nutrition, consistent housing, quality medical care, and costly orthodontia, routinized physical training in the form of youth athletics is now a common feature of bourgeois childhood. It may be that the growing role of youth sports in upper-middle-class life is part of a larger project of privileged parents, and the schools they patronize, to prepare children for adulthoods in a class stratum characterized by increasing social competitiveness and physical longevity.

All American

Observers from other countries often are startled to discover how much attention U.S. colleges and universities give to sports. People around the globe are passionate about competitive athletics, but no others weave sports into academic culture and institutional identity to the extent that Americans do. The place of athletics in our national academic life has a long and complicated history that can be only briefly summarized here. Nevertheless, only in light of this past is it possible to fully understand the place of athletics, and particularly football, in selective admissions.[4]

Athletics have long been a part of the American college experience, but until the late nineteenth century their role was peripheral to institutional life. They were typically initiated and controlled by students, and were largely informal. Intercollegiate athletic competition began in the mid-nineteenth century, when boat racing first gained popularity. Baseball developed a following during the Civil War, and track-and-field events soon afterward. But football was the sport that indelibly changed American academic culture and the entire status order of U.S. higher education. The first recorded intercollegiate football match occurred between Rutgers and Princeton in 1869 (a Rutgers win), and within the space of thirty years the primacy of the sport in college athletics was definitive. The excitement, danger, and masculine character of the game are what made it revolutionary.

Football drew avid fans from its very beginning. Throughout the 1880s and 1890s, universities in every region of the country fielded teams and sent them on competitive expeditions to other schools. The matches provided novel opportunities for student, alumni, and community revelry that seemed immune to class distinctions. Football was widely embraced by ruling families of the eastern establishment. Through the game's early decades the nation's most prominent schools, specifically Harvard and Yale, developed what became national models for fielding and supporting competitive intercollegiate teams. They received enthusiastic support from the alumni cream. In 1893, for example, New York City hotels were jammed for a Thanksgiving game between Yale and Princeton. Banners bearing the schools' colors competed for recognition as they fluttered before the Fifth Avenue homes of the city's upper crust.[5] But the game also quickly developed eager followings far afield from eastern elites. One reason William Rainey Harper heavily supported a winning football team at the brand-new University of Chicago was to capture the attention of the eastern schools it sought as peers. And administrators at public universities throughout the Midwest soon learned that winning football teams were excellent public relations devices for taxpayers who might otherwise have little concern for higher education. Perhaps the clearest evidence of football's broad popularity and institutionalization is the facilities built to house the game. By the 1930s an important mark of an institution's stature was the size and impressiveness of its football stadium.

Football has always been a physically dangerous sport, and the numerous deaths and countless serious injuries inflicted on the field during the game's early years were an important impetus for intercollegiate coordination and regulation. In a testament both to the dangers of football and to the social prominence of the game, President Theodore Roosevelt summoned the coaches and physical directors of Harvard, Yale, and Princeton to the White House in 1905, where he admonished them to get "the game played on a thoroughly clean basis."[6] The schools sought solutions to their athletics troubles with the same tools that were animating the larger Progressive movement around them: innovation, organization, and regulation. That same year saw the founding of the Intercollegiate Athletic Association (IAA), the organization that would evolve over the subsequent decade into the National Collegiate Athletic Association (NCAA), the primary regulatory mechanism of intercollegiate sports today. Among the IAA's first football reforms was the introduction of the forward pass, a technical change in the game intended to diminish some of the tactical importance of brute force.

Merely tracing the early history of intercollegiate sports, however, begs the question of just why academics and athletics became intertwined in America in the first place. Historians suggest two answers to this puzzle. First, sports lent a macho air to a college life that was popularly regarded as bookish and effete. They provided a means whereby school leaders could make their institutions more appealing to the sons and fathers of wealthy families. Doing so was important because college administrators were eager to expand their client base and their cultural influence in the post–Civil War era. They wanted to expand well beyond their established job of producing teachers and ministers. The most ambitious academic leaders wanted none other than to manufacture a truly national upper class for a rapidly expanding society.[7]

Pursuit of this ambition at this particular point in history gave academic leaders some peculiar challenges. In a nation characterized by western expansion and rapid economic growth, the importance of postsecondary schooling for young men's futures was far from certain. Why would a father send an ambitious son to college for several years of book learning in a dry classical curriculum, when there was money to be made in the family business and wide opportunity on the American frontier? Sensing their precarious cultural authority, college leaders set out to make higher education more relevant and student life more lively. On the academic side, the classical curriculum, with its heavy emphasis on ancient texts and languages, gradually gave way to a diversified array of electives that included the natural, physical, and new social sciences. On the social side, college presidents increasingly accommodated students' desires for an undergraduate life that was more comfortable and more fun. Fraternities and literary societies were tolerated and even encouraged; student revelry, lubricated by alcohol, came to be more or less taken for granted by school authorities. And from the late nineteenth century onward, athletic activities received increasingly generous administrative support.

University presidents' worries about the effete reputation of higher education during this period paralleled a larger cultural anxiety about the fate of masculinity in a rapidly changing social order. The technological and organizational innovations of the late Industrial Revolution had transformed the character of business leadership. The work of building fortunes became an increasingly bureaucratic activity as corporations grew larger and business generally became more administratively complex. People who enjoyed national reputations as men's men—President Teddy Roosevelt perhaps most prominent among them—increasingly found themselves working behind desks and beholden to paperwork. In response to such changes in the character of working life, men of the nation's ruling and middle classes created new forms of manly recreation. Distant retreats in the Adirondack wilderness lent an aura of rugged outdoorsmanship to even the most well-heeled city men. The Boy Scouts organization was conceived and flourished as a means of enabling boys and adult Scoutmasters to enact an explicitly masculine gender role. And competitive athletics of all kinds drew more and more adherents. It is in this cultural context that college football—perhaps the most explicitly and elaborately macho of all American sports—moved from a modest student pastime to a national obsession in an astonishingly short span of years.[8]

Just like higher education more broadly, intercollegiate sports were largely a male purview well into the twentieth century. During the same historical era in which competitive football was eagerly embraced for college men, female athleticism was the object of considerable debate and concern among educators. On the one hand, many believed that mild exercise was a good way to manage female "nervousness," a problem widely perceived to be pervasive among white women of the more privileged classes. On the other hand, educators worried that excessive athleticism could bring about a host of physical and moral ills: fertility problems and a loss of femininity among the athletes, and erotic stimulation for both the players and their male spectators. By the early twentieth century, women educators had developed a settlement among these warring convictions. Women would participate in athletics, but only alongside other women, and the competitive aspect of sports would be strictly curtailed. Thus for much of the early twentieth century, female college athletes did not participate in intercollegiate *competition* per se; their intercollegiate play often took the form of meets in which no winners or rankings were declared. Mirroring the broader gender order, female intercollegiate athletics was essentially a separate sphere. Additionally, the most avid sportswomen were the subjects of wide suspicion, because sports generally were regarded as masculine, not gender-neutral, endeavors.[9]

It was not until the rise of liberal feminism in the 1960s and 1970s that the notion of gender parity in higher education was widely acknowledged as a legitimate goal. That goal received its most powerful realization in the form of Title IX of the federal Educational Amendments Act of 1972. This legislation, a highly contested and major political victory for feminists, outlawed any form of sexual discrimination in schools receiving federal aid. Title IX posed a deep challenge to virtually all intercollegiate athletics programs, which typically both segregated men's and women's programs and supported them unequally.

In the three decades since the passage of Title IX, university leaders, athletics directors, and women's advocacy groups have struggled continually over just what gender equity in intercollegiate sports should look like. In evidence of the depth of cultural presumptions that there are innate physical differences between women and men, the idea of integrated sports teams has been given little serious consideration. Schools have tended to demonstrate gender equity by supporting programs for men and women with relatively equal amounts of funding, personnel, and physical plants. And they generally have done this not by reducing commitments to men's programs but by increasing investments in women's teams. Culturally, too, women's sports have come to approximate the male model, not the other way around. Very soon after the passage of Title IX, women's programs adopted the logic of intercollegiate competition and the NCAA regulatory infrastructure that had first been developed for male teams.[10]

The net effect of Title IX, then, has been to expand the scale and cultural prominence of intercollegiate sports generally. Gender equity in college athletics has been pursued in the form of investment equivalency, and in the expansion of an explicitly competitive sports culture that is now regarded as gender-neutral. Whether or not this version of gender equity is a good thing remains a matter of debate. In their celebrated study of intercollegiate sports at selective schools such as the College, for example, James Shulman and William Bowen lament the demise of the female sports culture in favor of the winning-is-everything orientation long dominant in men's sports. And although few would advocate supporting men's and women's sports unequally, the Bowen team and others are deeply concerned about the costs of maintaining what is often called an "arms race" in sports expenditures.[11]

But because institutional identity is so deeply linked with the opponents one meets on the playing field, because the current system of intercollegiate play enjoys powerful political support, and because youth sports are such prominent features of upper-middle-class culture, intercollegiate athletics are unlikely to lose their central place in American higher education anytime soon.

Status Clubs and Status Rivals

Intercollegiate athletics, particularly football, have played a definitive role in coalescing America's myriad institutions of higher learning into distinct status groups. Efforts to regulate and coordinate sports first enabled schools to imagine themselves as *groups* of more or less similar institutions, and provided new practical mechanisms for creating intercollegiate linkages.[12] In the process of figuring out how to manage sports, colleges and universities also fashioned the basic architecture of an organizational status system that has endured into the present.

A central insight of sociology is that status—the prestige that people or organizations enjoy relative to others—is a potent social incentive and form of power.[13] Status is perennially interesting to sociologists for at least two reasons: it is a distinctively cultural social resource, and it rarely is trumped fully by other kinds of power. These features of status make it both an endlessly renewable human resource and a complicating feature in virtually all human affairs.

Consider, for example, the status systems that young people create among themselves, beyond the pale of adult control, in school. A cafeteria in a typical junior high school is an elaborate status world. Any competent citizen of that world will be well versed in its status rules. She will be able to tell you about the particular tables that athletes, preppies, intellectuals, and stoners lay claim to each day; the relative amounts of general regard or approbation each group suffers or enjoys from the others; the sartorial sign system natives negotiate when getting dressed for school each morning; and the particular students who are upwardly, downwardly, or laterally mobile between various status niches. Consider as well that the status individuals enjoy in any particular cafeteria is virtually meaningless in the lunchrooms of a different school district—a fact that goes far in explaining why household moves are often traumatic for young people, and why teenagers (who have invested years of effort in securing their position in a particular status order) can be particularly averse to changing schools. And, as many grownups learn the hard way, these status systems are highly resistant to even the most sustained efforts of otherwise powerful outsiders (such as parents, teachers, and law enforcement officials) to change the rules.[14]

Status is a particularly important feature of higher education, because the fundamental social power of colleges and universities lies in their ability to confer status, in the form of academic credentials, to graduates. Colleges and universities ultimately derive their license to confer status from governments, which one way or another have the final word on whose degrees are officially recognized in a particular national context. In many nations the central government directly regulates virtually all of the degree-conferring institutions in the country, assigning different functions to particular institutions and also, thereby, giving institutions varying kinds of status and capacities for conferring it to graduates. The French system of higher education is perhaps the paradigmatic case of a state-managed status regime. In France the highest-status schools are the grandes écoles, which are generally regarded as having the most elite academic faculties and the most competitive admissions. Different écoles confer rather different kinds of status, which parallel the intended futures of their graduates as technical professionals, government officials, or academics and intellectuals. Beneath the grandes écoles are the numerous French *universités,* which have less-competitive admissions profiles and confer degrees that are generally regarded as having less prestige.[15]

One of the distinctive features of U.S. higher education is that its status system has been left largely unregulated by any central state authority. Instead, and rather like young people in a school cafeteria, American colleges and universities have been left to create their own status systems, largely without government oversight. In the decades after the Civil War, America's educational leaders gradually assembled their own status systems, which are in large measure internationally distinctive. Two of these systems were discussed at length in Chapters 3 and 4 and have received extensive attention from both historians and economists. The first entails using measures of admissions selectivity as indexes of relative organizational prestige. One way we know a "top" school is by its low admissions rate and high average SAT scores. Similarly, we know that a school is gaining prestige or losing it by looking at annual migrations of these same numbers. The second system is a metric of the relative national representativeness of the student body. Part of the reason admissions officers travel nationally to recruit for their schools is to generate applications from as many states as possible. The holy grail of this second status system, representation of all fifty U.S. states in the student body, is regarded as one mark of national prominence.

Considerably less attention has been given to the third system for ascertaining status in American higher education: athletic league affiliation. To wit: we assess the status of any particular institution by looking at the status of the schools it meets in formal athletic competitions, especially football games.

Consider that many of the schools typically regarded as among the most prestigious in the country are members of a common athletic association: the Ivy League. This league began as a football consortium in 1945 and nine years later was extended to govern all other intercollegiate competition among its member institutions. Today the term *Ivy League* is virtually synonymous with high institutional prestige. But it is not just the Ivy schools that accrue status from their league membership. The same is true for virtually all institutions in the field of American higher education. In the Northeast, the Patriot League and the New England Small College Athletic Conference (NESCAC) are generally regarded as groups of high-status institutions. The same pattern obtains in other parts of the country. It is no accident that most of the member schools of the Big Ten are the flagship public research universities in their respective states. We find similar status agglomerations in the Southeastern Conference (SEC) and the Pacific-10 Conference (PAC-10) in their respective regions.

Perhaps the clearest example of the relationship between league membership and academic status is the University Athletic Association (UAA). Organized in 1986, the UAA currently has eight member schools: Brandeis, Carnegie Mellon, Case Western Reserve, the University of Chicago, Emory, NYU, Rochester, and Washington University in St. Louis. As with other athletic leagues, the UAA links schools that are comparable in many ways: all are private; all have a few prominent graduate programs and small but selective undergraduate colleges; and all are relatively close to one another in academic stature. What makes the UAA a particularly interesting example of a status club is that its member institutions are very dispersed geographically. It is hardly convenience that encourages these institutions to compete athletically. Quite to the contrary. The UAA schools devote considerable time and expense to physically moving their teams around the country so that they can compete with comparable schools of roughly equal prestige.[16]

This general insight about the relationship between status and athletic competition clarifies some otherwise puzzling features of American academia. Most importantly, it enables us to explain why athletics and academics are so tightly interwoven in the organizational fabric of our higher education system. In the absence of authoritative state control, educational leaders worked out their own mechanisms for determining relative organizational prestige. Two are quantitative and formally rational: measures of admissions selectivity and national representativeness. The third is categorical, physical, and often deeply emotional: league membership and intercollegiate athletic competition. Indeed, the embodied nature of athletics lends vivacity to the other two status systems: you don't just know that yours is a good school, you feel it, too, and should your school be dropping in its ranking you feel a tug to do something about it. The athletic component of the status system compels behavior in ways that mere reason cannot.

The fact that our academic status system is partly an athletic system has an important additional consequence for the landscape of institutional prestige in the United States: it means that schools in the Northeast continue to enjoy something of a status halo, even though the economic fortunes of this region have diminished considerably over the twentieth century and individually excellent schools are now found throughout the country. Northeastern institutions enjoy the distinct advantage of being geographically clustered. This proximity facilitates the athletic contests through which status parity is performed. For the same reason, geographic location elsewhere is disadvantageous. Individually excellent schools far from the Northeast often complain about the paucity of "appropriate" rivals available to them.[17]

One piece of evidence about the relationship between institutional status, athletics, and geography surfaced during a dinner for academic policy makers and admissions officials that I attended in the course of my research. One of the guests was director of admissions at a highly selective private college on the West Coast. When the conversation drifted to intercollegiate sports, this director explained how his school recently had initiated a "fly-in season," in which the school competed with institutions geographically distant from it. In football, the director explained, "we play several schools in [our region] that have a very different admissions profile. . . . And some of these schools have huge squads and it's like, they back a school bus up to a jail and load it up," he said with heavy sarcasm. "So this year we had some fly-in play," he continued, naming competitions with schools in other states that had comparable admissions profiles and academic reputations.

The general relationship between athletic and academic status illuminates why some athletic rivalries are particularly intense, and why the lack of clear rivals arouses suspicion. Schools that view one another as longtime opponents on the athletic field are very often close competitors in the game of institutional prestige. The enduring athletics rivalries of Berkeley and Stanford, Harvard and Yale, Williams and Amherst, Army and Navy all are similar in that they vivify on the playing field the enduring status competition between the opposing schools. Conversely, the lack of clear rivals has its own status meaning. The University of Notre Dame is famously anomalous in that it has an extraordinarily good football program, but no football league affiliation and no specific gridiron rival. Notre Dame football's rogue status lends it a kind of dark glamour: outsiders can only be impressed by what they see on the field, even while they often are not quite sure what kind of institutional creature the Fighting Irish represent.

The use of athletic competition as a means of defining status boundaries also creates conditions for the thrilling usurpation of those same boundaries in competitive play. The NCAA basketball play-off system, for example, enables schools occupying very different status niches to square off as competitive equals. The national championships temporarily disrupt the clear distinctions that usually sort schools into different kinds and calibers. So, for example, in the 2006 NCAA Division I national basketball play-offs, genteel Duke University lost to Louisiana State—a flagship public university, but an institution with a very different status pedigree than the tobacco merchant's Gothic paradise in Durham. Highly selective Boston College was bested by its otherwise less prestigious Pennsylvania cousin, Villanova, 60–59 in an overtime game that same year. Such competitions enable the entire field of higher education to enact a fundamental commonality despite deep status distinctions. In much the same way that carnival rituals generally offer temporary reprieve from status distinctions and thereby reaffirm underlying group solidarities, national play-offs enact a trans-league institutional community by temporarily suspending league borders. This is how cross-league sports contests of all sorts generate a distinctive kind of excitement and pleasure for players and spectators alike.[18]

It may be that Americans have been amenable to athletic competition as a way to define status in academia because of the populist character of sports themselves. University athletics programs often generate deep affection among a wide range of constituents, providing nonacademic incentives for people to care about colleges and universities. As historian Christopher J. Lucas writes regarding the surging popularity of football at the end of the nineteenth century, sports enabled colleges and universities to

> become genuinely "popular," but not because of the academic endeavors that purportedly represented their raison d'être. On the contrary . . . popular support for higher education drew its strength from the entertainment value of activities formerly consigned to academe's outermost periphery.[19]

Athletics also are regarded as meritocratic fields of human endeavor. Individual athletic talent is easily measurable and team success easily quantifiable. In a country historically skeptical about inherited privilege, athletics appears to provide mechanisms for mobility, both individual and institutional, on the basis of hard work and demonstrated ability.[20] However, as we will see, the meritocracy of sports is more fiction than fact.

A Coach's Ambition

Supporting the athletics status system is an entire occupational world of skilled athletes who make careers in college coaching. The College employs approximately two dozen paid coaches to recruit and train players for its twenty-eight intercollegiate varsity teams.

Generally coaches' work is of little interest to the academic faculty, who tend to see athletics as, at best, a spirited adjunct to academics or, at worst, a drag on the school's intellectual ambitions. In other words, if all of the College's workers were to eat together in the same cafeteria, few professors would share tables with coaches. In a sobering paradox of occupational politics, the coaches, who are elemental components of American higher education's status machinery, enjoy considerably less occupational prestige than their colleagues on the academic faculty. Indeed, the term *colleague* is rarely used to describe workers across the academic/athletic divide. This occupational stratification may go far in explaining why coaches' work is not well understood or appreciated by many scholars of higher education.

Much media attention is showered on coaches of star programs in particular sports (most commonly, NCAA Division I men's football and basketball), but most coaches work far outside the public limelight. The nation's legions of assistant and associate coaches, often fresh out of college themselves, typically work long hours on modest wages while developing their teams and their own careers. For in fact the fate of a college team and its coach's next job are indivisibly linked. Unlike many jobs in academia, in which accomplishment is difficult to assess objectively (just how does one assess the quality of an administrator? a teacher? a librarian?), in coaching the metrics are clear. Win records, league standings, and the numbers of team members sent to national competitions are among the many straightforward indexes of how well coaches are doing their jobs.[21] Coaches know that their career progress is predicated on such numbers. That is why ambitious coaches work hard to recruit top performers for their teams.

Among the ambitious ones is Mike Abell, an assistant coach for the College's men's lacrosse team. One summer afternoon I met him in his basement office adjacent to the locker rooms, a space that he shares with several other assistant coaches. Mike assumed his current job after leaving a similar position at another highly regarded liberal arts college. But that school had a significantly weaker lacrosse program, so the College was a step up for him professionally. The happy culmination of Mike's second year at the College had been his team's good standing in the NCAA Division III national play-offs.

Our meeting was in June, which meant the academic year and the playing season were behind him, but Mike assured me he was busy all summer long. "As soon as the season is out I'm working on next year," he said. "I like to go to see the kids who are coming to play [on the team next year]. That's sort of how it's done, you keep in touch with them after they've been admitted," he had told me in a casual conversation a couple of weeks earlier. Now, on our way to lunch, he explained further:

> [You're trying to] sort of work on the relationship, laying the groundwork for the next year. And you're also looking at the guys who you might be recruiting in the fall. I watch them, and I take notes, and I'll get their parents' cell phone numbers, because their parents are usually at the game . . . and I'll call them on July 1. You can't call them until July 1, that's an NCAA rule. So I'll start calling them at 8 A.M. on July 1, and I'll keep calling them all the way into the fall. [When I call] I'll try to personalize it, take notes so I can talk about something they do really well, or a particular game. [It's] easier [to do this] at the College than at [my previous school] because people have heard of the College. We're good. We're on the map.

By "on the map," Mike was referring to the cartography of college lacrosse. If anything, Mike's previous employer enjoyed more prestige among academics. But lacrosse is a different world.

Later in the summer Mike would be working at several sports camps for high school athletes. The camps usually pay Mike's travel and living expenses, and also compensate him for his work, which makes the appointments an appealing way to augment annual income. But Mike also does it for "networking," by which he means meeting other coaches, and recruiting—meeting rising seniors and even rising juniors whom he might keep an eye on as potential recruits a year down the road. Camp organizers understand that their programs are important mechanisms for brokering relationships between high school players and college coaches. "Sometimes [the sports camp people] will do this for us," Mike explained, showing me a bound booklet of Xerox pages, each of which featured the name and basic athletic statistics of several players, along with their photographs. He said that this material helped him keep track of the players he met. As we flipped through the pages, I noticed that entries for a few of the athletes had already been circled.

Kendra Dixon, the College's head women's basketball coach, concurs with Mike Abell about the importance of securing new talent for her team. "A lot of the job is about recruiting. If you want to have a team that wins, you have to have the talent, and in order to get that talent you have to go out and find it. You can't really have much of a program unless you recruit. That's kind of the bottom line." We were talking in her windowless office, located in an older campus building that had previously been occupied, and derided as unsatisfactory, by an academic department. Athletics staff had moved in after the professors had departed to freshly renovated quarters. Kendra told me pointedly, in a tone of complaint mixed with pride, "I put 92,000 miles on my car, in three years, largely driving around the Northeast to see girls play hoops." She said she would have traveled farther if she had been able to: "the Midwest, Texas, Oklahoma, South Carolina. . . . Those are all big hoop states with a lot of talent in them, but I don't have the time and the budget to go find those kids." As it is, Kendra spends a good bit of her own money on recruitment. "[The College] will pay my registration for . . . tournaments, and gas and tolls. But I sleep on people's couches. They don't pay for hotels or meals. So a lot of it is what the coach wants to do, how many people you want to see, how much you're willing to do, more or less on your own."

Recruitment involves a lot more than finding talent. Talent also must be enticed to even consider the College, then to apply, and then must be accepted in the formal admission process. In some ways, then, the recruitment work of coaches is similar to that of admissions officers. Both scour the country, looking for highly accomplished prospective students and courting their applications. But there is a crucial difference in the recruiting goals of admissions officers and coaches, one that has significant implications for the character of coaches' work. Admissions officers recruit *classes,* while coaches recruit *individuals:* perhaps a fourth swimmer to complete a relay team, a seasoned goalie, or a couple of big guys to beef up the defensive line next year. Coaches' specialized needs mean that their recruitment efforts are rife with unsettling contingencies. How far should the recruitment net be cast? In which particular players should the most recruitment effort be invested? Which applicants will pass muster in Admissions? In contrast with admissions officers' recruitment process, which may be described as a sieve through which thousands are sorted and most are eliminated over time, athletic recruitment is more like a gauntlet, in which coaches carry particular recruits through a sequence of trials, each of which can steal a coveted individual away.

Coaches hedge their bets for this gauntlet in a variety of ways. For example, they try to begin each recruiting season with a very large number of contacts. In this they are much like admissions officers, even though the intent of their effort is somewhat different: coaches keep their eyes out for good athletes in general, but they also are looking for particular players with the right mix of attributes. They often have some help from third parties, such as the summer sports camps Mike Abell described, or larger databases that further rationalize the search for talent. Terry Taylor, an assistant football coach, explained that his team uses an independent data delivery service that compiles information supplied by high school coaches across the country. For football, the service provides information on players' positions, height and weight, and recent academic statistics. The College's football coaches purchase this information in a searchable form and then sort potential recruits according to whatever criteria they like. Terry claimed that they contacted "a hundred guys for every one we actually get. . . . And I'm not talking a hundred *names,* I'm talking a hundred *contacts.*"

A second way coaches improve their chances is to make sure from the beginning that potential recruits are "admissible," that is, that their academic accomplishments are either within, or not far below, the College's typical admission profile. As Mike Abell, the lacrosse coach, explained:

> Right away we start talking about academics. Because I can't get them in if the academics aren't there. Plus, it's not really good, for anyone, to get someone here and they can't handle the academics and they drop out or they just get benched, can't play [because of academic probation]. So, I'm not going to bring a kid here with 900 SATs. It's just not going to happen. But 1100, maybe we keep talking.

Coaches sometimes also become ad hoc admissions consultants, advising potential recruits on how to enhance their admissibility. One of the reasons Mike might keep talking to a good player with an 1100 SAT, for example, is "because you know people can usually raise their score to 1200, 1250. I might say 'OK, if you're serious about this, then I would suggest that you take an SAT prep course, that you study and take the SAT again and see if you can bring up that score.'"

Another way that coaches augment their recruitment efforts is by making sure that their relationships with the Admissions Office are in good working order. Coaches understand that Admissions, not Athletics, has the last word on who will receive admission offers. Savvy coaches understand that laying groundwork for good communication and mutual regard across this organizational divide is worth the investment. "I gotta tell you, during the school year I'm over in that Admissions Office every day," Mike Abell told me:

> Just about every day I'm over there. I'm talking to [names of officers] about the team or about particular players or about whatever. But I'm over there. I'm working with them. And here some of the coaches, you know, they never go over to the office, or they only go over there when they have some bone to pick, or they have reputations for being cranky. Well, you know what? Guess what's going to be harder for you next time around?

Securing admission for top players is hardly the end of the recruiting process, however. Once they are admitted, recruits also must be convinced to accept the College's offer of admission over all others. And the more attractive the recruits, both athletically and academically, the more options they have and hence the more difficult they are to hold on to once the admission offers have been mailed. "I have to admit it can be a hard sell," Coach Terry Taylor confessed about football recruitment at the College:

> I mean, first of all we don't have a winning team right now. So that's right there. But also, we're good but we're not at the very top academically. So if a kid is good enough to get in [here], he's probably holding out for a [peer school name] or a [peer school name] which is stronger than us academically and also has a stronger football program. And nicer facilities.

It is in the nature of this highly competitive recruitment game that, despite a coach's best attempts, other schools often win the best players. The perennial effort and routine disappointments of recruitment are among the most onerous parts of coaches' work.

"Mitchell, it's horrible, it's just horrible. It's the worst part of the job, and I imagine other people would tell you the same thing." This from Coach Wilcox, the College's former swim coach and director of athletics:

> It's the part of the job that is most like being a salesman. It takes a lot of time. I mean, you work all day, and some of us have morning practices so maybe you started your day at 6 A.M., and you're teaching [usually physical education classes] and doing your other responsibilities all day, and then at the end of the day you need to get on the phone and talk to people for two hours a night. And you may be calling hundreds of kids. And some of them have never heard of your school and some of them don't know the process at all, so you have to explain that to them. And it's ongoing, it's just constant. And then you're traveling, driving to watch kids play. . . . You work so hard for a very small number of players. In swimming—it's been a few years since I did recruiting, but I clearly remember—I'd work all season and I'd get five kids to go Early Decision, and then I'd keep working on the regular admits and none of them would come. So I'd work all year for five swimmers.

An extraordinary amount of effort, perhaps, but nevertheless what it takes to field winning teams and thereby move up the career ladder of college coaching. Wilcox would know. He took his first coaching job when he was right out of college, twenty-five years ago, at his alma mater. "I remember the pay was $1500 a year. And I took it, and I tended bar and I did whatever I could to make it happen. And I loved it. I really did."

Competing Capacities

For admissions officers, the athletics program cuts both ways. On the one hand, the breadth and relative quality of the College's athletics offerings are important draws for many potential students. On the other hand, officers differ from coaches in how to prioritize applicant qualifications, and this difference creates chronic tensions between the two departments. Like two partners in a stormy marriage, Athletics and Admissions are deeply intertwined even while they often drive each other crazy.

Critics of the role sports play in college admissions tend to overlook the extent to which the goals of athletic and academic recruitment are in alignment. Coaches and admissions officers share the important interest of needing to make their school attractive to high-caliber applicants. And because so many otherwise qualified applicants also are interested in athletics, admissions officers make sure that information about the College's sports teams is presented in the best possible light. I learned quickly that the organizational distance between Admissions and Athletics was short. In Admissions there were colorful publications touting the College's sports programs. There were wallet-size season schedules on hand for virtually every varsity program. Specialized brochures for particular teams could easily be obtained from Athletics if a prospective student requested more information. The campus athletics facilities were included in every official campus tour, and home games were often prominently advertised during open-house events. The College's Web site featured the sports program prominently.

When I delivered oral information sessions to prospective students and their parents, I followed the example of the seasoned officers by consistently mentioning the College's twenty-eight intercollegiate varsity teams and the names of the prestigious schools with which we competed. I mentioned the popular, well-organized intramurals program. If a prospective student I was interviewing indicated that she was considering playing on a varsity team, I would have her fill out a special "athletic interest" form and encourage her to be in touch with the coach for her sport—unless the athletics contact had been made in advance of the admissions interview, which frequently was the case. On several occasions I looked up the name and contact information of the coach myself and gave this information to the applicant. I was hardly alone in my efforts, and I thought little of them at the time. My job was to make the College as appealing as possible to applicants, to answer all of their questions, and to help them accumulate institutional contacts that would encourage their identification with the school. In doing this job I relied on the athletics programs as components of the College's overall recruitment machinery. I was not terribly surprised to learn, then, that an independent survey commissioned by the senior administration found that almost half of a recent year's entering class had had some sort of contact with the College's coaching staff.

Workers in both departments concur that their jobs are interrelated. Regarding the start of his recruiting season each fall, Terry Taylor, the assistant football coach, explained to me: "I'm basically working for Admissions. . . . I'm telling [potential recruits] about the College, all the good things about us. And I've got to know, because at that point I'm the one who is getting all the questions. So I'm basically selling the school at that point." Admissions officers also understand the extent to which coaches act as emissaries of the school. For example, Liam Rizer publicly thanked the coaches for their recruitment efforts at a meeting of the board of trustees: "I have to give a lot of credit . . . to the good efforts of our coaching staff. They help us a lot. . . . They have just been very aggressive in attracting good student athletes for us, in getting them to look at the College and then choose it."

The College was similar to its academically selective peer institutions in its reliance on sports to recruit applicants. In *athletics* terms, the College compared poorly with some of the most *academically* competitive liberal arts colleges in the country. In other words, several competitor schools were widely regarded as better than the College both on the playing field and in the classroom. The College did not have a reputation as a "jock school." It traditionally had been strong in a handful of sports, but league championships and national titles were rare for it. Still, like at most other academically selective institutions, varsity sports were a pervasive feature of student life at the College. Well over a third of the student body participated in intercollegiate sports.[22] Many more participated in intramurals.

While athletics are a big part of the College's student culture and overall recruitment efforts, they also create chronic obstacles to admissions officers' goal of recruiting the numerically strongest classes they can. Admissions officers must mind the numbers, specifically SAT scores and the percentage of each entering cohort completing high school in the top 10 or 20 percent of their classes. These figures are important to officers because, along with the overall acceptance rate, they are primary metrics with which class quality is assessed by internal parties such as senior administrators and the board of trustees, and by external ones such as *U.S. News & World Report*. But alas, in the aggregate, and especially in the "high-profile" sports of football and men's basketball and hockey, applicants' athletic ability is inversely related to their academic achievement.[23]

Coaches see the inverse relationship between athletic and academic accomplishment as a fact of life. Terry Taylor, the football coach, indicated as much when he described how he tries to assemble his team roster each year. We were talking about having enough players to successfully field a football team. He talked about "practice players," explaining that these were guys who were good enough to enable his top players to practice competitively, but not strong enough to win games on their own. "Those are some of my strongest recruits academically, the practice players with the 1450 boards who won't see a lot of game time," he said. "And those are good kids, you need those guys—for practice, and it doesn't hurt that they help you keep your [academic] numbers up." Mike Abell, the men's lacrosse coach, volunteered to me, "The kids who are athletic recruits are just weaker academically. That's how it is, and so Admissions needs to understand that and work with that. . . . If you're going to have a winning program, you've got to work with these kids."

Admissions was well aware of the general statistical relationships between academic and athletic ability. Liam Rizer once said to me, "It's always a tension there, with the coaches. I tend to feel that if [the coaches] are really happy with what we're doing [in Admissions], then we're probably being too generous with them. So you want to meet their needs, but, you know, they're always going to be wanting more help from you."

I suggested that this sounded like a chronic tension.

"Yeah. Yeah. I think that's right."

He talked also about how relationships between Admissions and particular coaches become quid pro quo over time. "We know when we've gone out of our way with an admit, and they [the coaches] do too. So you sort of hope that, well OK, we did this one for you, so, now, keep that in mind the next time around."

I asked him if this quid pro quo ever was explicitly discussed.

He thought for a moment and then said, "No. No, I wouldn't say so. It's more like it's understood. Now some coaches, you'll never give them enough, they're always calling you to the table. But I'd say for the most part it's not like that."

One person who had a reputation in Admissions for never getting enough was Al Schwartz, the head coach of the men's ice hockey team. Officers regularly complained about the way Coach Schwartz recruited players and negotiated with Admissions. I got a fuller explanation for Coach Schwartz's reputation one winter day in the office from Alan Albinoni, the officer assigned to manage admissions for men's hockey. Alan had just finished a meeting with "Schwartz," as he was known in Admissions. When Alan wandered in to the room where I was working, I got the sense that he wanted to talk. I asked why Schwartz had such a bad reputation in Admissions.

The problem, Alan explained, "is that the guy just doesn't seem to care about bringing us schlocky kids. Now to be fair I have to say, a lot of it has to do with hockey. It's the helmet sports in general, but somehow it seems to be the worst with hockey. The kids who can play are just not very [academically] good kids. But it's also, the [high school] counselors tell me, that Schwartz doesn't recruit very hard at the prep schools."

"Which is where you might get better kids," I inferred.

"Which is where we might get some better kids, right. So, what happens is, he and I sit down and we go over all of the kids that he wants, and we talk about who's [tentatively] admitted and who's not."

The various contingencies summed to quite a puzzle. First of all, many of Schwartz's top picks were Canadian, which Admissions regarded somewhat differently because international students were expensive in terms of financial aid—they did not qualify for federally subsidized grants or loans. In addition to this international problem, according to Alan, Schwartz consistently put at the top of his recruiting list kids who were weak academically. Alan showed me Schwartz's recruiting list, which was arranged hierarchically. Schwartz's prime picks were near the top of the list. While we were talking, Alan moved his finger downward, motioning to names of players who were lower priority for the coach. "And we're thinking, why can't he want these kids instead, who are stronger academically but may not be quite as good as these other kids for the team?"

Another factor was the likelihood that the recruits who ultimately were accepted also would accept the admission offer. On his recruitment list Schwartz had marked in yellow all of the applicants he thought were likely to come if they were admitted. Also on the list were the Admissions Office's preliminary decisions on the admit status of the hockey recruits. Provisional admits had been marked with the letter "A," provisional rejects with "Z." Out of the twenty-five or so names on the list, only a few had the magic combination: marked in yellow (likely to come) *and* marked with "A" (likely admit). At that moment it became clear to me just how difficult the matching process and the inter-office negotiations could be.

Alan reiterated that the process was especially tough for the "helmet sports"—football and hockey. "It's different in other sports," he said. "Soccer, totally different story. I'll sit down with [the soccer coach] and he'll have twelve recruits and we'll already have accepted eight or nine of them." Here was further evidence that admissions officers understand that talented players of different sports tend to have different academic profiles.[24] But coaches' recruitment strategies also vary in consequential ways. As he continued with the comparison between hockey and soccer, Alan said of the difference, "Some of it is George." George Carroll, the College's charismatic men's soccer coach, enjoyed a place at the other end of admissions officers' love spectrum from Coach Schwartz. Carroll was known for making officers' lives easier. He had a reputation for recruiting athletes who were academically strong. And he was willing to go the extra mile for a particularly desirable kid. "That one soccer player we gave [an academic merit scholarship] to this year, George sat down with that kid for four hours, to talk with him about the College. He really puts out for us." He also did the little things, like bringing an offering of junk food to officers during a long day of committee work.

There were other reasons why all coaches, or all sports, were not regarded as equal by Admissions. As Liam Rizer explained to me one day over lunch, "Within athletics there are differences. I mean, there's football and hockey and basketball . . . " While he talked, he used his hands to create an imaginary vertical scale. With one palm he put these three sports on a notch near the top. "And then there's women's softball," he said, motioning low. "So," he said, on the question of how much pull Athletics has in Admissions, "it depends. It depends on the coach, the team, how much alumni support there is for a particular team." I asked which teams had strong alumni support. "Well, football. The *New York Times* posts all the football scores, so the guys . . . see those, they don't see the scores for the other teams."

High Profile

One January Friday I was in the office helping out with prospective-student interviews. There was a lot of interview traffic that day, somewhat unusual given the season, and I was not sure why. Issa Laurence, a student intern from California, explained that it was a "recruiting weekend" for football. Aha, I said, and we had a chat about it, exploiting the privacy of the back office, a closed door between us and the bustle of guests. "I'm fine with recruiting for football, but do we have to have *seven* weekends?" Issa asked with campy emphasis. Football alone, apparently, had scheduled seven recruitment weekends that year. "And all the recruits are followed around by the assistant coaches. Talk about boy toys. It's really something else. And they're running a shuttle for the candidates between here and Athletics." She embellished the news with wide, incredulous eyes. I had to concur that the shuttle service did seem a little over the top. Yes, it was cold outside, but the athletics facilities were perhaps five hundred yards away from Admissions.

We continued to talk, about a highly publicized change in the football team's coaching staff. A brand-new head coach had just announced, at the end of his inaugural season, that he was leaving the College for a school with a larger football program. The resignation had sent a shock wave through various campus offices. Senior administrators knew that many trustees kept a careful eye on the football program. Further down the pecking order, both Athletics and Admissions had banked on the promise of the new coach: Athletics had hoped he would raise the win record, and hence the profile, of a recently lackluster program; admissions officers, knowing that athletes make simultaneous decisions about teams, coaches, and schools, worried about what the resignation would do to recruitment efforts and numbers this year. It was impressive if not surprising, then, in light of all the linked interests, that the College hired a new head football coach from another school in a matter of weeks.

This change in staff is just one example of the difficulties inherent in fielding a competitive football team. Issa conjectured, "I say, just get rid of football. It's so expensive and it's so big with recruiting. But I made the mistake of saying that at an [Admissions] intern meeting, and everyone just about bit my head off." Why? I asked. "They're like 'no way, not football.' They all love it."

In their definitive study of intercollegiate athletics at selective private colleges, James Shulman and William Bowen found that football was favored by more than mere affection. Supporting winning football teams requires investments in physical plant, coaching, and transportation that far exceed the necessary expenditures for many other sports programs. Additionally, talented football players tend to be among the least academically qualified applicants to the nation's top schools, which means that recruiting strong players necessarily requires stretching academic standards for admission. But because football is so tightly woven into the fabric of particular institutions and into American higher education generally, Shulman and Bowen argued, changing the game's privileged status will likely be difficult.

Gary Wilcox concurred that football "is just very different in a lot of ways from the other sports." First, there are the numbers of players required to field a competitive team. In the College's league a full roster is seventy-five players—enough to run two sets of plays simultaneously in practice, Terry Taylor explained. The College has a relatively small number of students, so fielding a full roster means that approximately 10 percent of the male students need to be football players. From the standpoint of Admissions this is no small task. The large numbers, coupled with the game's strategic complexity and grueling physical demands, means that not one but several coaches are required to sustain a competitive team. Then there is the equipment, and the costs inherent in transporting and housing the large squad for away games. But despite these expenses and a string of lackluster seasons, football enjoyed favored status among the athletics programs at the College.

In the wake of the turnover of the head football coach and the College's unimpressive recent win records, the president assured a trustee committee on admissions that the College remained committed to fielding a football team that was both athletically competitive and academically competent. "We don't necessarily need a star team, but we certainly need a team that is strong enough to go out on the field every week with a reasonable chance of not getting clobbered," President Evers explained. "So I have made it clear to the [new] coach that we remain committed to strengthening football at the College." He continued that it was important to support the players academically as well as athletically, because, he said, attrition rates for football players at the College were higher than the general attrition rate. "We need to do everything we can to make sure that these athletes are successful on the field and in the classroom. And I am confident that with a sustained commitment we will be able to do that."

Those seven recruitment weekends in Admissions were, it seemed, part of a broader institutional effort to heat up a tepid football program. But why? Why not distribute the considerable resources devoted to football to better sustain the College's twenty-seven other varsity sports programs, or enhance its intramural or fitness programs? Although my research does not provide a definitive explanation for why football retains peculiarly strong commitments from institutional decision makers, it does enable me to suggest that the game's historical legacy and its quintessential masculinity are factors in its continued prestige.

By virtue of its early role in coalescing intercollegiate athletic competition, football tends to have deep roots and strong support among older alumni—many of whom graduated when their schools were all-male or had only recently become coeducational. Few older alums attended college when gender equity in varsity sports was a legally mandated imperative. These simple chronological facts mean that those who are most likely to serve as institutional trustees— older men—often remember rather different, more thoroughly masculine alma maters than the ones whose futures they currently direct. It is easy, therefore, for trustees to equate the fate of a school with the fate of its football team.

In the wake of the gender revolution in college athletics brought about by Title IX, football has become the only high-profile sport that is the sole purview of men. And of course, football is not only demographically male. It is also culturally masculine. It is hard not to notice the macho aura that made football popular more than a century ago. There are the pads and pants and helmets that exaggerate players' male physiques. There is the emphasis on strength and weight, the organized physical violence, and the bodily experience of playing the game. As Gary Wilcox put it to me, in football

> you're asking someone to voluntarily endure pain on a regular basis. . . . Think about that. To endure physical pain voluntarily. . . . You're asking someone to go out onto the field on a regular basis and face someone who may be larger and stronger than they are and endure physical pain.

It was easy for me to make warrior associations—from the physical pain of our team on the gridiron, to battle and bravery and honor.

Paradoxically, football's physical costs may facilitate its continued support by institutional decision makers who feel responsible for students' well-being. No one, and certainly not President Evers, wants our boys "getting clobbered" by the competition, so everyone does what they can to beef up the team. Trustees, administrators, coaches, and admissions officers all cooperate to give football players a fighting chance. In doing so they perpetuate a significant bastion of male privilege in the increasingly gender-equitable world of college sports.

Nurturing Athletic Talent

Among life's little inconveniences for the admissions officers were visiting students who were not the right age. High school juniors and seniors were the typical and ideal visitors, because it was they who contributed to any given year's application numbers. Younger prospects, who didn't help on this year's statistics, were regarded as a chore. But of course these visitors never knew this. All of them were greeted with the same smiling faces as their age-appropriate brethren, and their interview write-ups were placed in a holding file.

The first aberrant sophomore I interviewed was a hockey player with a gentle demeanor and a strong midwestern accent. When I asked him what led him to consider the College (an easy question, one I often used to get an interview going), he told me that his father had made the choice of schools. When dad found one that might be suitable, he passed word on to son. Hockey was part of the picture. By the time I met him, the young man had visited already with hockey's Coach Schwartz.

This boy and his dad were hardly alone in their simultaneous pursuit of athletics and college access. While it is admittedly limited to observations at a single institution, my research is highly suggestive of a formidable organizational system linking athletes, their parents, coaches, and colleges in ways that facilitate the ambitions of all four parties. The student athletes who ultimately become applicants to selective colleges are the products of an increasingly elaborate machinery supporting youth sports in America. This machinery creates the contexts in which nascent athletic skill is identified and nurtured. It supplies the leagues, game schedules, and regional finals in which the dramas of competition are enacted by athletes and enjoyed by parents. It connects ambitious coaches with ambitious players, and their often equally ambitious mothers and fathers, across the very blurry boundary between youth and college sports. In addition to the many intrinsic pleasures of team play, the organizational machinery of youth sports provides nontrivial advantages to talented student-athletes when they commence the college admissions process. And because, as with most social advantages, this one is disproportionately enjoyed by the relatively affluent, the machinery of youth sports raises serious questions about the relationship between athletic ability and social inequality.

A common myth about athletic ability is that it is somehow innate. The myth of natural talent is comforting to those of us who are poor athletes in a society of sports enthusiasts, but it does little to explain why some people are extraordinary athletes. A widely cited study of competitive swimmers by sociologist Daniel Chambliss takes us a long way from myth toward a robust sociology of athletic accomplishment. Observing swimmers at various competitive levels, from country club youth teams to Olympic medal contenders, Chambliss found that speed in the water is largely a function of technical variation in how swimmers execute minute components of their task. Faster competition times are a result of *how* one swims; champions swim faster because they swim differently. Speed does not come from innate ability. It comes from skills that are learned, meticulously mastered, and doggedly attended to over months and years of practice.[25]

Like any skilled capacity (the ability to read, say, or fix carbure-
tors, or assemble a perfect pastry), athletic capacity is acquired. Like
other skills, it is likely to develop faster under conditions in which
the skill builder can watch and emulate more-accomplished practi-
tioners and get instruction from capable teachers. And just as volumes of educational research tell us that academic learning is facili-
tated by encouraging parents, so too is learning a sport much easier
when parents care about and attend to the game. Athletic ability can
be nurtured more or less, and we should expect that ability will vary
directly with the amount and quality of athletic nurturing children
receive.

Recent sociological scholarship makes it clear that upper-middle-
class children receive the lion's share of athletic support in America.
In her detailed examination of the parenting practices and daily
schedules of affluent and low-income families, Annette Lareau
paints a stark contrast between the lifeworlds of children across the
American class spectrum. Working-class and poor children participate in few organized extracurricular athletics. They are much more
likely to play sports informally than to be involved in coordinated
league play. By contrast, many upper-middle-class families' lives revolve around children's organized sports. Parents often lament the
difficulty of ferrying multiple children to multiple athletics practices, juggling competition schedules, and traveling great distances
to watch their kids play. Along with investments of time, parents
make considerable investments of money in children's sports—paying for uniforms, league fees, and frequently expensive summer
skills camps.[26]

Parents' involvement in their children's sports activities tends to
continue into the college admissions process and through the undergraduate years. My interview with Kendra Dixon, the College's
head coach for women's basketball, made this clear. When I asked
Kendra how she went about recruiting athletes for her team, she

volunteered that cultivating good relationships with parents was an important part of the work:

> Especially with the women, I think, you're really entering into a relationship with their parents too. You're talking to them a lot, and they need to feel like they can trust you to provide their daughter with a good experience. They're sending them off to college and they want it to be right for the daughter. As a coach you know that. You know that if you're recruiting this girl from the Midwest and she can't afford to go home at Thanksgiving, then she's probably having Thanksgiving at your house.

Parents also follow the athletic progress of their children on the intercollegiate circuit—often literally so, traveling many hours to watch sons and daughters compete. But just as students of parental involvement in classrooms and hospitals have found, the presence of mom and dad has its downsides.[27] Parents cause problems for coaches when they challenge coaches' authority. "There will be some parents who want to talk with [me] during games about strategy, and some coaches will do that but I won't," Kendra told me. "I've got an assistant coach, sixty years old, he'll go up in the stands and talk with the parents, and I tell him, 'If you want to do that, great, but I'm not talking to the parents during the games.'"

Sometimes, though, unwanted parental involvement is hard to contain. Kendra offered the example of one telling incident:

> Last season I was cornered once in a restaurant by a father—and this was a big man—cornered me in the restaurant while I was eating out with some of my friends, and [he said], 'Why isn't my daughter getting court time?' Well, I'm sorry, but you don't come up to me and intimidate me on my own time, in front of my friends and colleagues. . . . And you know I can understand part of it, here the guy and his wife have driven three hours to watch their daughter play a game, and she barely plays at all and we don't win, I mean that can be disappointing. But that's just the way it is.

Note that Kendra was empathetic about the source of the father's frustration: *I can understand part of it, here the guy and his wife have driven three hours to watch their daughter play a game.* Coaches appreciate that parents are heavily invested in their children's athletics even when that investment becomes a problem.

The bottom line is that the distinction between athletes and their parents is often fuzzy for coaches, just as it is for the larger institutional administration. I made note, for example, of a serious conversation that took place among admissions officers and trustees at one spring meeting. The chair of the board's committee on admissions reported that an officer had told her of one of the College's recruiting handicaps: the campus is located far from the northeastern urban centers from which many of its students are drawn. The trustee explained that the distance makes it difficult for parents of varsity athletes to attend home-field games, while many of the College's competitor schools enjoy more proximate locations to big cities. "Well, given that we're not going to move the College . . . ," Liam Rizer offered in jest at the meeting, his comment trailing away into silence. Unfortunately the problem of the school's physical location was not something amenable to repair by either administrators or trustees.

Ultimately the parents of the College's athletes deserve the consideration that coaches, admissions officers, and trustees try to show them. Parents are the ones who pay the year-to-year costs of nurturing athletic excellence in their children. Parents invest financially, temporally, and (as Kendra's example of the angry father indicates) emotionally in their children's athletic careers. In the process, mothers and fathers do much to create the talent that coaches rely on to field winning teams. To the extent that skilled athletes are essential fuels of the intercollegiate status system, institutional leaders would be unwise to dismiss the desires of athletes' parents. Even a decent sports program requires a consistent flow of new players, after all, and it is always nice to have an impressive showing in the stands in games against status rivals.

Thinking about athletic talent as a learned capacity nurtured throughout childhood enables us to ask new questions about the relationship between youth sports, family wealth, and college access in America. Selective institutions like the College rely on an elaborate infrastructure of youth sports programs to supply their teams with skilled players. Ambitious coaches need those players to maintain the athletic respectability of their current employers and move forward with their own careers. But athletic skill is not, like some random genetic trait, evenly distributed among the U.S. population. We have good reason to suspect that it is pooled most deeply in the nation's most privileged families and communities. Parents who can afford the lessons and league fees and summer camps, the cars for rides to practices, and the houses in school districts with extensive sports programs are more likely to nurture in their children the athletic skill levels sought by competitive colleges.

Additionally, affluence supports a wide palette of sports in which young people can aspire to excellence. With its twenty-eight varsity teams, the College accommodates a great many athletic ambitions. Still, the College disappoints more than a few jocks each year. Prospective students who were excellent at water polo, alpine skiing, or equestrian sports, for example, were obliged to look elsewhere for competitive varsity programs, while young golfers who had built their skills on world-class greens would not have been impressed by the College's course. Some of these limitations were regarded as genuine recruitment problems by admissions officers. During my fieldwork I heard laments that the College's limited support for golf and equestrian sports took it out of the running for some of the wealthiest and socially glossiest prospective students. As top colleges seek to accommodate the athletic ambitions of the nation's most coveted applicants—the variously accomplished high schoolers whose parents can afford to pay full tuition—they only elaborate an organizational machinery that systematically favors relatively wealthy families.[28]

By contrast, young people from low-income backgrounds will be less likely to receive the sustained athletic nurturance throughout childhood that sums to exceptional talent at the point of college entrance. They will be more likely to attend public high schools with tighter budgets and fewer resources devoted to "extracurricular" varsity athletic programs. They will be exposed to fewer people, such as the College lacrosse team's Mike Abell, who regularly traverse the blurry divide between youth and college sports when they coach at summer sports camps, and who are able to serve as college admissions brokers for exceptionally talented players.

In comparison with student populations in affluent suburbs and private schools, athletic skill attracting the notice of college recruiters will be a relatively rare event in poor communities. This fact will strike some readers as counterintuitive, because American sports mythology contains so many heart-warming stories about talented but disadvantaged young people being "discovered" by college recruiters and using their subsequent educations to move up in the world. The stories posit that midwestern farm boys and the sons of southern sharecroppers have football as their golden ticket, that urban blacks have hoops, and that soccer is the magic key for Latin American and African kids. This mythology is a product of the huge amount of media attention directed to a few extraordinary cases at the very top of competitive athletic hierarchies. Outside this limelight are the tens of thousands of only pretty good teenage athletes who constitute the vast majority of every sport's recruitment pool. This vast majority is systematically produced by the organizational machinery of adult-sponsored youth athletics. Most college players are groomed by socioeconomically comfortable families.

Certainly, luck and pluck will combine for a few top athletes from modest backgrounds every year, demonstrating, especially for those eager to believe it, that college sports can be a vehicle of upward educational mobility. But for the vast majority of college athletes (the rank and file, the practice players), a college application charmed by placement on a coach's wish list will be another one of many admission advantages disproportionately enjoyed by the well-to-do.

Keeping in Shape

Americans first embraced college athletics in the nineteenth century in the hope of making campus life more masculine and more fun. In contrast with the cerebral work of the classroom, sports exercised the physical and sensual sides of the human organism. This was the essential appeal of sports, first to students and subsequently to savvy school officials. I have argued that this peculiarly American mix of academics and athletics is an important inter-organizational status system, peopled by ambitious coaches who pursue their own careers by fielding winning college teams. In order to do their work, these coaches rely on the elaborate organizational machinery of youth sports in America. And because this machinery is maintained largely by the relatively wealthy, it tends to enhance class privilege in the transition from high school to college.

All those sports have consequences for the physical bodies of the young men and women who play them. It should not go unremarked that the College's students were, in the aggregate, a handsome lot. One campus legend held that the College's mail center received the largest single delivery of J. Crew catalogs of any college in the country. That story was never to my knowledge verified, but I can confirm that on warm spring days a stroll across campus offered the surreal impression of a world engineered by J. Crew, Banana Republic, and Abercrombie & Fitch. The look was athletically preppy and generally tidy, though a bit of just-out-of-bed rumple was *de rigueur* for the men. The physiques underneath the clothes often approximated a fashion-catalog ideal. Skin was unblemished, teeth were braces-straight, bodies firm and trim. Not all of the students were physically attractive, of course, but there was an overall impression of comeliness. New students sometimes confessed to being impressed, and intimidated, by the good looks of the student body. "A candy museum" is how one young faculty member wryly described it. Look, please, but do not touch without expressed permission.

Where did these bodies come from? Certainly many arrived beautiful—the products of years of careful grooming and investment by families doing everything they could to keep their children healthy and attractive. But the varsity practices dutifully attended by the third of the students who were on intercollegiate sports teams probably had something to do with the slender waists and confident strides, as did the hours logged at the campus fitness center by many students who never engaged in competitive play. Then there was the official PE program, run by the athletic department and a requirement of graduation, and the optional yoga, aerobics, and swing dance lessons, and the student-run outdoor club, which sponsored weekend hikes and bicycle trips. Body management and physical recreations of all sorts are integral parts of the College's main business.

We might suspect that the collateral effects of these activities on physical appearance are not lost on the students, or on the adults who invest so carefully in young people's futures. The school is preparing its graduates for lives of privilege, but also of physical challenge and social competition. Ever-lengthening life expectancy among the upper middle class means that bodies must be kept serviceable for longer stretches of history. Habits learned early on may serve alumni well decades hence. And it is no secret that college is a very important determinant of marital patterns.[29] Because college athletics have long been associated with male virility, and because women continue to be evaluated by others on the basis of their physical appearance, we should not be surprised if young people of both genders exploit college sports as a means of enhancing their appeal to sexual and marital partners. Additionally, the ubiquity of serial monogamy means that many of today's undergraduates will enter the market for mates at multiple points in their adult lives, perhaps being evaluated well into old age on the basis of their looks and sexual capacity. Additionally, social science confirms what many know from experience: looks matter to employers.[30]

It may be that parents and educators support sports so avidly in part because they provide means of working on young bodies in publicly legitimate ways. Few parents would want to confess to others that they worry about their children's physical appearance. Ideas about the health advantages and "life lessons" of competitive athletics are easier to say out loud. Likewise academic leaders, who know as well as parents do that looks are consequential for most matters of love and money in a competitive society, can easily justify athletics expenditures in the name of fitness and the teaching of teamwork and personal discipline. In maintaining the athletics programs that are so central to the organization of higher learning in America, adults help young people shape their bodies in accord with prevailing erotic and aesthetic ideals.

chapter five

RACE

It is classic liberal arts. A roomful of eager students is seated around me in a horseshoe of seminar tables. The windows are open to admit the mild summer morning. The student/teacher ratio is luxurious. A cohort of thirty has been split into two groups of fifteen, making it easier for me to learn names and offer individualized instruction in the writing workshops I have volunteered to conduct as part of this year's "Start-Up," a College program designed to acquaint high school students of color with liberal arts schools in general and with this one in particular. I have a hunch, soon proven correct, that helping out in the program will give me a fuller sense of the task of recruiting "multiculturals," as the school's administrators officially describe students who are both U.S. citizens or permanent residents and who claim a racial identity other than white.

I am struck by the energy that visibly percolates through a group of high school sophomores—the ceaseless body movements, the giggly communications, the mix of curiosity and wariness with which a new teacher is received. Almost totally absent are the poker faces and listless composures of the undergraduates I have left for a few semesters in order to do this research. I am reminded that the detachment so common in college classrooms is a learned skill.

Today's session, about the composition of college-level essays, has gone well. My charges have been attentive, and I have more or less pulled off my preferred classroom performance, an ad hoc mix of academic sobriety and "learning is fun!" esprit. Near the end of the period I ask for help compiling a list of first names. Though I do not say this, I plan to use the names as pseudonyms for the authors of the student papers I will later distribute to the class as examples. On the blackboard I have put two columns, marked "boys" and "girls." The students quickly deliver a shower of contributions: Jose, Jorge, Jamila, Shannequa, Veronica, Tiarra, Terrell, Aloke. But, problem, I do not know how to spell several of the names, and they are uttered in accented Englishes that make it difficult for my Anglo ear to parse phonetically. Additionally I cannot discern the gender designation of some of the offerings. "Shannequa," for example, is both problems in one. Upon its utterance I hear "Shanneek" and gamely start to spell out what I have heard in the column marked "boys." The students enthusiastically point out that I have gotten both the spelling and the gender of the name incorrectly. "OK, white boy needs help with that one!" I confess with a smile. But my charges already realize that my linguistic shortcomings extend well beyond these particular errors. Instead of spelling *Shannequa*, the student who offered the name instead tosses out, in a tone colored with subtle shades of respect, resignation, and ridicule, *"Mary."*

"No, I want Shannequa, you just have to help me spell it." Even though I sauce it with teacherly sternness, the mea culpa is heard and accepted. I get a patient spelling of S-h-a-n-n-e-q-u-a. The students do me the unsolicited favor of spelling out subsequent names.

Such was our inheritance, that sunny morning, of four decades of work by civil rights activists, administrators, and educators to integrate America's colleges and universities. My inheritance, that day, was a roomful of students both similar to and different from the kid I had been at their age, students whose grandparents could scarcely have dreamed of attending schools like the College, let alone being wooed into attendance by expenses-paid summer workshops. My students' inheritance was a little universe of selective schools that avidly courted minority kids' attention with flattering letters, free college counseling, and a professor who had trouble spelling black people's names.

The College's Start-Up initiative and the many programs like it at selective schools across the country are the fruits of two formidable and contradictory national legacies: a deep faith in the promise of education as a vehicle of social mobility, and a long history of racial segregation, stratification, and institutional exclusion. On the one hand, Americans have long looked to college as an important means of securing the good life. Millions of tax dollars have been spent to grow our higher education system, millions more on aid programs intended to ensure college opportunity to people from a wide range of financial means. Courts and legislatures have created elaborate legal mechanisms to ensure college access regardless of race or gender. During the years in which my students' parents came of age, the United States built the largest, most organizationally varied, and perhaps the most broadly accessible higher education system in world history.

On the other hand, students of color remain relative newcomers on campuses initially built to serve Anglo-Europeans. The basic character of American higher education evolved over two full centuries before African American young people, let alone Latino and Asian American students, were welcomed to attend college with whites. A great deal, but far from everything, has changed at schools like the College in the forty years since students of color were first invited to attend them; the curricula, religious traditions, student cultures, and even the locations of the schools serving the national upper classes continue to bear the imprint of their exclusionary history. A more sociologically consequential problem is that the organizational systems that deliver students to the point of selective college entrance remain structured in ways that systematically favor white and Asian American applicants over black and Latino ones. As copious scholarship makes clear, black and Latino students remain considerably less likely to become candidates for admission at the nation's most prestigious schools than their presence in the general population would have us expect.[1]

These dual legacies are evident in the organization of admissions officers' daily work. Most officers express a desire to create opportunity for deserving kids who, for one reason or another, have not had as much opportunity as they deserve. And as an occupational group, officers are committed to facilitating access to college for all young people, irrespective of socioeconomic background. Their professional associations proclaim as much.[2] But even if they were without these ethical commitments, officers at the nation's most prestigious schools would be obliged to work hard to admit students of color, because a racially varied student body is now an important index of institutional quality among colleges and universities in America. In much the same manner that nationwide geographical representation became a signal of institutional prominence a century ago, a racially heterogeneous student body is a marker of a school's national reach and academic caliber today.[3] So ethical convictions mix with institutional ambition to sustain rigorous minority recruitment efforts at the nation's most elite schools.

The College's own efforts were a complicated mix of ethical conviction, stubborn demographics, academic fashion, and organizational culture. There was officers' genuine desire to create opportunity for minority students, but there were also the challenges of finding black and Latino kids who might seriously consider the College, of finding sufficient numbers of them who met baseline academic criteria, and of convincing those who applied and were accepted to attend the College rather than some other school. There was the lofty goal of "diversity," but there was also the more self-interested imperative that the College *appear* diverse to outsiders. And there was the uncanny way in which organizational routines worked at cross-purposes with the diversity everyone said they desired.

The Strange Career of Affirmative Action in College Admissions

The color line in American higher education was stark well into the twentieth century. Northeastern institutions like the College had by and large been designed for a racially exclusive clientele. Indeed, their ability to coalesce and sequester young people with desirable social attributes was a big part of what made private residential schools appealing to eastern WASP families in the first place.[4] A handful of relatively radical places, specifically a few midwestern schools with abolitionist founders, made efforts to enroll African Americans, but everywhere the numbers of black college students remained small. A new universe of schools built specifically for blacks appeared in the wake of the Civil War, but most of these institutions were located in the South even when they relied on the support of northern philanthropists. Westward expansion of both the nation and public higher education created opportunities that, with few exceptions, only whites were able to exploit. And in the heart of Yankee country, with its high concentration of the nation's oldest and most respected schools, academic entrepreneurs were primarily concerned with establishing a prominent role for their institutions among America's leadership class.[5]

The College participated in this exclusionary history. Only six black students attended the College during the first century of its existence. The archives indicate that these few did not have an easy time. A letter signed by several black students and sent to a trustee in the early 1920s carried a troubling complaint about the racial climate on campus:

> We know that the entrance of four Negro students last year did not meet with the unanimous approval of the Faculty. Frequently throughout the year there occurred certain demonstrations on the part of students which certainly cannot be overlooked by us. [Name] played basket-ball on the varsity team, he sacrificed his time and gave his efforts to make a name for the College. On one occasion, a College man on the sidelines used the term 'nigger' referring to [name]. Is that the proper spirit for a College man? The term 'nigger' was used in the College Literary Magazine last year. The . . . Glee Club, at a smoker, sang in our presence a song about "the nigger went fishing one day."

The authors of the letter left no question about their own position regarding these events.

> For generations this term has been applied to the Negro. It is not a nick-name. It is not to be compared or likened to the nick-names given to other nationalities. To the American Negro of to-day, it is a gross insult. . . . Since we realize the wide breach which exists between the races and the effect which the slightest agitation has on the race problem, we cannot but feel that a little diplomacy should be exercised in the use of this detestable term.

The trustee responded promptly. "I hope that I should be among the first to deplore any conduct on the part of the student body . . . that seemed calculated to humiliate or provoke you or your friends because of your race," he wrote. But he discounted the extent of institutional responsibility for the untoward events. Perhaps the racial slurs were "isolated instances," the products of "the thoughtlessness and insufficient experience of youth," he suggested. "What you must consider is whether the College *as a whole* has treated you with the politeness and kindness with which . . . you undoubtedly deserve to be treated."[6] It would be almost fifty years before the archives included evidence of more proactive institutional efforts on behalf of black students.

Providing for the educational ambitions of African Americans was not a serious concern of northeastern schools generally until well after World War II. Priorities changed in the 1960s when civil rights activists, black militants, and many faculty members began to demand greater representation of African Americans in the enrollments and curricula of the nation's elite schools. It was the beginning of what political sociologist John Skrentny has called "the minority rights revolution," a broad swath of grassroots protest, cultural change, and institutional adaptation that made America a more officially diverse place during the middle decades of the twentieth century.[7] The revolution was not inevitable. For higher education, the historical record leaves little doubt that most institutional leaders required the push of protest and political crisis to move the academy toward racial pluralism. Schools became integrated in the shadow of urban race riots and often within earshot of campus demonstrations.[8]

Far removed from major urban centers and generally a conservative place, the College was not a site of violent protest during the 1960s, but it was hardly immune to the minority rights revolution. The admission of women, coupled with a virtual doubling of institutional size, brought rapid change to the College in the space of a very few years.[9] And the racial turbulence that was transforming the consciousness of the rest of the country was felt at this school as well. A memo to trustees from the College's president in 1969 included an assurance that "especially in light of the disrupting and often violent tactics which characterize the behavior of students on many campuses, it should be a source of great pride to us all that

[our] students, black and white, have expressed themselves . . . in an orderly, rational, and civilized way on issues on which they feel just as deeply and strongly as students on other campuses."

The students were not violent, but many of them were intent on seeing racial change come to campus. At least this is the sentiment depicted in a student essay written in 1970:

> The College is a small, isolated, private liberal arts college. . . It is a name school, a socially acceptable school, and very much a rich man's school. As such, it has been resistant to change, a last bastion of the white Anglo-Saxon, his mores, his genteel country gentleman liberalism, in essence, a defender of the status quo. But infusions of young blood in key administrative offices, the change in the younger generation, and a need to justify its very existence in the face of rising social and financial pressures have forced the College to re-evaluate herself and her role carefully. And slowly, in this most comfortable of ivory towers, things have begun to change. While the students of the 1950's and early 1960's were outstanding in their apathy, today's student has begun to find social consciousness. First came [the admission of women]. Next was a widesweeping series of curriculum reforms that offered freedoms in thinking and development. . . . Finally, the College began to examine her admissions policies and realize that she was not doing her share for the Black in America.

The school this author had entered his freshman year was overwhelmingly white. Not a single black face appeared in the photo-laden viewbook of 1964. Testament to the marginal place of race in institutional priorities, annual admissions reports did not even distinguish minority applications and enrollments at the time. Though there is record of an organized black student presence on campus by the late 1960s, the actual number of black students was small—by one 1969 account, only seventeen.

But by the time the author graduated, his alma mater was paying considerable official attention to black students. In a speech to the campus in the spring of 1969, the president announced plans for an "African-American Cultural Center," a new facility "where the black perspective can be presented through discussions, lectures, art exhibits, and similar educational, cultural, and social events." He said the decision had been prompted by discussions with the College's Black Union, and also by the "tragic fact . . . that our educational programs in this country largely ignore the history and culture of the 11% of the population who belong to the Negro race." Additionally the president promised that the College would "actively seek out black candidates who might qualify for administrative openings" and develop teacher-exchange programs with predominantly black colleges and universities. Though the president apparently made no mention that day of minority recruitment efforts in admissions, the alumni magazine's coverage of the speech reported that black enrollment was expected to double the following year.

From this point onward the archives indicate a sustained effort to shift the College's image in the direction of racial pluralism. In 1970 the local town newspaper reported that the College's black student organization had scheduled "a Sub-Freshman Weekend for prospective black students," to which some two hundred had been invited and fifty to a hundred were expected to attend. The weekend's events included interviews with admissions officers, panel discussions, and an afternoon lecture by black activist and intellectual Franklin Williams. Publicity got at least as far as New York City, where the story was given a few column inches in a prominent Harlem newspaper. The next admissions viewbook, published in the early 1970s, featured photographs of black students. Women and political activists also were represented for the first time. Viewbooks later in the decade made proud reference to campus visitors such as Alex Haley and Shirley Chisholm, and the facility announced by the president in 1969 was described as a vital, even historically significant, campus presence. A late 1980s viewbook listed full academic programs in African American, Asian, and women's studies. A memorial to the College's first black graduate was unveiled a decade later.

Why did the College, a school that saw very little campus turbulence in the 1960s, nevertheless begin to change significantly during the civil rights era? The answer to this puzzle lies in seeing the College as a group player. Organizations rarely make changes on their own, because doing so comes with considerable risk of failure or embarrassment. Instead of taking big risks though innovation, organizations more often hedge their bets through imitation. They keep their eyes on what *other* organizations—particularly the large, influential, highly visible ones—are up to, and then model their practices in the direction of where the big players seem to be headed. Favoring imitation over innovation can prevent an organization from making history. But because imitation also is a lot less risky than changing first or not changing at all, it can be a good strategy for organizational survival and even prosperity.[10] This is why the College began its slow mutation in the direction of racial pluralism in the late 1960s. It started to change because virtually all of elite higher education was changing.[11]

It is notable that in his 1969 speech, the College's president claimed that serving the needs of racial minorities was not a particularly exceptional policy for the College, and that doing so would benefit all students, not just African Americans. The planned center was akin to "all kinds of cultural centers" sponsored on college campuses; the president cited "Newman Clubs, Hillel Societies, Methodist centers, and Baptist centers" as examples, and suggested that the new facility was comparable to these others. "It seems to me . . . that the logic of this case is not radically different from the logic of the cases of similar arrangements regarding other groups." Additionally the president went out of his way to assure his audience that the new center would not be built for blacks alone. "It should be emphasized once again that the center will be designed to meet the needs of *all* members of the College communities," he said.

The speech implied that honoring difference was something the College did as a matter of course, and it suggested that there would be clear benefits not just for the subjects of this recognition but for everyone on campus. Read in the present, these claims seem unextraordinary. But the notion that honoring *racial* difference might be a typical and beneficial thing for a college to do was, in the 1960s, a novel idea. That we now take it for granted is testament how deftly, in the wake of protest, academic leaders defined the meaning of race in higher education on their own terms. Indeed, a full explanation of the College's own history through the civil rights era requires that we see it as part and parcel of the larger minority rights revolution, because it turns out that institutional leaders like the College's president were collectively instrumental in creating a new language for how Americans conceive of racial difference.

John Skrentny writes that "by the mid-1970s . . . university elites clearly were committed to reaching out to minority groups, and with zeal and creativity developed reasons why it was a good idea."[12] Some of their zeal and creativity was displayed in the legal system, specifically in amicus curiae briefs for the case that ultimately became the U.S. Supreme Court's landmark ruling in *Regents of the University of California v. Bakke* (1978). The case garnered attention throughout academia because it implicated racial preferences in admissions programs under way, in one form or another, at selective schools across the nation. Its outcome has informed how academic personnel think and talk about race ever since.

The case had its origin in 1973 when Alan Bakke, a white Californian, was denied admission to the recently opened medical school of the University of California at Davis. The following year Bakke again applied and was again rejected. The ensuing lawsuit charged that Bakke's measurable academic credentials—his grades and MCAT scores—were higher than the average marks of those who were admitted to the medical school under a special program for "disadvantaged" applicants. Though the program used no specific definition of "disadvantage," in practice the program was a racial affirmative action initiative: in 1973 and 1974, no white applicants were admitted to the medical school under the auspices of the program. As the case made its way through the courts, it garnered considerable attention from higher education leaders, because the ultimate judicial ruling on the case promised to set the terms by which colleges and universities might pursue racial integration.

A widely cited amicus curiae brief on behalf of Columbia University, Harvard University, Stanford University, and the University of Pennsylvania laid out the basic components of what would quickly become a standard argument for racial affirmative action in selective college admissions. The argument is notable for its deployment of a novel term in educational jurisprudence—*diversity*—and for its unabashed claim that elite schools like the College shouldered the task of producing national leaders.

The argument began with a mea culpa: many institutions had long excluded nonwhites:

> Up to about a decade ago, it was the fact (not designedly, but the fact nevertheless) that the student bodies of the amici institutions were overwhelmingly white, and their faculties almost exclusively so. . . . By not enrolling minority students in significant numbers, the amici were continuing to deny intellectual house room to a broad spectrum of diverse cultural insights, thereby perpetuating a sort of white myopia among students and faculty in many academic disciplines.[13]

But, the brief continued, educational elites had been apprised of their error and now were working vigorously to enroll greater numbers of minority students. "It was to alleviate . . . serious educational deficiencies in their training and research programs that the amici (and numerous other colleges and universities) developed admissions programs designed to increase minority enrollment." The amici claimed that doing so required considering nonwhite racial status preferentially in admissions protocols:

> Intensive recruitment of minority applicants could not of itself begin to insure a diverse student body in institutions as selective as the amici institutions. . . . Admissions decisions based on racially neutral criteria, which take no account of the educational deficit under which America's non-whites have labored throughout our history, would not yield a large enough number of minority students to achieve substantial diversity.[14]

In other words, racial affirmative action in admissions was a necessary strategy for maintaining a necessarily diverse student body.

Just why this diversity was essential had to do with the important role elite schools claimed for themselves in the creation of the nation's leaders—of all races:

> By our [racial affirmative action] admissions programs, we are not merely contributing to the cause of increasing the numbers of minority leaders and public servants—although we wish very much to do that. We are also broadening the perceptions of our majority students, and we believe that this will be reflected in qualities that they will retain for the rest of their lives. A central function of the teacher is to sow the seeds for the next generation of intellectual leaders, and this, indeed, is a main reason why many university instructors find that an ethnically diverse student body helps them to fulfill their teaching roles. In short, we hope that by these efforts, the leadership of the next generation—majority and minority members alike—will be the better, the wiser, and the more understanding.[15]

As we have seen in earlier pages, academics had long dreamed of controlling the production of national leaders, and by the mid-twentieth century that dream had largely been realized. An entire organizational firmament of higher education had been built in

America by then, and at its summit was a charmed circle of predominantly private, eastern schools that were popularly assumed to choose, train, and certify the best and brightest. But the civil rights and black power movements called the basic integrity of this system into question. Were the best and brightest necessarily the whitest? Affirmative action in selective admissions, and the diversity arguments with which it was framed, were educators' bid to maintain the legitimacy of the entire enterprise. It worked.[16]

The Supreme Court ultimately ruled that the specifics of the Davis program made it an unconstitutional quota system. Alan Bakke was to be admitted to the medical school. However, Justice Lewis Powell made it clear in a famous swing opinion that it was constitutionally permissible for schools to consider race in selective admissions in the interest of diversity. Justice Powell's rationale directly echoed the academics' diversity argument:

> The attainment of a diverse student body . . . clearly is a constitutionally permissible goal for an institution of higher education. . . . The atmosphere of "speculation, experiment, and creation"—so essential to the quality of higher education—is widely believed to be promoted by a diverse student body. As the Court noted in [an earlier case] . . . it is not too much to say that the "nation's future depends upon leaders trained through wide exposure" to the ideas and mores of students as diverse as this Nation of many peoples.[17]

Racial diversity has been part of official business at U.S. colleges and universities ever since.

The *Bakke* decision affirmed the academic goal of racial diversity, but it left unspecified just how race should be defined. In a nation characterized by massive immigration and religious and ethnic pluralism, the question of what constituted a *racial* as opposed to some other kind of group could have been difficult to answer. But as it happened this ambiguity had largely been settled by federal agencies' standardization of racial categories years before. The provisions for nondiscrimination in employment in the Civil Rights Act of 1964 had presented federal bureaucrats with the deceptively mundane task of specifying race categories on the reporting forms it required of certain employers. Officers in various federal agencies ultimately defined racial "minorities" as those U.S. citizens of African, Hispanic, Asian, or Native American descent. The scheme made it much easier to standardize procedures across multiple government offices and to measure compliance with federal employment guidelines in a predictable way. Government officials created the categories to solve accounting problems and to appease particular political constituencies, but the categories quickly became official themselves. Despite the multitude of cultural and socioeconomic differences obscured by these simple terms, official understandings of race hardened into a system of five general types—African American/black, Hispanic, Asian, Native American, and white. It was a profound instance of unintended consequences. In the process of creating compliance standards for affirmative action employment programs, the federal government invented the four "minority groups" whose existence is now largely taken for granted.[18]

Academic administrators solved their own problem of defining diversity by simply adopting the government's category scheme for use in their own institutions. This took care of the same accounting problems for colleges and universities that it had solved for federal bureaucrats. The categories made diversity easy to define and easy to measure. They made it possible for schools to set diversity goals, mark progress toward their attainment, and advertise success to critical outsiders. Despite the wide range of differences in educational opportunity and economic advantage obscured by these simple terms, official diversity very quickly came to be measured by the proportion of a student body that fell into the official minority categories of African American/black, Hispanic, Native American, or Asian. "Diversity" became a number.

From 1973 onward, the tables in the College's admissions reports feature data for a group called "minorities," and in the years after the *Bakke* decision the tables further differentiate the group into four component groups: Asians, Hispanics, blacks, and Native Americans. The numbers gradually grew as the office devoted more resources to minority recruitment. The 1984 report betrays its author's pride that 8 percent of the next entering class would be "American minorities . . . we believe this to be the highest percentage in the history of the College." Credit for the success was shared with a minority student organization whose members had lent a hand in recruitment. A letter written in the mid-1980s from the head dean to an alumnus promises that the College has

> increased our pool of [minority] applicants over the past couple of years and we have been matriculating a few more students each year. We work very hard at this and spend a lot of time visiting minority schools, running a minority weekend and working with accepted students in the spring. While we have had some success, it is never enough and we continue to try very hard to increase our pool and the number of students who matriculate.

In the space of twenty years, minority representation at the College had been transformed from a marginal concern into an official institutional priority. It began as a modest administrative response to modest campus pressure and the broader civil rights movement. It became a sustained official effort to recruit not only African Americans but Latinos, Asians, and Native Americans, too.

The College of Many Colors

Like virtually all elite U.S. colleges and universities, the College had an explicit commitment to racial diversity. Considerable effort was made to ensure that all official representations of the institution included a bit of rainbow. Admissions publications enthusiastically described "a diverse community." An entire section of the Web site was devoted to students of color. Black, Latino, and Asian faces frequently smiled out from photographs in promotional literature, and the several organizations for campus racial and ethnic groups were well publicized. The president routinely mentioned the goal of diversity in his speeches and writings. Local cynics noted the regularity with which at least one of the honorary degrees conferred each spring at commencement went to a person of color.

But while the College was officially a rainbow, in its history, demography, and general character it was a rather monochromatic place. Founded by ministers, the school developed its early clientele among the sons of affluent Protestant families. Catholic and, in lesser numbers, Jewish students gradually came to make up considerable proportions of the undergraduate population as the twentieth century progressed, and coeducation brought women to campus during the civil rights era. But racial homogeneity proved to be more enduring. During the years that I conducted my research, the student body was approximately 85 percent white. Politically liberal faculty and students often used the low minority numbers as evidence for claims that, despite the official rhetoric, institutional commitment to racial diversity was shallow.

As palpable as the numbers, but less often discussed, was the Anglo feel of the place. Prospective students who had grown up in the wealthier precincts of suburbia or who hailed from rural areas might fail to see the campus through the lens of race. But for urban kids and especially people of color, the whiteness of the College was hard to miss. It had something to do with the fact that most of the people on campus were physically white, of course. But it was many other things, too: the stiff, cushionless pews in the chapel, the endless lawns and perennial beds, the Saabs and Volvos and Range Rovers driven by more than a few of the undergraduates, the conservative clothing favored by most everyone, the kinds of music heard through dorm room windows, and the specific flavor of English encouraged in the classrooms. It was no one thing in particular, but many things together, that summed to an impression, a character, a *culture* that was preponderantly white.[19] It was what some of the students who accepted the College's admission offer and enrolled in one or two anthropology courses might learn was sometimes called the *unmarked category* of whiteness, the central reference point, falsely presumed neutral, against which other kinds of people and practices were comparatively "diverse."[20]

This overall character was paradoxical for Admissions. On the one hand, officers realized that the College's close approximation of a New England postcard was one of the school's top selling points. The place looked and felt like many people's idealizations of what a traditional liberal arts college should be. That was the good part. But the hard facts of U.S. educational history also meant that the private eastern schools, long regarded as the nation's best, also were traditionally white places. The enduring Anglo character of the College was hard to reconcile with contemporary expectations that elite higher education be "diverse." That was the bad part, and it was a dilemma not only for the admissions office I studied but for virtually all of the nation's most prestigious colleges and universities. How could traditionally Anglo-European institutions retain their essences while also accommodating—celebrating—racial difference?[21]

While philosophers and college presidents debated that question, the College's admissions officers faced it as a workaday problem. As the organizational window through which consequential outsiders viewed the College, Admissions was obliged to accentuate the school's official racial diversity. And because the essential racial character of the school was rather different from this official one, officers tended to enhance the pictures they drew for the world with carefully chosen bits of color.

One way officers did this was by hiring as colleagues people who were themselves racial minorities. In the late 1990s Admissions hired Danesha Adams, a black woman from the Midwest, for the position of director of multicultural recruitment. In addition to covering a few general recruitment territories, Danesha headed up the office's varied efforts to attract minority applicants. Once when the departure of an officer required a new hire, several people told me that the replacement, Terrence Carter, would be an asset in terms of multicultural recruitment. Terrence brought good experience in this regard from a nearby state university, and he was black. Additionally, each year officers were happy to find minority students to fill vacancies in their staffs of student interns and tour guides. In these highly visible positions, minority presence was a good thing.

A second way to color the picture was to highlight those aspects of the College that conformed to the official story about diversity. Information sessions for prospective students invariably included mention of the racial composition of the College. The number was chosen carefully. One officer explained that it was better to say that "15 percent of the student body is multicultural" than to break down that already small number into the individually less impressive statistics for black, Latino, Asian, and Native American students. And officers knew how to surround that 15 percent with other information that summed to a stronger impression. You would move quickly on to state that the College's students came from dozens of foreign countries and that half the student body received some form of financial aid (a figure officers sometimes described as "socioeconomic diversity"). When delivering information sessions myself, I made it a point to mention the full range of religious activity on campus: the interfaith chapel services, the Hillel and Newman chapters, the Muslim, meditation, and evangelical Christian organizations. One of my own favorite additions to the info sessions was an account of recent back-to-back events of the gay/lesbian and evangelical Christian student groups. The calendar week dubbed "Celebration of Sex" had been followed directly by one called "Here is Jesus." Such stories accentuated the varied components of campus culture while placing the one unimpressive statistic into an overall image of student diversity.

A third technique was to prevent less flattering assessments of the College from coming into public view. Just as a harried host might squirrel dirty laundry under the bed when company comes, admissions officers sometimes took care to ensure that campus visitors were not exposed to unsavory views.

High school guidance counselors are among every college's most important external audiences, because they serve as institutional status arbiters for prospective students and their families. Counselors are tutors for status-conscious parents about the relative prestige of various institutions, and they are matchmakers who help prospective students and their families find schools whose attributes fit the predilections of particular kids. This is why admissions officers use care in managing guidance counselors, particularly the ones from schools serving wealthy families. So it is telling that when counselors came to campus, as, for example, on the motorcoach tours coordinated by the College and some of its regional neighbors, officers were thoughtful about who the visitors would see.

Early in my fieldwork I helped Val Marin coordinate the on-campus details for a motorcoach tour. It was one of my first work assignments in the office, and I was eager to do it right. I leaned heavily on Val, an old hand in the office and an extremely skilled one, for advice. One part of my job was to secure student talent to entertain the counselors during a wine-and-cheese hour. Val typically asked a student singing group to perform a few of its locally famous campy numbers. Part of the show involved the singers introducing themselves to the audience; Val was careful to give stage directions on this point in advance. "Let's have them say their name and what their major is. Not where they're from. That happened last year and it was 'Hi I'm from Connecticut, and I'm from Connecticut, and I'm from Connecticut too.' It doesn't make the best impression.'"

I also was to recruit faculty to chat with the counselors during the reception. For this Val cautioned that we needed to invite "people who aren't introverted" and to steer clear of certain faculty who couldn't be trusted in such settings. One minority professor with a reputation for her critical views of campus race relations was at the top of Val's no-way list:

> I cannot trust her. I can't trust what she will say. I mean, once she told some counselors that she would not be comfortable advising a person of color to come here. She said that right in front of high school guidance counselors! And another time I heard her say that she doesn't feel safe on campus. That she walks around afraid that someone is going to hit her over the head with a hockey stick. I mean, come on. We simply can't have that.

Needless to say, this professor received few invitations to hobnob with guidance counselors.

Lest some of these representational strategies appear inordinately deceptive, it is important to remember that all of us tend to high-light our most impressive attributes while obscuring unflattering ones. Disciplined impression management is a benchmark of social maturity for both individuals and organizations. Tending to appear-ances, and adhering to the official rules of a game, are things about which we want both our children and our institutions to be con-cerned.[22] In working hard to appear "diverse" at this point in his-tory, the College is engaged in a process fundamental to all collec-tive life. It is trying to play by the rules that now define good behavior in elite higher education. And even while at times this im-pression management means that officers emphasize the convenient truths while hiding less flattering ones, I never saw College person-nel engage in the kind of sorcerous spin that apparently is par for the course in Washington and in corporate America.[23] Quite to the contrary: officers were consistently thoughtful about how to represent the College in the best possible light without being dishonest. As Danesha Adams said to me, describing her efforts to recruit students of color, "My job is to paint a picture for them, to tell them as positive a story as I can about the College. But I'm not going to lie."

Hard to Get

Beyond the official rhetoric, most of the officers seemed to care genuinely that the College grow its multicultural enrollment. One day Liam Rizer volunteered to me that the College's incremental successes in recruiting more students of color was "one of the things that I'm most proud of doing [during my time here]. . . . I think that's just the right thing to do." Other officers made it clear that enhancing campus diversity was an important professional goal for them. In the course of my fieldwork I never heard an officer even suggest that the College was devoting *excessive* attention to minority recruitment. And in fact the College's many efforts to represent itself as a diverse institution were paralleled by an ongoing commitment to realize racial diversity in the form of greater numbers of black, Latino, and Asian students. Despite genuine commitments and more than a little organizational muscle, though, the task of recruiting students of color in general, and black and Latino kids in particular, was a tough one.

It is tempting to think of college entrance as a beginning, a mark of the transition to adulthood. But in sociological terms this point also marks the end of a complicated educational process. College applicants are not just out there in the population, waiting for the requisite deadlines to approach before they submit paperwork to their schools of choice. They are, rather, delivered to the point of application by social systems that send children from different groups to this particular destination at different rates.

Imagine the journey toward adult prosperity as a crowded automobile freeway. In each vehicle there is a parent driver keeping an eye on the young passengers in the backseat. Eventually the kids will do a lot of the steering, but the change of drivers is very gradual. This is a one-way road. Everyone is moving forward, but the quality of the vehicles they are navigating varies directly, if imperfectly, with the amount of money they have. Relatively wealthy parents enjoy the latest technologies, the most comfortable rides, and they have the means to keep their machines running smoothly. Poorer parents are more likely to drive the older models, or economy versions with weaker engines. They can be intimidated by the fast movers, and so they often stick cautiously to the slower lanes. And because they have fewer resources to keep their machines up and running, these drivers tend to deliver their cargoes less predictably and less far. This has big consequences for children's life outcomes, because prosperity in adulthood now virtually mandates that families deliver their children at least to the point of college entrance—a feat that requires years of mindful navigation even under the best conditions. What is more, children's arrival at prosperity is somewhat better ensured by an even farther exit: admission to a highly selective school.[24]

Let us presume that all of the drivers want their children to reach prosperity, and that they do whatever they can to enhance their children's chances of getting there. Despite everyone's best efforts, the traffic thins out as the years progress, for reasons having largely to do with social class. Parents from different class groups raise their children with different amounts and kinds of resources, and these differences result in variable academic and extracurricular attainments. Relatively affluent parents are more likely to reside in communities with academically rigorous public schools rich with athletics, music, arts, and forensics programs. These are the kinds of schools that consistently produce the exemplary achievements favored by selective colleges: the debate champions, the all-state swimmers, the transcripts quilted with numerous honors and AP-level courses. When affluent children confront problems at school, their parents, who are likely to be skilled in the language and rhythms of white-collar workplaces, know how to get teachers and administrators to pay attention to them. Dissatisfied mothers and fathers may remove their children from the public sector entirely, opting instead for private schools. It is as if they take a costly alternative, a toll lane, past the slower paths of mediocre public schools.

Students from economically modest backgrounds face cumulative impediments on the journey toward adult prosperity. First, the educational lanes in which they travel are not so smooth. Lower-income families are more likely to reside in communities whose schools have weaker academic programs, thinner extracurricular offerings, and weak or nonexistent college counseling. Individual drivers cannot improve the road themselves. The best they can do is try to keep their own machines running and avoid the most formidable obstacles in the road. But often these families' own household machinery is far from luxurious: tight finances, chronic indebtedness, and job loss are more likely to be facts of life. Additionally these families may be unskilled in negotiating through their troubles with administrators, teachers, and social service providers, because the parents' own jobs have not equipped them to be deft with the linguistic and strategic tools of white-collar workplaces. In short the task of moving children forward can in itself be a significant accomplishment, because many of the drivers have sketchy road maps, unreliable machines, and thin insurance for the troubles that almost inevitably come up along the way.

Many of these less-privileged families have the ambition to take their children far, but the generally difficult conditions and the slower traffic around them inhibit their progress. And then there are all those tempting alternative destinations, the splashy billboards along the roadside advertising more proximate satisfactions: direct entrance into the labor force; community college; military service;

early motherhood; crime. In light of these relatively more attainable ambitions, and the difficulties less-privileged families face on the long road to selective schools, the idea of a prestigious degree will be a distant dream for many children and their parents—a fantasy, if it is considered at all.

Because they are, in general, enjoying fairly comfortable rides, affluent families are more likely to stay on course to elite colleges. They also are insulated from many of the tempting amusements and necessary pit stops that pull many parties off that road. Affluent children enjoy childhoods less troubled by the financial uncertainties that make life unpredictable in poorer households. The neighborhoods in which they grow up are likely to be physically safe and geographically removed from the glitter of urban street life. As they begin to imagine their own futures, affluent children will tend to assume that college will be a part of the picture. They and their friends will devote considerable time to thinking about where, not whether or how, to attend a highly regarded school. In this they will receive elaborate assistance from college guidance professionals.[25]

The road to college is not race-neutral. Black and Latino households are disproportionately represented in the lower tiers of the class system, which means that black and Latino children are carried toward adulthood by social processes that render them considerably less likely to make it to an elite college or university.[26] The nation's long history of residential segregation by race is an important part of this pattern of racial disadvantage, because it has concentrated low-income blacks, in particular, in central urban areas with ailing schools. The legacy of racial segregation means that middle-class black families tend to live adjacent to poorer rather than wealthier neighborhoods; this makes it more difficult for black families to accumulate the property wealth that facilitates social mobility, and it exposes black children to a wider gamut of costly temptations—

criminal activity, drug abuse, early pregnancy—than one finds in wealthier suburban communities.[27]

All of these factors contribute to a situation in which highly selective schools like the College open their doors to welcome minority applicants, only to find that relatively few of them have made it to the point of readiness for admission. They have gone directly into the labor force, joined the military, or dropped out of high school. They have entered community colleges, perhaps staying close to home in order to take care of younger siblings, support their parents, or raise their own children. Astonishingly large numbers of black and Latino men have been sent to prison.[28]

To be sure, many black and Latino young people stay on course to the point of college entrance. Some come from affluent families and enjoy the toll roads to college. Some apply smarts and determination to modest circumstances and travel as far or farther than many more-privileged students. Nevertheless, in the aggregate, African American and Latino high schoolers do less well than whites and Asians on virtually every measure of college readiness. One of the most consequential indexes, earned SAT scores, reveals the general pattern. While average SAT scores tests have risen for all students over the years, aggregate scores for whites and Asians are consistently the highest. The racial disparities are most pronounced on the SAT math test, in which average scores for blacks trail those of whites by more than 100 points and of Asians by more than 150 points. But the difference is significant on the verbal test as well, where the difference in average scores between blacks and whites, for example, also comes close to 100 points.[29] Especially troubling is the fact that significant racial disparities in aggregate test scores remain even after researchers control for students' socioeconomic status and family background.[30] This is especially consequential at schools toward the top of higher education's prestige hierarchy, schools where officers like Danesha Adams and her colleagues are obliged to make fine distinctions among large numbers of highly qualified applicants. As Danesha put it, "Nationally the average SAT score is [about] 1050. The kids we are looking for are not normal. They are so many standard deviations above that. That's who we're dealing with, so we take it for granted. But it's a very small niche."

The relatively few minority students who are in that niche are coveted prizes in an intense competition among the admissions offices of the nation's most selective schools. There are only a limited number of minority students available in each year's pool of applicants to selective institutions, and this hard demographic fact compounds the already competitive dynamics of the system. Literally every selective college in the country is after the same small number of minority kids each year. Danesha illustrated the problem succinctly when she described how the competitive dynamic played out at the College:

> There is this idea out there [on campus] that we're just not doing enough, or we're not going to the right [high] schools and getting the right kids. But what they don't know is that the kids we want, the kids we are considering for the College, also have lots of other options. A kid that we take with 1200 boards might be comparing us with Harvard, Stanford. . . . I was talking with an administrator here the other day, and she [said] that we should take kids . . . who have SAT scores 150 points below our class average. Well, if our class average is [about 1350] now, that means kids with 1200 boards. Well, these kids with 1200 boards have lots of other options, and they'll look at them and they'll go to the place with the most prestige. Just like any other kid.

Just like any other kid, Danesha said, minority applicants tend to choose the most prestigious school to which they are admitted. And because all the very top schools want these students, schools that are only near the top, like the College, often lose minority applicants to institutions farther up the pecking order.

For any skeptics, Danesha had evidence from a recent admissions cycle to support her claim.

> I had [name of secretary] run off a list of the multicultural kids we accepted, but who went elsewhere, and their SAT scores. And the SAT scores are 1200, 1150, 1100. And they're going to Yale, Stanford, [name of a highly selective liberal arts school, a competitor]. You know what . . . we'll accept them . . . and we'll get a letter back saying "well I'm going to Dartmouth."

When Danesha talked to me about this problem, which she did on several occasions, it was typically with a tone of frustration. "It's like, what do we have to do to get these kids?" she said to me once in a long car ride. "It's at the point where some of the kids we are turning down, because of their grades and test scores, are being accepted at [names of more selective schools]."

Given the high demand, we should perhaps not be surprised by the proliferation of service programs designed to facilitate minority students' transition to college. The programs have names like Upward Bound, TRIO, One Voice, GEAR UP, COACH, Posse, and Link. They function like roadside assistance programs on the journey to college, supplying missing parts, mechanical advice, and substitute rides to kids whose families are making the trip on bumpy roads or with modest equipment. These programs tend to support students during the crucial last years of high school, when academic accomplishment and guidance counseling can make or break a shot at admission to a selective school. Admissions officers like these programs because, much like the good reputations of affluent public and preparatory schools, service programs for educationally disadvantaged kids provide college admissions officers with proxy assurance of applicants' academic seriousness and general preparation. They reduce the search costs inherent in finding qualified applicants.[31]

Some selective colleges have gotten into the business of developing their own assistance programs for minority students, selecting promising kids who are a few years away from college and helping them navigate the final distance. The College's Start-Up program was an effort of this kind. Generously supported by the private foundation of a wealthy College family, Start-Up was intended to provide college prep advice to minority students and get them thinking about the goal of selective admission in general and the College in particular. Participants were brought to campus for seven days and put through a crash course in college-level academics and the selective application process. In addition to my writing workshop, students took mini-courses in philosophy, world politics, and a kind of college-application 101. They were introduced to the lingo of admissions *(Early Decision, matriculate, student/faculty ratio)* and given advice on such things as How Good Candidates Get Denied *(deadlines, bad attitude, senioritis, lack of information)*. The College covered all expenses, including travel to campus, and provided participants with modest stipends.

Start-Up was regarded locally as an innovative recruitment effort, but I learned from one of my own Start-Up students that it was hardly unique. At the end of the class session I described above, one girl lingered over her paper after the others had left for lunch. If it was a flirtation, a bid at having the teacher all to herself, I took the bait. I walked up to her and said playfully "D-O-N-E. Done!" She submitted her paper and we chatted a bit. I learned that this was only one of several college prep programs that Krystal, from Chicago, was attending that summer. She had just returned from a week at a private college in downstate Indiana, where the emphasis had been on media ("It was kind of cool, we got to make our own videos, that's what it was, kind of media studies"). After Start-Up she would be on to her third commitment, in Wisconsin: "I'm missing the first part of that program because I said I was doing this one, and they said 'Oh that's OK, come anyway.'" One of the programs carried a stipend of over a thousand dollars.

In addition to such programs, academically accomplished minority applicants could expect generous financial aid packages, expenses-paid recruitment visits, and other perks from the many schools eager to enhance their minority numbers. Some of the effects of this competitive system struck Danesha Adams as perverse.

> It's interesting how quickly these kids develop a sense of entitlement, just like the other kids [at the College], that once they're here it's not supposed to cost them anything. Like they're owed the education for free. And they complain about leaving school with loans, or they ask for some money for some particular program and they get turned down and they say, 'Well, there you go.' And I have to say that some of them are encouraged in this by some faculty and administrators. Well, you know what? I don't think that kids are owed a $35,000 education. They may be entitled to a college education, that's what public universities are for. But they are not entitled to [this particular] education. So I find that very problematic, that for some of the students they see this as something they shouldn't have to pay for. . . . I said this just the other day in Start-Up, college education is the only product where people sometimes expect not to have to pay for it. I said to them, *imagine you're at a Lexus dealership, and you told the dealer, "You know what, I would look good in that car, I think you should give it to me for $500."* We would never say that. Or *"I think you should just give it to me."* That would never happen. But somehow with college sometimes kids presume that they should get it for nothing. And they'll go into debt for other things, credit debt for the fancy stuff. But not for college.

It is a sobering dynamic. Virtually every selective college and university in the country has an official commitment to racial diversity, yet at the top of the college selection pyramid there are very few black and Latino students to go around. So elite institutions that routinely send thousands of qualified applicants away go out looking for qualified applicants of a certain sort. They start the hunt even when the kids are years away from college. If the bounty needs a hand along the way, hunters are armed with all of the relevant expertise. They can waive application fees. They might even negotiate on tuition. But even with all of this effort there are not enough minority students left on the road to selective schools to meet demand. So students like Krystal can fill up their summer calendars by accepting multiple invitations.

The dearth of minority candidates making it into proximity of selective college entrance is especially profound among black and Latino men. Danesha Adams offered some grim figures in this regard when she described the challenge of recruiting boys for Start-Up. For the first year of the program Danesha sent out twice as many invitations to boys as to girls. She knew from experience that academically accomplished minority boys are harder to locate, and she figured the disproportionate invitations would enhance her odds of getting a gender balance in the program. That first year she enrolled twenty-three female participants but only nine males. So the following year she sent invitations to even more boys. Three hundred invitations to males yielded only thirteen accepts. "I'm convinced that if I sent invitations only to boys, I'd still get a majority of girls," Danesha said. "They'd pass them on to their sisters. The parents would send their daughters."[32]

Beyond the general paucity of potential applicants in certain demographic groups, small liberal arts schools like the College face an additional recruitment challenge. Officers who work with minority families point out that different racial groups conceive of the institutional status order in different ways. I first learned about this when I happened to be working alongside Danesha Adams and Terrence Carter, stuffing envelopes for a mass mailing. I asked Terrence what he had found most surprising about his job at the College, compared with his last post in the admissions office of a prominent state university. "I suppose what surprised me the most was the low quality of our minority applicants," he said.

"Low quality," I repeated, just to make sure I had heard him right.

"Yeah. Low. I mean, at State, we had a lot of minority applicants who were a lot stronger. A *lot* stronger. And we would get them too. It's like they'd apply to Yale and Brown and we would be their second choice, their safety school. If they didn't get in to the Ivy, they'd come to State."

I noted to myself how different this was from how counselors at affluent white schools thought about academic prestige. They and their clients saw a fine calibration of status, with the Ivies at the top, good but less selective schools in the middle, and regional state universities at the bottom. One counselor from a private school in New York City had told me, for example, that schools in the SUNY system had "no cachet at all. None, really, for my parents." Apparently it was different in other communities.

"I think it's that black families just haven't heard of [the College], or they don't think about the whole liberal arts thing," Terrence continued. "It's like, they think of the big-name private schools, the Ivies, and then the public universities, and not as much in between. I think there are an awful lot of schools that minority kids don't even think of."

I ventured, "I wonder if liberal arts colleges are kind of a white thing, sort of a white preference, and it's not really the same for black kids." Both Terrence and Danesha nodded their heads, that there was probably something to that. Danesha went on, "Or like

with Asian families, a lot of them are really interested in name recognition, that's really important to them, and if you don't have that
you're a lot less compelling."

And there was the problem of the College's location. The officers
widely presumed, not without evidence, that the College's rural setting was a hard sell for many minority applicants. Minority kids
were more likely to hail from urban areas, where they were accustomed not only to racial and ethnic pluralism but also to schools
and neighborhoods in which they were not "minorities" at all. Prospective students from large urban centers sometimes betrayed in-
comprehension about just how far the College was from their
hometowns. Danesha frequently told a story about one prospective
student who assumed that she could travel to campus on the com-
muter rail system serving New York City, hundreds of miles away.

Additionally these students' parents were often wary of sending
their children across the cultural distance that sometimes needed to
be traversed when they attended the College. Mr. Carlisle, a veteran
administrator in the dean of students office who participated actively in multicultural recruitment, told me that it was actually
more difficult to recruit the parents than the kids. Parents, he said,

> are worried that their kids are going to go away to this place, and
> then they come home the parents aren't going to understand their
> kids anymore. They're afraid their kids will leave for a different
> world. That's the hard part for them. And so I spend a lot of time
> with the parents, working to gain their trust. I have them come [to
> campus] to spend time here, not just on special, parent weekends but
> just to spend regular time on regular days, so they know what it's like.

In the end there were several reasons it was hard for the College
to get minority students. The social processes that bring young people to the point of selective college entrance delivered relatively few
black and Latino students generally. Those who did get to this point

were objects of intense competition among the nation's most prestigious schools. Places that were good, but somewhat less selective,
like the College, often lost out to the Ivies and other more prestigious institutions in the race to land minority students. It seemed
that schools like the College figured less prominently in the educational aspirations of minority families. And the facts of geographic
and cultural distance often stacked the deck against the College's
bids to recruit these coveted students.

Still, it would be incorrect to paint the College's modest success at
minority recruitment as limited entirely by the spinning wheels of
larger social systems. The school's own machinery inhibited minority recruitment as well.

The Typical Student

Clearly there were important aspects of minority recruitment that
admissions officers could do little about. They could not rewrite the
history of higher education in America, which had created an organizational landscape in which schools traditionally serving Anglo-
European Protestants were now disproportionately the wealthiest
and most highly regarded. They could not by themselves change the
societal-level organization of wealth, race, and educational opportunity that brought relatively few black and Latino students into the
orbit of selective colleges. They could not easily ignore the fierce
competition for minority applicants when "diversity" is now an important marker of legitimacy and excellence in academia. And they
certainly could not change the College's zip code. Nevertheless,
there were things the school could do to move its demographic in
the desired direction.

The College did many of these things. There was the official diversity, broadcast over every possible medium from admissions literature to commencement addresses, which, many hoped, sent the

right signals to prospective minority students. There was the direc-
torship of multicultural recruitment, Danesha Adams's job. There
was Start-Up, and the periodic recruitment weekends during the
academic year targeted specifically to minority students. There were
special recruitment initiatives for students of color in Boston and
Chicago. There were designated staff positions in the dean of students' office, officially described as serving the needs of "educationally disadvantaged" students but widely regarded on campus as primarily serving the minority enrollment. And over the years there
were incremental changes in the racial composition of the student
body. On that one crucial statistic—percentage of students who
are nonwhite U.S. citizens—"our strategy is to creep that number
up a little bit each year," Liam Rizer told me time and again. And
they did.

From the standpoint of many admissions officers, the College
was doing virtually everything it could to recruit students of color,
and it bothered officers a little when concerned parties from other
parts of the institution—faculty, alumni—weighed in with big ideas
about how to improve the numbers. "We have a joke in the office,"
Danesha told me one morning over breakfast. "Every time someone
from outside the office approaches us with an idea about how to recruit minority students, we say, *Maybe we should get a bus and drive
[minority students] up to see the College. Maybe we should get a bus.*
Well you know what, we've tried that. We've tried the bus." The
general perception among officers was that it was easy for other people to blame Admissions for lackluster minority numbers because
outsiders knew so little about just how complicated minority recruitment was.

Still, it was difficult to disregard some of the contrarian opinions:
the Asian student who had accepted the College's admission offer
and then, once here, felt like she'd been fooled into believing the
place was considerably more diverse than it actually was; the young

admissions officer, a College alum, who subtly conveyed to me her uncertainty about just what her alma mater's official commitment to minority recruitment really meant. There was Terrence Carter's relatively rapid departure for a job elsewhere. And there was the tepid opinion of Mr. Carlisle.

Mr. Carlisle could make several claims to authority on campus, though in fact he rarely had to make them, since he was widely admired and occasionally feared by students, faculty, and administrators alike. He was an African American administrator in the Student Life division, a military veteran, and a longtime champion of higher education funding in the state capitol. He was so revered that, even despite the College's pervasive first-name culture, virtually everyone, including President Evers, referred to him as "Mr. Carlisle." Many believed that Mr. Carlisle more or less single-handedly maintained the College's stellar minority retention rate. He had a good track record, a regional reputation, and intelligence going for him on occasions when he wanted something to go his way. There was the time a few years ago, for example, when Mr. Carlisle had gone to the college president in a successful effort to overturn a negative admissions decision that had already been mailed to a black male applicant. There was the fact that Mr. Carlisle was annually extended the courtesy of perusing certain applications even after they had been evaluated by Admissions. He was the sort of person you wanted to have on your side.

So I took notice when Mr. Carlisle conveyed a considerably less rosy impression of the College's minority recruitment efforts than the one I had developed over many months in Admissions. Mr. Carlisle spoke at length about a time when he had worked with a colleague from Atlanta to assemble a list of contacts at private schools that enrolled large numbers of African American students. "Well-prepared, full-paying students who don't need financial aid," as he described them. The officer who was given the contacts made the Atlanta trip on other business but apparently never followed through on the contacts. Mr. Carlisle then said he knew of other liberal arts colleges that used their athletics programs in recruitment efforts specifically targeted to students of color, but he did not talk about any comparable efforts at the College. Then he spoke, again at length, about a new minority recruitment program for which the College had contracted with an outside agency, but somehow he managed to say nothing positive about it. Then I realized that, in the course of a two-hour conversation devoted almost entirely to minority recruitment at the College, Mr. Carlisle had said very little in the way of praise.

Like any politically touchy issue, the matter of whether the College was doing everything it could to recruit minority applicants depended upon who was asked. Those who answered the question affirmatively could point to a long list of admissions programs and initiatives and incrementally improving class statistics. Critics could point to the distance between rhetoric and reality, squandered recruitment opportunities, and other schools that were doing better in their minority numbers. But in time I came to suspect that what was most consequential for the racial composition of the College was something on which boosters and critics would agree: the typical student.

The typical student did not officially exist. When inquisitors asked for a description of this student, the automatic response was that there was no such thing. I said so, poker-faced, many times, to prospective students myself. It was part of the job, and in fact what I said was technically true. There was no single type of College student. But there was what statisticians would call the *modal case,* what humanists might call the *archetype.* Whatever to call her, virtually everyone—admissions staff, current students, faculty, alumni, and high school guidance counselors who were at all in the know— agreed that the typical student existed. Because of course the typical student was coextensive with the College's reputation. She was a big chunk of your enrollment, the kind of kid the alumni had been when they were her age, the type you saw so often on the brick-paved paths between classes, chatting happily with her typical friends. She seemed so at home here. She was the kid guidance counselors had in mind when they described the College to their clients, the kind who would be comfortable at a place like this. Like the College itself, the typical student was financially comfortable, athletically capable, academically respectable, and physically attractive. Very good academically, if perhaps not the best in her high school class. Usually from the urban Northeast or an area in the orbit of a few other large cities. More likely than not, suburban. And white.

It was this typical student that admissions officers talked about when they used terms like *fill* and *bread and butter* to describe the admits they could count on to take a big chunk of the seats in each year's entering class. Typical students appeared often at campus information sessions and at the recruitment events officers held on the road during fall travel season. Many had been handpicked by their guidance counselors to meet the College's reps when they visited high schools. Compared with most of the applicants called "multicultural," typical students were more likely to have traveled in the fast lane toward selective college entrance. They had been the beneficiaries of strong academic programs, summer sports camps, and SAT prep courses. Sometimes their application essays described an exchange year in Israel, a tour of Europe, or pursuit of an exotic hobby like capoeira or orienteering. They tended to have decent test scores. They tended to pay full tuition.

Typical students, in fact, were the human fuel preferred by the College's organizational machinery. They enabled the place to run smoothly in lots of ways. They sought out places just like the College and generally liked what they saw when they visited campus. They had a clear sense of what it took to be admitted, and they got a lot of help assembling their applications. They looked good on paper. Many of them never even filed the financial aid forms. Those typical students who were admitted and who enrolled (and a great many of them did enroll) tended to quickly identify with the place. They did not have to buy new clothes or fudge their family backgrounds in order to fit into the dominant student culture, and they were spared of minor embarrassments like having to spell out their names for professors. Long after graduation, many of these typical students would remember their time at the College as among the best years of their lives, and their affection for the school would be eagerly encouraged by personnel in the Development Office. At least that is what the overwhelming preponderance of white people in wedding portraits and reunion photos and necrology headshots in the alumni magazine led one to suspect.

The bottom line was that typical students were the sustenance that the College relied upon most heavily to maintain its financial prosperity. Just as physical bodies are shaped by their dietary histories, the organizational character of the College betrayed the steady richness of its human food. Over many years the College had grown fat by catering to affluent families and by nurturing affection for alma mater in the hearts of its most socioeconomically successful alumni. As is the case with any organization that has grown accustomed to long stretches of affluence, the College's employees were not predisposed to significant cutbacks or dramatic changes of intake.

This is why Liam Rizer could be justly proud of the consistently incremental movement of the multicultural numbers. On the one hand, Liam and his colleagues could be pleased that they were moving things in the right direction, gradually shifting the College's diet of students in accord with prevailing ideals about diversity. On the other hand, the changes were consistently marginal because the College pursued most of its business on the presumption that its primary clientele would continue to be typical students. A reliance on typical students seemed to explain why there were no systematic efforts to recruit among the sizable black communities in the region's nearby cities. It seemed to explain why there was no systematic effort to tap the growing size and wealth of Latino populations in California, Texas, the mountain West, and southern Florida. The reliance on typical students seemed to explain why I never heard anyone even suggest that the College should fundamentally rethink its applicant pool—should, for example, redirect its primary recruitment strategies away from wealthy white northeastern enclaves and toward other demographic groups. Like an addict in denial, the College kept its dependence immune to scrutiny.[33]

Ironies of Affirmative Action

Virtually all selective colleges are officially committed to increasing their minority numbers, and in general their efforts have been fruitful. Over the last forty years African Americans, the original beneficiaries of admissions preference initiatives, have enrolled in the nation's most selective schools in significantly greater numbers.[34] And there is solid evidence that they are academically well served once they enroll. Recent scholarship by Mario Small and Christopher Winship finds, for example, that institutional selectivity is strongly and positively related to college completion for black students: quite simply, the more selective the college black students attend, the more likely they are to graduate.[35]

It is notable that schools originally built to serve an Anglo-Protestant elite do such a good job of serving students from very different backgrounds. These schools continue to be exclusive, but they simultaneously are able to incorporate new kinds of personnel. What they might not yet be so good at is creating contexts in which students of color can enjoy their college years as much as their white peers. Research consistently shows that black students, in particular, often experience the social side of college life on predominantly white campuses as a struggle.[36] I was sobered to realize that administrators at the College tended to talk about the needs of minority students almost exclusively in terms of their academic progress and the necessity of keeping them free from explicit harassment or discrimination; the question of whether students of color were enjoying their educations was perhaps too luxurious a concern.

In addition to its incremental improvements in minority admissions, the College had an especially impressive record of minority retention. It had earned bragging rights among student-life professionals for the high proportion of its black students, specifically, who completed their degrees. Regardless of how one perceived the situation, the glass was half empty and half full. Whether the College's efforts to integrate its student body were reactionary or progressive ultimately depended on who was doing the perceiving and how they measured progress. But whatever its pace, change was probably inevitable, because the desires of the College's typical students had changed over time in ways that even a conservative school could not afford to ignore.

In the course of my fieldwork, I specifically asked several admissions officers just who the College's commitment to diversity was for. Danesha Adams believed that the consequential parties included "some of the more sophisticated prep school kids." "They'll say things in interviews like, 'Well, my roommate is from Trinidad, and diversity is very important to me.'" Danesha also pointed out that official measures of campus diversity had become unofficial markers of institutional prestige in the little universe of elite higher education. "I'd say that the College wants to encourage diversity, but even if they didn't want to they'd have to do it anyway, so they would. They want to but they also have to, because that's what's expected of a school of a certain caliber. It has to be diverse."

Liam Rizer thought that the demand for diversity was strongest among the most academically accomplished students in each year's applicant pool.

> The high performers, they look around and think, "I don't want to be at a school where it's all white upper-middle-class kids." They want a different experience than that, and we know that. So it's become important just to attract the kind of students we're trying to attract.

Liam confessed that the need to appeal to these top students was an important part of the incentive to grow the multicultural numbers. But he also believed that the shifting demographic improved the school's character more generally. "The College is a different place now," he continued. "I mean it's still, you know, the rich kids and the upper-middle-class kids and the cars and the clothes. But there's more here now. It's a more interesting place, I think." Another seasoned officer, Alan Albinoni, believed that racial diversity was an important "marketing" objective among all the elite schools. "Part of what we are trying to do is to create diverse campuses, where people can go to school with people who are different from them, even if they hardly interact with them, to go to a school with a diverse student body," Alan explained. "People don't realize the marketing aspect of that. At some level it's just really important, from a sheer marketing standpoint."

Officers cared about minority admissions for several reasons, then: because they thought that admitting minorities was the right thing to do; because the national reputation of the College was linked to its minority numbers; and because the school's typical students increasingly demanded a diverse student body. These findings suggest that among the most enduring effects of the rights movements of the 1960s was a shift in cultural presumptions about what counts as a good education.[37] The academic leaders who invented the idea of educational diversity and the strategies for achieving it also created a new standard of academic excellence. Those schools that claim to be the best now work hard to be racially diverse, because their institutional peers and their most sought-after clients now expect as much. This is an irony of affirmative action that has not been fully appreciated by previous observers: admissions practices that originally were intended to insulate elite schools from accusations of racial exclusion have acquired a very different meaning. "Diversity," as measured by the numbers of students in sharply defined categories, is now an index of academic prestige.

A second irony, and a more troubling one, is that the strategic importance of these categories encourages selective schools to distribute opportunity in peculiarly circumscribed ways. I was present on many occasions when admissions officers expressed ambivalence about how various definitions of race, diversity, and educational disadvantage fared in the applicant evaluation process. It troubled officers when budget exigencies and the official definitions of diversity made it hard for them to admit many deserving students who lacked the right mix of skin color, citizenship, and financial need. As Beth Cole recollected to me, looking back over her two years of experience in the office:

> Some of the hardest decisions were about, say, these hardworking immigrant kids from New York City. They may have been from Latvia, Russia, Eastern European kids. Not very good public high schools, but great grades and they're working very hard. Obviously they've overcome a lot, they've worked hard, they would do so well at college. But their SAT scores wouldn't be great, that was often the case, and they'd be very expensive, just as expensive as the multicultural kids, but we couldn't take them.

I had a good sense of the reasons why, but I asked Beth directly rather than filling in the blanks on my own. "Because we couldn't count them as multicultural, and because they would have weak SAT scores, which they often did, and because they cost [financial aid] money," she told me squarely.

Every year there were kids like this, lots of them: international students from a rainbow of racial backgrounds who nevertheless did not count in the official statistics for minority students (they were tallied instead in the less consequential "international" category); Afro-Caribbean immigrants with stellar academic records whose parents had never completed the paperwork that would have rendered their children U.S. citizens and hence countable on the minority numbers; pale-skinned valedictorians from rural New England or Brighton Beach. Officers took as many of these students as they could, on the various consequential dimensions, afford. But there were always more who were turned away.

Forty years ago, the nation's academic leaders created a morally weighty language of diversity to explain their race-specific interventions into the social processes that deliver young people to college. While the diversity talk was vague and expansive, the measure that came to serve as diversity's proxy was narrowly, even arbitrarily, precise. That the number of nonwhite U.S. citizens in its student body became the primary yardstick of a school's diversity and, however implicitly, its commitment to educational opportunity, is an accident of affirmative action's strange career. Today the official measure encourages the inclusion of some worthy applicants and the exclusion of worthy others. This is why affirmative action is controversial.

chapter six

DECISIONS

In the summer of 2003 the United States Supreme Court handed down two decisions regarding selective admissions. At issue in both cases was whether and how admissions officers could consider race in the assessment of applicants. In one case, *Gratz v. Bollinger,* the Court ruled that the affirmative action system used at the University of Michigan's undergraduate college was unconstitutional. That system added a fixed number of points to applicants from certain racial groups on the numerical scores used to make undergraduate admissions decisions. The Court's ruling in the other case, *Grutter v. Bollinger,* regarding the University of Michigan law school, was a cautious endorsement of racial affirmative action when conducted in the context of what Justice Sandra Day O'Connor, writing for a narrow majority, called the "individualized consideration" of applications:

> We find that the Law School's admissions program bears the hallmarks of a narrowly tailored [race-conscious admissions] plan. As Justice Powell made clear in *Bakke,* truly individualized consideration demands that race be used in a flexible, nonmechanical way. It follows from this mandate that universities cannot establish quotas for members of certain racial groups or put members of those groups on

separate admissions tracks. . . . Universities can, however, consider race or ethnicity more flexibly as a "plus" factor in the context of individualized consideration of each and every applicant.[1]

The term "individualized consideration" was sprinkled throughout the *Grutter* decision, leaving little doubt about the kind of evaluation the Supreme Court regarded as optimal.[2]

Consideration of the Early Decision (ED) applications began each year around Thanksgiving. There was a palpable excitement in the office about it, this first of a long series of meetings called "committee," a sense of anticipation heightened by the coincidence of the winter holidays. After ED there would be weeks of reading, in December and January, when officers spent very long days and nights poring through applications and the office hired additional staff simply to open the flood of incoming mail. Committee recommenced for Regular Decision applications in late January and continued well into March, when the "fat packets" of admission and the "thin envelopes" of rejection were posted in time for delivery by the notification deadline religiously heeded by most selective schools, April 1.

Committee is the dramatic crest of the annual admissions cycle. It is when all of the many exigencies that officers are charged with managing get explicitly negotiated, and when officers do what the general public perceives them as doing primarily. The other aspects of admissions work—the travel, the courting of applicants and counselors and parents, the endless maintenance of databases and files—all seem a little mundane in comparison. The thrill of committee wore off long before it was finished, but in mid-November the job was as fresh and welcomed as the recently falling snow.

Previous accounts of selective admissions have tended either to over- or underestimate the importance of committee. On the one hand, journalists and admissions officers themselves often overplay it. They tend to see committee as the crucial moment for applicants rather than the conclusion of the years-long, incremental series of preparatory evaluations that it actually is. They tend to believe in the version of reality dramatized by committee itself, namely, that the evaluation of applications happens at a specific time and place by a relatively small number of people. On the other hand, social scientists have tended to discount the importance of committee in the overall architecture of educational transitions. Because they have been interested primarily in population-level relationships—in the characteristics of who is and is not admitted to elite schools in the aggregate—social scientists have not recognized the importance of the fact that, at the most prestigious institutions, admissions decisions are made about *individuals.* Consequently, they have scarcely considered the importance of individualized consideration to the structure of inequality in elite higher education in America.

My primary argument in this chapter is that individualized consideration creates peculiar and heretofore unacknowledged forms of class bias in selective college admissions. Considering applicants as individuals and not just as the attributes listed in their files obliges admissions officers to glue attributes together into coherent and aesthetically compelling composites—characters, in other words, with names. I call this glue *evaluative storytelling.* When applications are not accompanied by sufficient raw material for crafting compelling stories, they remain mere types that officers have seen hundreds or even thousands of times. As types, applications are easy enough to categorize. Types, however, have little that compels the making of exceptions, or what officers call "stretching," for them. This is why evaluative storytelling is most elaborate for borderline applicants. When decisions are tough calls, a good story can be a decisive advantage.

Coarse Sorts and Fine Distinctions

Not all decisions are the same. They vary in consequence, of course. Deciding what to have for dinner is a matter different from deciding where to live or whom to marry. Decisions also vary in kind. Sometimes the job is to separate, on the basis of relatively clear criteria, those cases that are acceptable from those that not. These are coarse sorts. Other times the job is to discern optimal cases from among multiple acceptable alternatives. These are fine distinctions. A simple illustration clarifies the difference between the two.[3]

Imagine someone intent on selecting a ring for her beloved. It is one thing for this lover to decide in general terms about the kind, quality, and cost of the ring she seeks, quite another to determine which particular ring she will buy. The first is a coarse sort. In pursuing it, the lover will have to decide what features a ring must have to be considered at all. It must have a gold setting, say. It must feature a single precious stone. It must cost somewhere in the neighborhood of a thousand dollars. And it must come from a jeweler reputable enough that the purchaser and her lover will be able to infer its quality merely by looking at the name on the box.

One way to sort acceptable rings from the rest would be to look at every single ring available and apply the chosen criteria: gold setting, single stone, a thousand dollars, reputable seller. But even in a small town with a handful of jewelers, shopping in this way would be a pretty big job. So instead the shopper relies on proxies to sort potentially viable candidates from all the rest. She categorically rules out pawn shops and discount retailers. She consults with friends who recently have made similar purchases. She surfs the Web for buyer testimonials. Armed with the knowledge gleaned from this homework, she simplifies her search by making coarse sorts. She eliminates all rings from consideration except for those sold by, say, two reputable dealers.

From here selection assumes a different character. The buyer will consider each remaining candidate individually. She will discriminate on the basis of little details: the character of each stone's cut and color, the shape and hand feel of each setting. The buyer will be more attentive to the aesthetic and emotional responses she has to the finalists. She may remove a few from further consideration because she "doesn't like" them. She may "fall in love" with one particular ring.

The difference between coarse sorts and fine distinctions is important in organizational life because the two kinds of evaluation have different resource requirements. Many coarse sorts can be made on the basis of a relatively small amount of salient information about candidates. They often can be made in a relatively mechanical fashion, even farmed out to subordinates (or computers) who can be trained (or programmed) to apply universal eligibility criteria to all the cases under consideration. By contrast, fine distinctions tend to require a lot of information. Each case must be known in detail if fine distinctions among cases are to be made. Fine distinctions also tend to take time, and they are harder to standardize, farm out, or computerize. This is because fine distinctions are pursued in order to discern precisely that which standard procedures are designed to ignore, namely, the peculiarities of individual cases.

In an important sense the U.S. Supreme Court rulings in the Michigan affirmative action cases were about marking the difference between coarse sorts and fine distinctions. The undergraduate college's system for giving a standard evaluative advantage to members of certain minority groups was organized around a coarse sort. Applicants falling into particular categories received a categorical advantage. The law school's system, by contrast, was organized around fine distinctions. Minority status mattered, but only through the mechanism of individualized assessment in which race was considered in the context of particular biographies. The Court ultimately ruled that only the latter form of evaluation was a constitutionally acceptable way to consider race in selective admissions. Fine distinctions through individualized assessment were OK. Coarse sorts on the basis of racial categories were not.

However precious the human beings described inside of them, college application files are not diamond rings. They are amalgams of many prior evaluations: standardized test scores, grades on transcripts, recommendation letters, and athletic ratings, for example. Every assessment inside an application folder may reasonably be thought of as something an applicant has earned, of course, but it also is an assessment that some other party has *produced*. Some of these assessments are the product of elaborate bureaucracies. SAT scores are manufactured by a huge testing organization; GPAs and class ranks are administrative summaries of multiple teacher assessments in the form of grades. Then there are the more "personal" assessments: recommendation letters written by teachers and guidance counselors; e-mail messages from alumni and other friends in high places, dutifully printed out by the staff in college admissions offices and added to the application files. When admissions officers sit down to read applications, they do not assess applicants directly. They coalesce prior assessments into an overall evaluation. In this sense the moment of evaluation in admissions offices is only the end point of a process that anthropologist Edwin Hutchins has aptly called "distributed cognition." Each applicant has been observed and evaluated many times through the course of his or her biography; the college application is the paper trail of this widely dispersed evaluative work.[4]

The organizational machinery that produces all of these prior assessments and delivers them to selective colleges is a crucial mechanism of class privilege, because it is not equally distributed throughout the population. This is why individualized consideration does little to mitigate class privilege and, indeed, exaggerates it.

Out of public earshot, officers often described the students they were considering as "apps" or "kids," a practice I mimic below. In doing so they inserted a bit of distance between applications and the human beings represented inside them. Like workers in other settings whose jobs require fateful decisions about other people (in hospitals and welfare offices, for example), admissions officers had a language that enabled them to bracket the emotional difficulties inherent in the work. An app or a kid could be described as "great" or "lousy" or "a dud," accepted or rejected at less psychic cost than the young men and women behind the files.[5]

This psychic distancing was useful because officers were obliged to evaluate hundreds of applications each year. Simply making one's way through the paper was a large task. Letting oneself have feelings about each applicant as a human being was a luxury for which the admissions calendar did not allow sufficient time. Between November and March, each officer at the College typically completed primary reads on four hundred to five hundred applications. Even the most seasoned officers told me that it took at least fifteen minutes of undivided attention to read each file. It all added up to many long days and nights, but by the standards of the admissions profession the College's reading load was a cakewalk. At the big schools—the Columbias, the NYUs—standard loads easily topped one thousand files per person per year. Offices like the one I studied, then, were the places where the kind of individualized consideration the O'Connor court deemed ideal might most plausibly be deployed.

A common axiom in selective admissions is that decisions are not made about applicants, but about applications. The distinction is subtle but important. Evaluation is not of persons but of files. How much and what kind of information is inside those files, and the extent to which readers are able to place that information in the context of its origins, are the primary bases of evaluation.

Reading and Rating

At the College, evaluation was a three-stage process: reading and rating, storytelling, and class crafting.[6] Each stage had components of coarse sorts and fine distinctions, but their mixture varied. Reading and rating was largely a coarse sort. In this stage officers applied standard evaluative criteria to the applications and scored them with a summary number that made it possible to group the applications into three large categories: easy accept, easy deny, and a large middle category. Yet reading and rating also entailed some fine distinction, because officers always read each file individually. They never categorically rejected an application on the basis of a single attribute. Instead each app was assessed on its own, in light of a large battery of standard criteria, and rejected only if multiple indications summed to a composite case for elimination. In other words, reading and rating took the form of a very inefficient ring buyer, someone who takes the time to assess every piece of jewelry individually and regardless of its source of origin. The work quickly became tedious. Officers often took it home, fifty or so files at a time, where they could nurse themselves through it with creature comforts like pajamas and hot tea. They made their way through each application using two standardized forms as their guides.

The form titled "Applicant Rating" was a worksheet for a quantitative evaluation system indigenous to the office and honed from year to year. The nine-point scale (1 = low; 9 = high) was a rough numerical estimate of the desirability of each candidate, and itself was a composite of other estimates. The worksheet featured subsidiary scales with which to estimate the quality of the app's *high school* (measured by the percentage of its graduates who attend four-year colleges); the strength of the app's chosen *curriculum* (measured by the number and difficulty of academic courses, including the number of Advanced Placement [AP] courses); the app's *grades;* and *rank* in high school class. Values on these four scales subsequently were averaged to determine the "Academic" component of the overall score, worth 4 of the total 9. SAT/ACT scores also were converted for incorporation into the 1–9 overall scale, worth 3 of the 9. Accomplishment in extracurricular activities was summarized in the "Personal" score, worth 2 of the 9. The final score was referred to as the app's *fin rating*—short for *financial aid.* The score was used partly to distinguish the most desirable candidates for merit scholarships and to facilitate the hard choices that the limits of institutional budgets always made inevitable.

Determining the fin rating was actually simpler in practice than in theory, as two examples from the approximately one hundred applications I read and rated myself will illustrate. I met both of the applicants rated below during my recruitment trip to the West Coast in the fall of 2001, and I produced the initial ratings of the apps back at the College a few months later. Another officer made second reads of the files when I was finished. Of course, all information that might identify the people represented in these files has been changed here.

There was Hal Cohen from Irving High, an urban public school whose catchment area included one of the wealthiest neighborhoods of the large city in which it was located. In the parlance of the College's Admissions Office, it was a *79 percent high school*—meaning that 79 percent of its graduates went directly on to four-year colleges. Officers used this figure as a proxy for a school's academic caliber, on the presumption that the higher the number, the more likely the school was to offer a rigorous college preparatory curriculum and to have an academically-oriented school culture. Irving's 79 was at the high end for public schools. I rated it 3/4 (3 out of 4) on the *high school* score, because it was clearly geared toward college preparation but probably did not have the uniformly excellent academics of many private and a few of the very best public schools. Hal had a grade point average of 6.51 on a scale, now common in public schools, that granted additional metric weight to grades earned in certain advanced-level courses. Irving High took things a bit further, offering the prestigious International Baccalaureate (IB) diploma for its most ambitious and accomplished students, a group that included Hal. This transcript earned him a 4/4 on both the *curriculum* and the *grades* scores. Because he was at a public high school, the guidance office had provided Hal's rank in class: 21st out of 325 students—clearly in the top 10 percent, so I assigned him a 4/4 on the *rank* score. To compute Hal's overall "Academic" rating, I computed a rough estimate of *high school, curriculum, grades,* and *rank:* (3 + 4 + 4 + 4) ÷ 4, or 4.

Hal was a good tester, too. His combined SAT score was 1400, which put him in the highest quartile of the rating form's SAT component. He earned a 3/3 in the SAT category, bringing his fin rating to 7.

Hal played football and tennis throughout high school, but at an information session I conducted at Irving High he told me that he was not interested in college-level varsity sports. He had other things on his plate, specifically, heavy involvement in Irving's theater program and some commercial acting work on the side. It was easy to imagine Hal's striking good looks on a stage, perhaps even in the ad pages of a glossy magazine. But the fin rating figured in only demonstrated academic and extracurricular accomplishments, not physical appearance.[7] The Applicant Rating form took account of extracurriculars with the "Personal" score, which could have the values 0 (below average), 1 (average), or 2 (outstanding). The great majority of apps received a rating of 1 on the Personal score, but Hal was in every way a standout, one of those exceptionally accomplished young people from urban public high schools with whom admissions officers tended to fall in love. His primary extracurricular was a not-for-profit organization he had started at the age of fifteen when, after an encounter with a young family living on the street, he became passionate about the plight of homeless children. With the support of local merchants Hal created a store at which indigent families were able to buy new clothes, books, and educational toys using a fictive currency disbursed to participants in the form of monthly stipends. Hal's was one of only a handful of the applications I read during my research to which I assigned a Personal score of 2/2, bringing his overall fin rating to a full 9/9.

Hal's 2/2 Personal was left unchanged by the admissions officer who reviewed my work. Not so for Brian Scott, the soft-spoken young man from the Richardson School, just over the hill from Irving High, with whom I myself fell in love. My affection was not all Brian's fault. His school and his guidance counselor charmed me first. Richardson was one of the most exclusive private schools in its city, a status its physical plant did not advertise crassly. The campus was tucked into a glen of old evergreens that fragrantly shaded its modest but thoughtfully designed wood-frame buildings. I received a warm welcome from the head counselor at Richardson, too. She was so pleased to meet me. Had I had trouble finding my way? After several visits to public high schools where I had felt like a name on a roster or even an intrusion, the warm welcome was a nice thing. So too was the appointment the counselor had arranged for me in advance with this particular student, Brian Scott, who, I was told in advance, had himself sought out the College specifically because of its noted environmental studies program. My recollection warmed by this context, it was perhaps a little easier for me to overestimate the assets in Brian's application back at the College months later.

His academic numbers were easy enough to calculate. Richardson was a 100 percent school—entirely college prep, and with a good reputation to boot, so it received a 4/4 on the *high school* score. Brian's curriculum, which included courses in global climate change, ethics, honors calculus, and honors chemistry, received a 4/4 *curriculum* score. Brian's grades did not match his courses in quality, however. His transcript was heavy with Bs and also contained a couple of Cs, most recently in a senior-year math class. I scored Brian's *grades* at 2/4; his marks were weak, but the school and curriculum were strong, so I gave him a little more credit. The same grades earned through a standard curriculum at Irving High School likely would have rendered Brian inadmissible at the College. As it was, this kid probably was getting one of the best high school educations in the nation, regardless of his middling grades. He remained at least a decent candidate academically—even though I could only guess about his rank in class because, in a practice common at private schools, Richardson did not report it. The practice of withholding class rank was usually and officially explained as a means of mitigating competitiveness among students. Its real purpose was widely presumed to be to hide all ranks outside the top quintile so that admissions offices with an eye on the *U.S. News & World Report* rankings would not have a low class rank as a mark against an applicant. I took a guess that Brian Scott was in the middle of the pack at Richardson and assigned him a *rank* score of 2/4. But even with his low *grade* and *rank* scores, the quality of his curriculum and his enrollment at a highly regarded private high school put his overall "Academic" score at 3/4. Brian did well in the SAT category, too, earning a 1410 combined score and hence a 3/3 on the College's SAT rating. His fin was up to 6 (3 + 3).

After that, I overestimated. I was too impressed with Brian's family history, which included several timber merchants, and Brian's own ambition to write a new and different chapter in this history, which was the subject of the well-crafted personal essay Brian wrote for his application. I was too impressed by how Brian had spent his three previous summers, doing manual labor—rare for applicants from affluent families—in order to get close to the eco-friendly survey and harvesting techniques under development by a regional timber company. The whole application had a nice coherence about it. The high-end science courses and the training in ethics and climate change fit nicely with the summer work, which fit nicely with Brian's own ambitions, which in turn fit nicely with one of the College's academic strengths. All of this, topped off with my memories of the nice counselor and the nice campus under the trees, added up to my too nice 2/2 personal rating for Brian Scott, which subsequently was overruled by one of the admissions officers (I do not know which one), who, with a heavy black marker, changed my rating of $6 + 2 = 8$ to a $6 + 1 = 7$.

The fin ratings enabled officers to make coarse sorts among applications. Apps with very high and very low ratings were decided relatively quickly in a process called "rounds," in which apps receiving fin ratings of 0 to 3 were rejected upon a confirmatory read by a second officer, while apps with ratings of 8 or 9 were, upon a second confirmatory read, accepted. The fate of approximately 20 percent of each year's applicant pool was decided this way. Officers also used fin ratings when they talked about applicants in committee meetings and informally among themselves. Hal Cohen, *a 9 from Washington,* who might be a candidate for one of the College's most generous merit scholarships; Brian Scott, *the timber kid, a 7 from Richardson.* Like the Apgar scores used to assess newborn infants or the performance statistics that describe baseball players, fin ratings summarized the vital characteristics of applications.[8]

In addition to calculating the fin, officers also completed a "pink sheet" for each applicant that summarized the case in more detail. Printed on two sides of pink paper, it contained designated spaces for approximately thirty pieces of information that could be culled from each file. The pink sheets were crib notes for oral discussions about apps, and they contained most, but not all, of the information that was the basis for final decisions. Grades, class rank, and test scores were on the pink sheets. So too was fairly detailed information about high school transcripts and extracurricular activities. Pink sheets carried descriptive information about households—parents' educational backgrounds and occupations; number of siblings in college and the names of their schools; race/ethnicity; and whether or not paperwork had been filed with Financial Aid. The aid question allowed only for answers of *yes* or *no;* amounts were specified in other documents produced by the financial aid officers. Apps for which the answer to the aid question was no were described colloquially as "free," because their acceptance would not "cost" the College any of its financial aid budget. Those who would need a lot of financial aid to be able to attend the College often were colloquially described as "expensive" or "needy."

There were spaces on the pink sheets where officers could describe the content and quality of the personal essays. There were lines for summarizing the content of recommendation letters sent from teachers and guidance counselors. There were spaces for the name of the applicant's high school and for the percentage of graduates from that school who went directly on to four-year colleges. There were spaces for filling in the athletic ratings supplied by the College's own coaching staff. There was a place for indicating whether the app was the son or daughter of a College alumnus.

When they were thoroughly filled in, pink sheets represented virtually every asset of an applicant that mattered to the College. A story could be told about a kid on the basis of the pink sheet alone.

Storytelling

One day in the winter of 2000, I stopped by Val Marin's office to touch base with her about a grant proposal I was writing at her request. The grant, which the College ultimately was awarded, was to provide scholarship funds for academically accomplished applicants from the new Eastern European republics. When I poked my head through Val's door, I found her with Beth Cole, surrounded by several stacks of applications through which they seemed to be making their way rather quickly. "Watcha doing?" I asked.

"Z-ing incomplete international apps," Val said. *Z* was office code for *deny*. Val and Beth were trying to cut down on the committee workload by rejecting many, but not all, of the applicants from abroad whose files were lacking vital information. The sorting was not being done carelessly. I watched as Beth put a Z on one of the folders, paused over it for a moment, then handed it off to Val.

"I think I may have Z-d this one too quickly," she said.

Val looked through the file for a minute and said, "Yep, too fast. I'll follow up on it." I don't know why that particular application was reconsidered, but Val did convey some clues about the kinds of attributes that got files second looks. She flipped through one app from a small African nation. The kid attended a boarding school in northern Italy. "That school is fifty thousand dollars a year. Yep. Fifty grand," she repeated, plunking the file back on its stack. "They take all the kids in the school, every year, from November to January, and move the entire school into the mountains so the kids can ski. It's incredible."

While I took a moment to drop my jaw at this, Val picked up the file again and said, "I bet the kid's father owns half the country." She flipped through the papers, looking for dad's occupation. "What do you know, 'prime minister.' Interesting, huh? I know the counselor [at the Italian school], she's a nice lady. I'll give her a call and see what's up with the file."

About a week later when I was in Val's office again, she asked me to look through a half dozen of the applications the office had received that year from Bulgaria. "I've narrowed it down to six," she said, "and they're all excellent. Don't even look at their grades because they all have [the equivalent of straight A's]. They've all got great test scores. I'm wondering if you can help me distinguish them." Val knew that she would be able to advocate for only one of the six Bulgarians in committee, because all of them would need more or less full scholarships to attend the College and officers were loath to admit students unless they also could offer the necessary financial aid. In a tone flavored equally with admiration and regret, Val often said that the College could fill each year's entering class with Eastern European valedictorians. Academic numbers were not the only data to which Admissions was obliged to attend, however, so my eyes and fingers sought out aspects of the six Bulgarian files that might enable me to read beyond all of the uniform statistics. I looked for the recommendation letters, the personal essays, and any other evidence that might enable me to make fine distinctions.

Both of these visits to Val's office were occasions for what I call evaluative storytelling: the work of assembling narratives about applicants that become the basis for fine distinctions. Once cases have been placed into a category (incomplete international apps, the top six Bulgarians), discrimination among them tends to take the form of stories about how one or a few cases should be distinguished from all the others. Evaluative storytelling often happens at the tops of decision hierarchies, after coarse sorts have weeded out all of the cases that do not meet baseline criteria yet there are still more candidates than there are goodies to award. This is what Harvard sociologist Michèle Lamont and her colleagues find in their studies of the blue-ribbon panels assembled to select the winners among finalists for prestigious scholarly fellowships. Because all of the candidates who make it to the final rounds of consideration are good or excellent, judges tend to distinguish the best from the rest by crafting moral accounts about winners that distinguish them in kind from the others.[9] Evaluative storytelling also happens when the attributes of a case make it difficult to categorize. Its mix of assets and deficits puts it in the grey zone between yes and no, admit and deny. Under either condition, evaluators' abilities to tell compelling stories about a case are consequential for its ultimate fate.[10]

Evaluative storytelling is *always* a collaborative endeavor, because it requires not only the participation of the story's teller but also the producers of the narrative raw materials from which the story is made. If admissions officers are going to tell stories about college applicants, there must be things for officers to say, and those things are supplied by others: external testing agencies, high school guidance counselors, and the applicants themselves. Val Marin got some of the material for her story about the African kid from his application. There she found the name of his school, which was the beginning of the story. Val filled it in with material from her own prior knowledge of the place: that it was extraordinarily costly; that it sent all of its students skiing each winter. The next piece of material came from the application, which listed the app's father's occupation. *Prime minister* added sufficient intrigue that Val decided to seek out information for another chapter. *I know the counselor . . . she's a nice lady. I'll give her a call and see what's up with the file.*

The stories Val would be able to tell about the six Bulgarians would be less intriguing—not because the applicants themselves were less compelling or worthy, but because Val would have very little material with which to craft distinctive stories about needy Bulgarians. She would not know guidance counselors at the high schools the Bulgarians had attended, so there would be no counselor calls. She would not have visited the Bulgarians' high schools, so there would be fewer details of setting and circumstance with which to embellish the narratives. And because none of the six Bulgarians had made the trip to the College for a campus interview, features of the applicants as embodied people, with appearances and gestures and personalities, would go missing from the stories, too. So a story about one of the six Bulgarians would get told in committee, but it would have a generic quality. It would be another story about another Eastern European valedictorian. Listening officers would recognize that they had heard stories just like it many times before.

Previous students of elite college admissions often have recognized that applicants from privileged backgrounds tend to have many advocates lobbying for them through the evaluation process. High school guidance counselors, in particular, are crucial brokers of applicants at selective colleges because they have enduring and reciprocally beneficial relationships with admissions officers.[11] But previous observers have tended to presume that it is applicants, and not information about them, that high schools and colleges are brokering. My observations suggest that information is the essential medium of exchange between guidance counselors, admissions officers, and indeed a wide web of college personnel. All of the parties in this evaluative economy use information as a form of currency to buy respect, curry influence, and direct the outcomes of those decisions in which their own interests are implicated. Evaluative stories are the glue that binds all of this information together, creating a narrative subject—the applicant—whose ultimate fate can be adjudicated by a single, summary admission decision.

The primary forum for evaluative storytelling in the office was committee, the weeks-long series of meetings during which officers consider and collectively determine the fate of applications. In contrast to the quiet solitude of reading and rating, storytelling was collaborative and often highly theatrical. Reading and rating quickly grew tedious, but committee, while exhausting, was fun. "It's like you do all this time getting ready and then, POOF!, they're gone," was how Tisha Adams once contrasted the two jobs.

Storytelling in committee took a fairly scripted form. Officers "presented" the files for which they had completed the initial reads. Working off their completed pink sheets, the presenter delivered an oral summary of each app, emphasizing its most important characteristics. By custom, information was presented in the order in which it appeared on the pink sheet:

Applicant name

Name of high school / rate of attendance at 4-year colleges

SAT scores; class rank; GPA

Financial aid (applied for = "yes")

If applicable, the amount of estimated financial need (from a different form)

Racial self-identification if not white; citizenship if not U.S.

Parental education and occupation; legacy status, if any

Number and age of siblings and the colleges they attend, if applicable

Summary of extracurricular activities, including athletics ratings if applicable

Quality and content of personal essay

Summary of high school curriculum and grades (often detailed)

Summary of recommendation letters

Summary of write-up of campus interview, if applicable

Officer's overall recommendation—Admit, Defer, Wait List, or Deny

Once the officer concluded his or her presentation, discussion was opened to the entire committee. By rule every committee session included a minimum of three officers. Also by rule, at every meeting either Liam Rizer or Susan Latterly was present. The most senior officer present had final authority over the decisions rendered in each session.

The majority of presentations were short and list-like—barely stories at all. The presenting officer would talk out the most salient details of the app fairly quickly, linking them with just a bit of narrative glue before opening things up for a collective decision, which usually was reached fairly quickly as well. So, for example, Bethany Leeds, an officer who read for a large midwestern territory, presented a Minnesota app named Nelson Kantor. Bethany reported Nelson's high SAT scores and tepid grades; his absent class rank (Nelson's school did not report it); his financial aid status—free; and his high rating from the College football coach. There was a brief discussion about whether he was "worth the A" (for *Admit*). Bethany made a succinct argument in favor: "If you think of him as a football player, he looks pretty good. He's got great SATs, he's free, Minnesota, and his school doesn't report rank so he's not going to hurt us there. He helps us in every way that's quantifiable." Nelson Kantor was admitted.

Kamiko Marumi, an Early Decision applicant and a U.S. national originally from Japan, was also an uncomplicated case. Kamiko was in the second quintile of her class and had pretty good test scores. The committee was told that Kamiko would probably cost some financial aid money, the dad had a middle-class job but the numbers from Financial Aid were not yet in. She was the student president of her regional youth musical association and chair of her school's Asian American interest group. There was a bit of discussion about Kamiko because she was not stellar in terms of her academic numbers. But Danesha Adams summed up what I suspected others at the table were thinking. "I don't see why we shouldn't lock in this great multicultural kid ED," she said. Kamiko Marumi was admitted.

Committee evaluations were an interesting mix of coarse sort and fine distinction. On the one hand, presenting officers ticked off each applicant's vital data in a way that emphasized their most salient and usually quantifiable assets: GPA, test scores, legacy status, amount of financial need, official minority status, and athletics rating. On the other hand, organizing consideration around named individuals created conditions under which officers could, if they wanted to or decided they needed to, fill out the presentations with richer narrative material. This is what happened when cases got complicated. The stories became more elaborate. Fine distinctions received more attention.

Consider the discussions I observed surrounding two Early Decision cases. Both of the apps under consideration had received initial hearings in committee, where their cases had been borderline between Admit and Defer (to the Regular Decision pool). The presenting officers, Alan Albinoni and Chris Winn, had subsequently gathered more information about the cases and then brought them back to committee for a second hearing. Both cases, in other words, were close calls.

Alan Albinoni presented his case first. "This is Katie Ethanbocker, from Roxton Academy. She's got SATs of 1240 and she's free. She's rated 3 for field hockey, she's a campus tour guide at Roxton, she's on the community service board there, too, which seems like kind of a big deal but I'm really not sure. I spoke with Bob Chinn, who's the counselor at Roxton." Officers routinely called the counselors with whom they had relationships after the initial ED committee session, letting counselors know the fate of their apps in advance so that they could prepare kids for disappointing news and, if they so chose, lobby officers for a second hearing. It was one of the many little advantages enjoyed by students at cushier high schools.

"And this guy, this is a guy who sends us good kids," Alan continued. "He likes us, he likes the College, and he's good to work with. He always treats us well. He says this girl really wants to come to the College and he thinks that if we want to get something going with Roxton she'd be a good one to do it with. He said her father went to

Dartmouth, he's a big contributor at Dartmouth, her sister's there now, her sister is a weaker candidate than Katie but she got into Dartmouth. Bob said if we don't take Katie now she'll apply Regular Decision to Dartmouth, and with the connections there she'll probably get in."

There was some discussion about the character of the counselor. Susan Latterly asked, "What do you think, is he being straight with you?"

Alan said, "I really like this counselor. Like I said he likes the College—you know we have a lot of counselors who are nice to us at other schools but they send us schlocky kids. From Roxton we get good kids, but they go elsewhere. But he does send us good kids, he was on the motorcoach tour last year, he likes us. And I got the impression that he wasn't just doing it for her [Katie, the app]. He sort of said 'This is how it is.'"

"What do you think?" Liam Rizer asked.

"Well, I think if we do it, he'll know that we stretched for her. He knows that we had a Defer on her so we'll be changing that."

The issue had now become whether to stretch for the app, given her hidden, and now revealed, attributes: her potential for the office to get something going with Roxton Academy, and the potential for the College to pick up a fresh donor. "He's generous with Dartmouth, who knows, he might be generous with the College too," Chris Winn said of Katie Ethanbocker's dad.

Alan continued, "And Bob said that this is a girl who really wants to come here. She did this on her own, shopped around and found a school that she really liked herself, didn't necessarily follow her father or her sister."

Liam said, "Let's do this one."

Multiple factors were responsible for the changed fate of Katie Ethanbocker's application. One of them, clearly, was Katie's father's apparent history of contributions to his alma mater, which officers hoped might be a portent of future gifts to the College. A second factor was officers' hope that Katie's admission might enable the College to get something going with Roxton, a school with lots of good kids from which the College had gotten few matriculants. An important third factor was Alan Albinoni's ability to get sufficient information about Katie Ethanbocker so that he could tell a good story about her varied attributes. The necessary material came from Alan's relationship with the guidance counselor. Furthermore the source of the information had some integrity. *He does send us good kids,* Alan pointed out. *He likes us.* The assets in Katie's file were not by themselves sufficient for admission, but the additional information from Roxton's counselor added enough good stuff to the story to convince officers that shifting the conclusion from Defer to Admit was reasonable.

Susan Latterly acknowledged as much when she added, with bemusement and resignation, "But I have to say, this is what bothers me about situations like this, and I am not saying that we shouldn't do it in this particular case, but it is the case that kids from these good private schools do have an edge with these counselors that the public school kids don't have. I mean, how many of the public school kids who look just like this one did we defer on, but because they don't have counselors like this, we'll never hear from them again? It just bothers me that here are these kids with so many advantages already, and then they have these counselors who do stuff like this and it works."

Next up was Jennifer Cable, an applicant who also had applied Early Decision. Chris Winn, another junior officer, had done the initial read on Jennifer and served as the presenting officer for her application in committee. Jennifer was from Highbrook High, a well-regarded public school in the affluent suburbs of a large midwestern city. Jennifer's hook was that her brother had become disabled in a car accident and the experience apparently affected

Jennifer so much that she went on to found an advocacy organization for disabled young people at her high school. Jennifer had only moderate SATs (about 1230) and only modest grades (GPA 11.50 on a 16-point scale), and had not taken any AP classes. On the initial committee evaluation Jennifer's file had been deferred to Regular Decision.

After that Chris had spoken with Theresa Jones, Jennifer's counselor at Highbrook. He had placed the call from Liam Rizer's office and had invited me to sit in. As he looked through the Cable file to refresh his memory, he volunteered that Theresa "does great write-ups on her kids. Just beautiful letters, you should take a look." Once he placed the call and obtained permission to do so from Theresa, Chris pushed the speaker button on the telephone so that I could listen in. She was silent on the phone while Chris conveyed the news about Jennifer's Defer, then expressed disappointment, talking about how much Jennifer wanted to attend the College.

"Just yesterday she came by the office with several of her friends to find out if I had heard anything, because she is so eager to hear," Theresa said. I remember thinking that this might be a carrot for Chris—a hint that Jennifer might be able to help him get something going with Highbrook. "She's a quiet person, a behind-the-scenes kind of person. But people love her. They love her. She's a great kid. And I think teachers [at the College] would really like her. She's a serious kid."

By call's end Chris had agreed to take Jennifer's case back to committee. After he had hung up the phone, he said to me that he would do so partly because he had presented Jennifer twenty-eighth out of more than thirty candidates, "so I may not have done everything I could for her. She's a tough call [Jennifer] . . . but she's worth talking about again. . . . And at the very least I can go back to Theresa and tell her that I brought her back to committee." I noted that it seemed important to Chris that perhaps the presentation itself had something to do with the disposition of the case. "I may not have presented her very well," he added.

So Jennifer was back in committee. The relevant variables were these: Highbrook was a very good school with a lot of well-qualified, free kids. Good kids applied to the College from Highbrook every year but, as at Roxton Academy, they tended to matriculate at other schools. What Jennifer had going for her, other than being from Highbrook, was that she was free and appeared to be a good citizen. In the argot of admissions, *she had strong PQs* (personal qualities). Against her were a lackluster academic record and a poor interview on campus—which Tisha Andrews, who had conducted it, was asked in this second meeting to recount for the committee.

"The thing that struck me about this girl is that she answered every question I asked with another question," Tisha began. "Academically she struck me as very unconfident. She did better when we were talking about nonacademic things, like the advocacy alliance, but she seemed rather shy and reserved overall. She was nice enough, but just not very confident about anything."[12]

Little things were starting to matter. Officers began talking about whether Jennifer was the sort of kid through whom they would want to get something going at Highbrook. Val said, "I have to tell you, the one thing that jumps out at me here is 'president of the science club.' I'm fine with science club, but to be honest it doesn't strike me as the kind of thing that a prominent person at Highbrook High School would be doing."

Tisha was pressed for more information about the interview. "It's quite possible she's popular," she said. This assessment seemed to be based on Jennifer's appearance. Chris said, "I met her out at Highbrook, she was the only girl there to meet me this year. It was the classic, here's the kid applying ED and they're the only one there waiting for you, front and center in the counseling office. And I liked her. She seemed like a very nice girl. You know, she's not beautiful but she's very pretty. And very nice."

I sensed bemusement around the table at the terrain on which the conversation had settled. On the one hand, people seemed to feel that things were getting a little tacky. On the other hand no one objected out loud.

"God, this is a tough one," Liam Rizer said.

Susan Latterly said, "You know, I have to say it again, here's another case of a kid having a big advantage because she has this counselor at a really good public school who can do this sort of thing for her. And all those kids at [name of modest high school] who effectively have no one to advocate for them just don't get this."

Perhaps because Jennifer Cable was such a tough one, discussion turned to the character of Highbrook's counselor, Theresa Jones. There was some concern about the kinds of kids Theresa had sent the College in the past.

Val said, "I'm sure I don't remember it [perfectly], but I bet that three years ago Theresa went out on a limb for that football player, and sure enough he got in but sure enough we got what we expected. I mean I like Theresa. I'm good friends with Theresa in fact, I see her all the time. But with a lot of these counselors that friendship does not mean anything in particular about the work end of things." Val asked what Jennifer's class rank was.

Chris said, "I asked Theresa and she said she didn't know."

"Oh that is such bullshit!" Val retorted. "I mean, I'm sure she told you that, but I'm sure she knows. All of these counselors know exactly where all of their kids are in the class."

"That's what she said!" Chris shot back. "Maybe she really couldn't tell me."

Val softened a little. "Maybe she couldn't, that's right. There may even be a district policy against it. But that's different from not knowing the rank. Of course she knows the rank." None of this was weighing in favor of Theresa Jones. In contrast with the presumed integrity of the news conveyed by Bob Chinn at Roxton, the additional material coming from Highbrook was being opened to question.

As the discussion continued, Val glanced at the counselor evaluation form that Theresa had filled out for Jennifer Cable. She found that Theresa had rated Jennifer only somewhat above average with her check marks in the categories printed on the form. "Well, what do you know, we have this glowing report about the kid but then the form isn't really glowing," she said cynically.

Alan Albinoni interjected, "I think this one should be Chris's call. We've discussed all of it, he knows the situation at that school better than we do. If he thinks we should do it then we should do it, if not, then . . ."

Discussion about the Cable app ended up consuming the better part of half an hour. It was not resolved by noon, when the committee decided to end its meeting and reconvene later in the day. Just before that next meeting I saw Chris Winn and asked what he had thought of the morning discussion. He agreed it was a tough call, but he also seemed to be getting weary of the case. Weary but not done. Between the morning and afternoon meetings Chris called Theresa again to ask about the modest check marks in her formal assessment of Jennifer Cable. Apparently Theresa had informed Chris that she tends to check conservatively. But Chris did not simply take Theresa's word for it. He headed down to the office basement where applications from previous years were archived and looked up old files from Highbrook High. When the afternoon meeting turned to the Cable file he was ready to report, "Theresa's a conservative checker. I looked at some of the other apps she's sent us, and it looks to be that way."

Concluding the discussion Liam said, "I don't think we need to talk about it any further. Chris, this one's up to you. If you think we should do it, let's do it."

Chris sighed but said, "Let's A her." He took the file, crossed out its D, and put an A alongside the blotted mark.

Jennifer Cable was a tough call partly because the attributes in her file—her grades and test scores, her Highbrook provenance, and her PQs—did not add up to a clear decision. This is why, to settle the uncertainty, officers resorted to other information: how Jennifer presented herself in the interview, for example, and what kind of character and social influence Jennifer might have at her high school. This information was derived from Jennifer's campus interview and her visit with Chris during his school visit, from Chris's phone call with Jennifer's guidance counselor, and from a critical perusal of how the counselor filled out her recommendation forms. When the counselor's trustworthiness was opened to dispute, Chris dug even further for material that might end the story definitively. Perhaps because the best he could do was report that Theresa was a conservative checker, the Jennifer Cable story was brought to a satisfactory, but not especially satisfying, conclusion.

For cases that were tough calls, the ability to tell at least satisfactory stories was a necessary but not sufficient condition for rendering positive decisions. Officers always needed to mind multiple bottom lines. Because summary statistics describing the overall academic quality of each entering class were only as good as the class ranks and test scores of the apps who were admitted, many kids with very low academic numbers were dismissed as "too weak for us." Because the College's financial aid budget was large but not inexhaustible, and because tuition payments were the school's primary source of revenue, the imperative of bringing the class in on budget meant that some of even the most compelling stories ended in denials.

Despite the omnipresent constraints on their evaluative discretion, officers sometimes told stories for apps they knew they would be unable to admit. Consider, for example, how Danesha Adams presented one case in committee:

> Here is a kid who is probably too weak for us, but I really want to argue for her. She has 1030 SATs and pretty good grades in a decent but not exceptional curriculum. She has a fairly significant learning disability and she uses the resource center at her school a lot. But she's worked very hard, all the way through high school, and really done everything she could to prepare for college.

There was considerable discussion around the table about the apparent extent of the disability. But Danesha concluded the storytelling by saying:

> She may be too weak for us. But I wanted to be sure and present her as best I could, because I feel like, here's a girl who really has done everything she could possibly do to get accepted at the College. I mean, if someone had set her down at the beginning of tenth grade and told her everything she should do to get into the College, they would have told her to do everything that she has done. So I feel like this girl at least deserved a fair hearing.

Danesha said up front that the applicant would probably not be admitted. Nevertheless she took the time to tell a story about her, making a point to *present her as best I could.* That officers told a few such stories even when the numbers preempted admission suggests the symbolic importance of the stories themselves. Officers wanted to make decisions for reasons they thought were the right ones. Storytelling enabled them to do that for tough calls that ended in admissions decisions but also, however paradoxically, for many of the most deserving applicants who nevertheless were denied admission.

There were many cases like these: applicants who seemed to have done everything they could to be admitted but whose categorical qualifications did not meet the College's baseline criteria. Many of these apps fell into a narrative genre all their own, one I came to call The Rural New England Valedictorian Story. This genre was reserved for applicants from rural parts of the College's broad geographic region who were the stars of their high schools but who were, relative to the College's national applicant pool, only average. Rural New England valedictorians had topped out their local high schools. They had taken all of the AP classes available to them, but these numbered only one or two. Rural New England valedictorians were the captains of their varsity sports teams, but in the context of national recruitment pools their skills were relatively modest. Because their parents were not wealthy, they required a lot of financial aid. They had excellent grades (hence their high class rank) but only middling SAT scores. Because they lived in the College's traditional service region, rural New England valedictorians brought no added geographic advantage to the school (indeed, comparable candidates from states underrepresented in the College's student body might be admitted easily). And because they were white, they did not enhance diversity statistics.

Officers accepted a few of the most accomplished of these applicants every year, and they did not like the fact that so many such stories ended in rejection. But the bottom line was that the exigencies impinging on each year's class obliged officers to turn most of these applicants away: because they cost too much, or their test scores were too low, or they had not made it to the top of the coaches' recruitment wish lists. Officers typically told Rural New England Valedictorian Stories in a tone that mixed resignation and regret, and they consoled Susan Latterly, whose regional reading territory obliged her to tell so many of them. That Susan was obliged to present a lot of deserving applicants who would not be admitted was regarded as a thankless job.

My observations suggest that the organization of assessment around individual cases has significant consequences for the structure of opportunity in selective college admissions. Individualized assessment obliges officers to make fine distinctions largely on the basis of the stories that can plausibly be told about candidates who are tough calls. This system of evaluation tends to exaggerate the socioeconomic variation in each year's applicant pool, because privileged young people tend to be embedded in elaborate machinery for delivering narrative raw material to admissions officers. However much officers might recognize and dislike them, the informational inequalities created by this machinery shape the outcome of admissions decisions.

An axiom common among admissions officers is: *The weaker the applicant, the thicker the file.* Some of the things in those thicker files could be quite exotic, providing fodder for much of the humor that leavened committee meetings. There was, for example, the applicant who had submitted her application rolled up inside a boot; she was giving one to the officers to preempt their "giving the boot" to her. There was the app who had convinced the owner of a fast-food franchise to post poems he had written on the restaurant's menu board, and had submitted photographs for proof. There was the app who excelled in an esoteric sport that involved completing gymnastic maneuvers while on horseback. As the weeks of committee progressed, officers let the material evidence of the more peculiar submissions accumulate in the conference room, transforming it into a kind of shrine to the extremities of youthful ambition.

To be sure, the U.S. Postal Service is a fairly democratic communication medium. Theoretically anyone can mail piles of narrative material to admissions offices. The ability to deliver the most compelling raw materials, however, is not equally distributed across the population. Neither is expertise in the genre of admissions storytelling, a skill that has increasingly been made available to wealthy families by a growing market of private consultants.

Amy Payne, for example, is the proprietor of her own admissions consulting business in a large eastern city. Soon after graduating from college, Amy went to work in admissions at an Ivy League university. After several years of experience there, she decided to combine her insider wisdom with a budding business sense. When I met Amy she was making her living as a consultant to families anxious enough about the college search to pay something in the orbit of $7,000 for her guidance. One evening over dinner she explained that much of the work entailed figuring out how to represent students' activities in such a way "that they make sense to admissions officers." I asked Amy what she meant.

> Well OK, one of the examples I give . . . is about poetry. I say, "Say you're a poet. You write poetry. Great. Now poetry is a solitary activity. It's something you do alone in your room. That's hard to talk about. In order for that to make sense to an admissions officer, you have to take it to the next level somehow. You write poetry, great. Well, maybe you should edit your high school's literary magazine. Or start a literary magazine. Or you and your friends should get together and start a 'zine. Or you should start a poetry blog. Or get your poetry published in a youth magazine." Or something like that. Now we're talking. Now that poetry makes sense to an admissions officer.

She continued. "You don't just want to be the list of activities. Because admissions officers have seen all of the activities. So you play the tuba. Great. *Why* do you play the tuba? So, that's what I try to do, fill out the picture so that it makes sense to a reader."

Amy's years in the Ivy League well prepared her to purvey storytelling wisdom because schools at the very top of the selectivity hierarchy receive far more qualified applicants than they ever accept. In the admissions offices of these schools, coarse sorts on the basis of baseline admissibility criteria eliminate only a portion of the files. "We used to say at [the school where she worked] that 40 percent of our applicants were academically admissible," Amy told me, "but we only take around 10 percent of them. So you're really needing to make pretty fine distinctions."

Most college applicants do not receive assistance from private consultants. Most of the affluent ones do, however, enjoy the services of professional guidance counselors whose jobs revolve around getting kids into college. Counselors at these high schools understand that admissions officers need narrative raw material. These counselors understand that it is easier for admissions officers to make tough calls in kids' favor when there are a lot of good things to say about their applications. This is why the recommendation letters that were posted from fashionable addresses tended to trail over multiple pages. It is why these letters often mentioned applicants' nicknames and their special niches in campus cultures. It was why they tended to make careful note of that unpleasant aberration in the transcript sophomore year—perhaps there had been a death in the family, or an undiagnosed learning disability, or a particularly intense and successful soccer season to explain away the low grades. The letters said lots of things, but they always said, *Trust me. I know this kid. Let me tell you how well.*

The benefits of detailed recommendation letters should not be underestimated. Anyone who has read such letters when hiring new faculty members or employees knows the advantages that flow to candidates whose respected elders take the time to write at length about them. Short letters, especially alongside long and detailed ones, can look suspiciously thin. This is why admissions officers were disappointed when strong applicants from weak high schools received counselor recommendations that were a mere few lines long. Officers knew that with so little information to work with it would be hard to craft compelling stories.

No doubt about it, the kids with counselors who had the time to be verbose on the recommendations were a little easier to like. In the fieldnotes I wrote when I was reading and rating applications myself, I wrote of the material in one folder:

Perrin Hammer from [name of school] was a little standout. On the counselor evaluation form that [the school] sends with all of its apps is a handwritten scrawl, "Great young woman—she'll light up your community as she has here." That stands out—just that little extra personalization of the app, different from filling in the grid or simply writing the stellar rec. . . . I note that such little bits may be the "extras" that well-supported guidance programs can supply that others can't.

Because officers relied so heavily on outside parties to supply the information they needed to tell stories and make tough calls, kids who had access to the most sophisticated information delivery systems were better off. They tended to get more and better reflections of themselves in front of admissions committees. Glint by glint, it all added up to more favorable impressions.

Admissions officers did not make decisions on their own. They were part of a campuswide system of distributed cognition. Applicants were crucial resources for the College, and the varied assets they brought were of value to multiple campus offices. As athletes, they were important to the coaches. As the children of more or less generous parents and as future alumni, they were important to the Development Office. Those who claimed membership in certain minority groups were important components of the College's claim to be a diverse institution. Because these different resources mattered to multiple parties on campus, evaluative authority was distributed beyond Admissions into several other administrative divisions.

Evaluation of certain applicants who were nonwhite U.S. citizens, for example, was shared with Mr. Carlisle, the director of what the College called its "opportunity programs." Mr. Carlisle got to weigh in on apps that might qualify for the scholarship initiatives under his purview before final decisions were made on their files. At a staff meeting near the end of the first committee season I observed, Liam

Rizer said cheerily that the time had come "to send the files of the minority kids we've rejected over to Mr. Carlisle." For kids whose demographic characteristics placed them within the range of eligibility for the programs he directed, Mr. Carlisle had what Beth Cole described as "right of appeal." "If he didn't agree with our decision, he could talk with Liam about it," she explained. Conversations with multiple officers and with the College's president confirmed that Mr. Carlisle's intervention could be decisive in changing admissions decisions. An interview with the man himself provided a particularly vivid example.

Mr. Carlisle recounted one spring in the mid-1990s, the first year in the tenure of Liam Rizer as dean of admissions, when an entering class included no black men—a situation Mr. Carlisle said troubled him greatly. So he looked again over the applications of several black men and decided to advocate to the new dean for one of them, a student named Jared Lamont. Mr. Carlisle asked Liam to look over the file one more time before he sent an official letter to Jared, and also to let Mr. Carlisle know of the decision before the official letter was sent. He heard nothing from Liam, but soon after received a call from Jared himself, asking, "'What is it about my application that kept me from getting in?'" Mr. Carlisle recalled:

> I told Jared that there must have been some mistake, that he had been admitted and to show up for [a special campus program] on June 15. So then I went to [President Evers] and told him what had happened. I said that the choice was his, he could either admit this student and give him aid, or he could take the money to pay the tuition out of my salary and take my resignation. And [the President] told me that I had put him in a rough position, what with [the] new director of admission. But he backed me up on it. So, I never told Jared about this, until [the end of his senior year]. . . . And that boy—when he walked across the stage to get his diploma, and shook the president's hand, he told the president, "You probably don't re-

member me, but I'm Jared Lamont, and I'm not supposed to be here." And then he came down the stage, and went over to . . . where [Liam Rizer] was sitting . . . and shook his hand and said, "You probably don't remember me, but I'm Jared Lamont, and I'm not supposed to be here."

Mr. Carlisle seemed to think that this story was emblematic of his own position in the College's order of things, because he finished the account by saying, "That's pretty much the story of my relationship with the Admissions Office."

The College was proud of its high retention rates for minority students, and many people on campus gave much of the credit for the good statistics to Mr. Carlisle. His well-burnished reputation almost certainly had a lot to do with the influence he was able to wield in Admissions.

The College also was proud of its high rate of alumni giving, which typically is measured as a proportion of living alumni who make financial contributions to their alma maters each year. In addition to the monetary returns, the College's high giving rate was good for the rankings. During the years in which I conducted my research, *U.S. News & World Report* used the alumni giving rate as a proxy for alumni satisfaction, an attribute it valued at 5 percent of each school's overall rank score. Here was one of the hard facts behind the Development Office's happy mantra that it was not the size of gifts but the "habit of giving" that mattered most. This did not mean that gifts could possibly be too large. Nor did it mean that the amount one gave bore no relation to influence over admissions decisions.

Consider, for example, another applicant who applied Early Decision, who was discussed in the same meeting in which Katie Ethanbocker and Jennifer Cable were considered a second time. Alan Albinoni presented the app.

"This is Marci Evans, we deferred her on Monday. She's on the

Development list. I talked with [name of administrator] over in Development and he asked about her. He asked if she would have a chance in Regular Decision. I said I would bring it to the committee. I can't tell how interested they are in her. Her uncle's a very dedicated College alum, long-standing friend of the College, active, but doesn't give very much. And there's a coach connection there somewhere. One of her relatives was a football coach here way back. She's DOA [daughter of alumnus]."

Bethany Leeds interjected, "But she's ch-ching, right?" *Ch-ching*, the sound of a cash register, was committee slang for an expensive applicant, someone who would cost a lot of financial aid money if admitted.

"Yep, she's needy," Alan said. "Her father is a regular contributor to the annual fund, but he doesn't give very much."

"What's she look like?" Susan Latterly asked—seeking a description not of the applicant's physical appearance but of her academic attributes, her documented accomplishments.

"She's got decent SATs, she's an OK student, A's and B's, some AP classes, but they're the weaker AP's, environmental science, and an English honors elective. She's got A's in her art classes."

There was a collective shrug about this. Officers presumed that art classes were easy A's.

"OK, I'll take out the A's in arts if you want. Outside of art she's got two A's, otherwise it's all B's."

After a few minutes of discussion, the quick consensus was that this kid was OK but not great academically, and needy, and that her importance to Development was far from clear. Ultimately the committee decided not to change the decision. "Let's leave this one where it is," Liam said.

In general, officers were not thrilled to admit legacies and "development prospects" whose files had few other attributes. Nevertheless (and, as the example above suggests, with some exceptions) officers occasionally decided to accept a weak but well-connected app right away "so it won't come back to haunt us" in the form of a phone call from a senior officer or a disgruntled trustee. For particularly difficult or politically sensitive cases, Liam would defer the final call to Tony Evers, the College's president, a strategy I observed several times in committee.

It might be easy to see such practices purely through the lens of nepotism, but it is important to remember how many institutional objectives big donors make possible: new buildings, new faculty, new scholarships. Admissions officers regarded a few of the College's more generous donors as among their office's greatest friends. Start-Up, the summer program that brought minority high schoolers to campus for summer boot camps in selective admissions, had been made possible by a wealthy parent. Tisha Andrews once told me about the time when the financial aid offers accepted during one year of especially good yield exceeded budget allocations. One trustee simply wrote a check for $200,000 to make up the difference. It was this sort of beneficence that led Liam Rizer to say more than once that he was always happy to take a call from a trustee.

Money certainly brought influence in Admissions, but by far the most elaborately orchestrated intervention into the work of the office was from the Athletics Department. Each year the varsity coaches supplied Admissions with two sets of rankings for their preferred applicants. Athletics recruits were rated by skill on a scale of 1 to 5, with 1 representing the most desirable candidates. They also were rated by relative desirability, on a "depth chart" that specified how preferred each recruit was relative to all the others for a given team. So, for example, a dozen hockey players might receive a desirability rating of 1, but only one of them could be first on the hockey coach's depth chart. As the coaches submitted their ratings and ordinal rankings, Admissions compiled them into a database that they used throughout committee season. The database was constantly consulted, updated, and consulted again. During the first admissions cycle I observed, printouts of the database were kept orderly for committee in a fat black binder. Even a few flipped pages betrayed their meticulous maintenance. The next year, officers rigged up a laptop so that the relevant data could be projected, for even easier perusal, on one of conference room walls.

Highly rated athletics recruits with prominent places on the depth charts could be admitted almost entirely on the basis of sports. Such decisions were made every year, particularly for the men's teams, where discrepancies between demonstrated athletic and academic accomplishment tended to be greater.[13] Decisions linked to the football team, especially, enjoyed positive endorsement at the senior administrative levels. Recall the trustee meeting I mentioned in Chapter 4, where President Evers had assured trustees that, despite the team's unimpressive win record in recent years, the administration remained committed to strengthening football at the College. Recall how Bethany Leeds successfully advocated for her app from Minnesota: "If you think of him as a football player." Recall more generally that a third of the College's students were on the roster of at least one varsity team, and that varsity coaches spent much of their time on the road each year: scouting out talent, drumming up interest, cultivating applications. Recall that athletics has been part of the DNA of elite higher education in the United States for a hundred years.

Class Crafting

The individualized consideration of committee took place in serial fashion over many weeks. Officers remained mindful, throughout committee season, of the exigencies that ultimately would inform the overall cohort of admitted students. They knew they ultimately would have to bring in the class "on budget"—attending to the numbers from Financial Aid while also admitting enough full payers to meet annual targets for tuition income. They knew that composite statistics describing the SAT scores and class ranks of admitted students were consequential for the College's academic reputation. They knew that broad geographic representation and official minority numbers mattered for institutional status, too. Finally, they knew that each admitted class would have to appease influential parties in other offices: Athletics, Development, President Evers, Mr. Carlisle. However it was difficult, if not impossible, in the thick of committee, to track precisely what the admitted cohort would look like as a whole. As soon as officers were finished with committee, evaluation moved to class crafting—a step designed to ensure that all of the various jobs officers needed the admitted classes to do for the College were taken care of, before decision letters were posted.

Class crafting took the form of highly consequential meetings called "F rounds" (for *financial aid*), in which officers honed the overall composition of the admitted cohort. In F rounds, some of the files marked for admission in committee inevitably were changed to Z, and vice versa. Previously accepted applicants whose decisions were changed through this process were said to have been "F-d." I did not directly observe F rounds. They were not scheduled in advance because it was impossible to predict precisely when the office would finish with committee, and they happened relatively swiftly. In my layman's life I already had unchangeable commitments elsewhere when F rounds took place, so I here rely on the firsthand accounts of College officers.

As their name implies, F rounds had a lot to do with money. "We'll go over [our financial aid budget] by a million [dollars]—or something like that, we always do," Susan Latterly said,

> and so what you have to do is go back through and revisit the kids getting aid and see who we need to let go. Which is very hard because

a lot of times you have already psychologically admitted the kid, and probably are happy about that, and now you have to go back and revisit that decision. It's very difficult.

They were not just about money, however. Susan continued:

And then after that we spend some time going over the admits trying to make sure that we have enough singers and enough athletes and enough whatevers, talking to the coaches and seeing what we've done with them—just really checking to make sure we've covered what we want.

Over lunch one day with Alan Albinoni, I made an early attempt at formulating the perspective on committee presented in these pages. I told Alan that I was intrigued by the performative aspect of committee evaluation, with how applicants were first assessed as bundles of quantifiable attributes, then transformed by committee into persons, then reconfigured as numbers in the form of composite statistics describing the entering class. From there, Alan took the discussion to the topic of F rounds:

In that meeting we work very hard to keep that process from happening, to keep them as numbers. Because it's much easier that way. It's much easier to deny the kid—especially after you already have accepted them—if you just see them as SAT scores and financial aid. The hard part about F-ing [financial aid rounds] committee is that you already have admitted them. And, you know, particular ones of us may have already committed to them. It's like you know them. So that makes it a lot harder. Which is why, in [regular] committee I always say, I always try to look at the bottom line, look at the numbers, because you know what? It doesn't get any easier to deny them later. It doesn't get any easier to say no after you have talked about them. It only gets harder.

Alan took it as good practice to keep in mind that applicants always were numbers as well as stories. It was harder to become emotionally invested in the numbers, harder to fall in love with numbers than with someone who had a story and a name.

The integrity of the characters produced by evaluative storytelling in committee should not be underestimated. "It's like you construct a hologram of the kid with the information in the file," I ventured to Alan, "and you discuss this version of the kid that you've created." To illustrate, I used my hands to sculpt a figure out of the air between us.

Alan agreed, adding, "In fact that's a part of the work that I really enjoy, because if it weren't for that I would have very little contact with the kids." He paused here, using his hand to gesture at the invisible figure between us. "That's a lot of my contact with them," he said.

Individualism and Evaluation

One of the happier aspects of each committee season was a practice I came to call the Rule of One Pick. Liam and Susan extended the Rule of One Pick to all of the junior officers; it entitled each of them to choose a single candidate for admission entirely at their own discretion. Talk about potential picks laced many committee discussions. People would sometimes ask officers presenting tough calls if they liked the apps enough to name them as their picks. Liam asked Chris Winn, for example, if he wanted to make Jennifer Cable his pick for that year. Chris deferred, opting to save his pick for some other candidate with whom he might be more taken.

The U.S. Supreme Court's decision in the *Grutter* case embodies the same optimism about individualized consideration reflected in the Rule of One Pick. In their admittedly very different ways, *Grutter v. Bollinger* and the Rule of One Pick both assert that individualized consideration enables decision makers to coalesce the myriad details of particular applications into more or less compelling wholes. Both assert that decisions made on the basis of what

Justice O'Connor called "highly individualized, holistic review"[14] have a different and higher value than decisions rendered on the basis of a few facts in each file. But the Rule of One Pick was an exception to everyday practice. *Grutter v. Bollinger,* by contrast, asserts the virtue of holistic review "for each and every applicant." This is problematic. My observations suggest that individualized consideration is neither as humane nor as remedial of social inequality as Justice O'Connor and her colleagues in the majority for *Grutter* might have hoped.

The Supreme Court's decision in *Grutter v. Bollinger* does not attend to two crucial features of evaluation in selective admissions. First, it does not attend to the fact that the storytelling essential to individualized consideration is dependent upon a generous supply of information, and that the social machinery that delivers information to decision makers is not equally distributed throughout the population. Socioeconomically privileged applicants enjoy the most elaborate information delivery, so their applications come loaded with lots of the raw materials evaluators need to tell individually compelling stories. This is how individualized consideration is discriminatory. It systematically favors applicants who are able to deliver the right kinds of information to the right parties at the right times, while systematically disadvantaging those without the necessary infrastructure to get word of themselves across.

Second, the Supreme Court's decision in *Grutter* fails to recognize the political implications of the fact that different kinds of assets coveted by schools are embedded inside each and every college applicant. Admissions officers usually do not have the luxury of making decisions entirely on the basis of their own holistic reviews, because influential people in the Development, Athletics, and President's offices, and on the board of trustees, also are invested in the outcome of admissions decisions. My observations suggest that, in practice, the individualized consideration of applications endorsed by the Supreme Court in *Grutter* serves as much to appease the demands of various intramural stakeholders as it does to preserve the integrity of the cases represented in the files. When the fate of applications is decided individually and narratively, over time, there is more wiggle room for negotiation among all of the parties who have a stake in the outcomes. This is why the Rule of One Pick was so special. It momentarily suspended all of the exigencies that otherwise constrained officers' discretion. Each year, the Rule of One Pick allowed each officer to be fully in charge of the decision for one application. The rest of the time officers were obliged to share the decision with others. It may be that the Supreme Court's endorsement of individualized consideration was predicated on the faulty assumption that admissions decisions are made by autonomous offices. They are not. My observations suggest that, in practice, individualized consideration is an intramural negotiation among multiple stakeholders about how particular decisions will turn out. When applicants come with assets valued by influential insiders—family wealth, trustee connections, official minority status, and athletic skill—they have advocates unavailable to others. The ethical implications of this fact are not trivial.

chapter seven

YIELD

An afternoon party marked the day the acceptance letters were mailed. The same table around which thousands of committee decisions had been made got dressed for celebration with strawberries and champagne. The committee months of quasi-isolation and casual clothing had once again come to an end, and the party marked a change of task and demeanor. It was yield season: time, once again, for neckties and dress clothes and the turning of sunny dispositions toward the outside world.

Yield season is important. American higher education is organized as a market in which students, not schools, have final say in who goes where. Many of the students with the top academic numbers, the stellar athletic and extracurricular accomplishments, and the most compelling PQs apply to several schools and end up with several good options. Even the most sought-after schools offer admission to many more applicants than they can admit, to insulate themselves from the uncertainties inherent in this market.

As if positioned on opposite sides of Alice's magic looking glass, during yield season students and colleges confront one another through the prism of two conjoined dilemmas. On the college side, the trick is to get many good or at least decent students to enter one's own institution rather than the competitors. On the student side, the trick is to choose which single invitation to accept from among several, often quite similar, options and, whenever possible, to play the choices off one another and secure better scholarship deals. During the four or so weeks between the extension of admission offers and the May 1 notification deadlines, perhaps a hundred top schools and thousands of highly desirable eighteen-year-olds negotiate who will go with whom. It makes for a heady case of spring fever on elite college campuses and in the hallways of the nation's most affluent high schools, as everyone scurries to secure the most optimal engagements.

Previous scholarship on selective college admissions has been rather stoic about this mutual selection process, tending to emphasize the more rational and measurable features of the sorting. The most impressive of this work has been written by economists, who ably have shown that students tend to enroll at the most prestigious schools to which they are admitted, even while all parties in these transactions attempt to gain relative advantage with Early Decision plans and deal-sweetening financial aid agreements.[1] While this scholarship offers valuable insights about the end results of the courtship between students and schools, it ignores very important features of the process. It ignores the fact that for many people, school selection is a deeply emotional experience. It is not merely a rational choice. Economic scholarship also tends to ignore all of the energy schools invest in managing the feelings of their clients.

Parents send their children to elite colleges for many reasons. They do so partly so that their offspring can acquire valuable credentials, of course. But they also want schools to help their children craft satisfying identities. They want their kids surrounded by interesting and challenging peers, and by trustworthy grown-ups who can assist their kids in the often difficult final years of adolescence. Little wonder, then, that parents do not think about schools exclusively in terms of rankings and tuition. Like many of the most consequential life choices—where to live or whom to marry, for example—the emotional aspects of school selection are as consequential for decision makers as the more objectively measurable ones. This is true regardless of how well economists and demographers are able to model aggregate outcomes on the basis of a few objectively measurable predictors (which, incidentally, they can do quite well for school choice, home purchase, and marital selection). Social scientists' ability to model choices in the aggregate should not lead us to forget, however, that for most people life's big decisions must not only be objectively reasonable. They must *feel* right as well. All else being equal, it is easier, and a lot more fun, to sign a mortgage or walk down the aisle after one really has fallen in love with this particular house, this particular person. The fact that people's feelings about life's big decisions so often parallel objective predictors of how they choose does not make the emotional side of choices secondary. Quite the contrary: it raises interesting and largely unanswered questions about just how facts and feelings are so consistently brought into alignment at consequential moments of discretion.

My observations of yield season at the College suggest that part of the answer has to do with the careful engineering of emotions by parties invested in the outcome of a choice. Because emotions matter so much to admitted students and their families, emotions also matter elaborately to schools. At places like the College, considerable investment is made in what Arlie Hochschild calls "emotion work"—the management of one's own feelings, and the engineering of feeling in others.[2] In selective admissions, the management and engineering of emotion is an important aspect of the job.

Getting Personal

Perusing the collection of old viewbooks in the College's archives, I was struck by how consistently the publications touted a few core assets of the place: the beauty of the campus, a sense of community, academic rigor, athleticism, sound career preparation, and individualized instruction. These themes are as prominent in the first promotional pamphlet in the archives, dated 1917, as they are in the glossy viewbook mailed out to thousands of prospective students in 2000.[3]

One significant change over time, however, is the manner in which the publications represent the relationship between students and the school. Those published between 1917 and 1981 speak to the reader in a distant voice. Like all of its predecessors in the archive, the 1981 viewbook is written in the voice of a single authorial narrator. Its tone is friendly, but uniform. The voice that introduces the College and its history at the beginning of the publication is the same as the one offering travel directions to campus at the end. Beginning with the 1987 edition, however, this single authorial speaker begins to give way to multiple voices. A letter printed on the first pages of the 1987 edition, signed by the College president and the dean of admissions, explains, "We have asked students, faculty members and alumni to share some thoughts about the College with you." Subsequent pages include color photographs and first-person testimonials of seven students. The 1994 viewbook also carries student testimonials; additionally, it explicitly encourages readers to imagine themselves as potential members of the College community. "Knowing which college to choose depends largely on knowing yourself," the text opens:

> Do you want to be challenged in a free-thinking but demanding intellectual forum? Would you like to become versed in the liberal arts, and prepared for not just one pursuit, but for anything? Are you seeking an environment where individual attention and a sense of community lead to lifelong friendships with students and faculty? If this is how you see yourself, we invite you to take a closer look at the College.

Unlike earlier publications, in which the College is presented as an institution separate from the reader, the 1987 viewbook encourages prospective students to 'see themselves' in the College.

Things get even more intimate in a mid-1990s viewbook titled *Collected Stories*. President Evers welcomes the reader with an introductory letter, which reads in part:

> Each person at the College has a story to tell. Mine began on a crisp, unusually bright January day. . . . I was a candidate for a faculty position. . . . The night before my interview with students, faculty members, the dean and the president, I walked wide-eyed around the campus. The library's lights illuminated the snow-covered quadrangle, and the stillness of the air was broken only by the muffled sound of boots crunching down on the snow as students hurried along shimmering campus paths. I could not have imagined a more idyllic setting.

By this point in history the congenial but distant authorial voice of the College had been relegated to the far back pages. Up in front were upbeat biographies. "Our stories are unique," President Evers concluded, "but our commitment to each individual's intellectual self-discovery is universal."

The viewbook in use during the period of my research maintained this emphasis on stories about individual students. The first words in the viewbook state:

> The following pages offer just a sampling of what's possible at the College, while introducing you to some of the ambitious, fun, and talented students who make this . . . campus their home. In their stories you may see the potential for creating your own.

This viewbook encourages readers to imagine the College as a collection, not of buildings and classes and activities, but of individual narratives, ones readers might use as models for advancing their own stories.

It would be foolish to posit a single cause for the rhetorical evolution in these viewbooks, but it may be more than mere coincidence that the College's promotional literature got more personal during the years when competition for top students among the nation's most selective institutions grew unprecedentedly intense. Economic scholarship suggests that the ecology of elite higher education was transformed in the 1980s and 1990s as the market for elite schooling became nationally integrated, as universal measures of institutional quality—specifically the *U.S. News & World Report* rankings—became more influential, and as demand for the seats at selective colleges grew.[4] As more good students began sending applications to greater numbers of schools, more found themselves obliged to make choices between multiple, numerically comparable institutions. Much like admissions officers, students found themselves doing some evaluative storytelling to make fine distinctions. Facing intense competition for the most coveted students, the College did what it could to help kids craft their narratives.

Dollars and Sense

At the champagne party, I had the chance to talk with Mitch Kraven, the junior financial aid officer, about his own work during yield season. "Oh, I'll start getting phone calls, probably on Monday, from parents who are surprised by their packages. And they may have things to tell me about their financial situation that we didn't know before. Like maybe there's been a divorce in the family, which is a big deal, or some significant change in income. And we'll try to take that into account, of course. But then we'll also get a lot of people who are just surprised by the amount of aid they got, but we can't do anything about it."

I nodded appreciatively.

"It's like, everyone believes that they are middle class. There's just a very wide range of people who are convinced that they are middle class, even when the numbers tell us that, well, they're not, that they're a lot more affluent than they think they are."

"So, a lot of face time, on the phone," I said.

"A lot of time on the phone, talking to parents. And it's very unpredictable work because you're doing paperwork on your desk but you're constantly getting phone calls, so it's hard to schedule, of course. But on the other hand, if people are calling us to talk about their packages, it means that they are interested in us. So the phone calls are a good sign."

I asked if the College extended more financial aid offers than the budget was able to cover.

"Oh yeah. Oh yeah. Say we're budgeted at around three million dollars, we've gone out with about eight million dollars in aid offers."

"So you're offering on the presumption that a lot of people won't come."

"Right. Which is [awkward]. . . . Sometimes on the phone parents will say, 'Well, maybe my kid can get the aid from someone who's gone elsewhere.' Well, it really doesn't work that way. And we'll tell them, 'Well, no, that's already been taken into account,' but it can be a little awkward."

"So the process is always somewhat uncertain, it sounds like—how much to offer versus how much is likely to be accepted?"

"Right, yes, it is uncertain to some degree, that's right."

April yield season is when the most dramatic round of what economists Michael McPherson and Morton Schapiro call "the student aid game"—the now widespread efforts by private colleges with status ambitions to buy academically accomplished students with scholarships—is played. On the college side, the objective is to acquire students whose SAT scores and high school class ranks will pull up the aggregate numbers submitted to college guidebooks and

U.S. News & World Report. On the student side, the objective is to get the highest tuition discounts possible from the most desired schools. Mitch Kraven's phone would be ringing for weeks as he and the parents and financial aid officers at other schools all played the student aid game.[5]

Minds and Hearts

It was not all about money, however. While Financial Aid answered its phones, people in Admissions arranged the open houses and overnight visits that they knew helped generate matriculations. Admissions officers knew that prospective students who actually visited the College were more likely than their comparably qualified peers to apply in the first place, and they knew that students who made campus visits after receiving their acceptance letters were more likely to make tuition deposits than those who stayed home or only visited elsewhere. I do not have any data about whether students tended to make their decisions before or after their campus visits, but I do know this: when it came to planning for visitors, Admissions left as little as possible to chance.

The schedule for the April 2001 open house included special tours of the campus residence halls. Officers knew that the generally high quality of the College's dormitories gave it a little edge over the competition; still, not just any dorm rooms would do for public display. Officers made sure that only relatively nice rooms, whose occupants kept them relatively orderly, were put on tour. There also was an "academic fair," which included representatives from all of the academic departments and programs. Officers made sure that each sign naming a department at the fair had a human being underneath it. Signs without professors beneath them were presumed to send a bad signal. There was a parents' reception at 5 p.m., with alcohol and hot hors d'oeuvres. Officers made sure there was plenty of food and drink and plenty of faculty on hand for chitchat. There was a special information session on the College's curriculum, an event at which I was invited to speak. I was flattered, because I knew how carefully officers tried to make sure that the talking heads at such events were trustworthy.

Throughout the prior eight months I had spent in Admissions, I had learned many lessons about impression management. I had learned to suppress my scholarly tendency to balance praise with criticism, to assess both sides of choices, to see shades of gray. I had learned how to talk only about positive features of the College without sounding too much like a real estate agent or an exceedingly enthusiastic salesclerk. I had learned to acknowledge any deficiencies of the College at the beginning of my answer to hard questions, but always to end my responses on a positive note. I tried to put all of these lessons to use in my presentation during the open house for accepted students. I concluded my little sermon, delivered at the pulpit of the College chapel, by discussing three students whom I had gotten to know personally in recent months. One had spent a semester in South America, studying indigenous women who earned lucrative incomes as market vendors on the streets of Bogota. One had been accepted to Harvard's law school. One, a sociology major and a budding novelist, had been tutored on campus by an internationally famous writer-in-residence.

Evidently I did pretty well, because when it was over I received warm compliments from Bethany Leeds and Alan Albinoni, who had been in the audience. They especially liked the part about the three individual students, so much so that they suggested I use it in presentations at future open houses. Along with her praise, however, Bethany offered a tip for future presentations: "The one thing, this is totally nitpicky, but all of your examples were of kids in the social sciences. If there were also a student in the sciences, that would be ideal. But maybe that's asking for the moon. It's a great story."

Despite their careful efforts to manage impressions, much of the information that got through to visitors fell outside officers' control. Officers wanted to give people a sense of what the College was "really" like, so they often encouraged visitors to attend regular events in the campus calendar. Doing so created conditions under which things might be heard and seen that were discordant with admissions' officers preferred points of view. For example, during the April 2002 open house, officers encouraged visitors to attend a forum sponsored by the College's philosophy department on the ethics of self-segregation in college housing. The forum's animating question concerned the conditions under which it might be ethically acceptable to allow or even encourage groups of students to self-segregate in institutionally-owned residence halls. The forum included a panel of several philosophers from around the country. One of the panelists voiced strong support for voluntary self-segregation by students who were members of racial and ethnic minority groups, but against traditional fraternities and sororities. This panelist forthrightly stated that in her assessment of institutional policy, the College took

> the standard liberal line of inclusion. It hasn't taken the next step. It hasn't said that, as an institution, identity matters, it matters intellectually and psychologically, that it's part of being a full person, and a fully educated person, to recognize difference and learn from it and celebrate it and struggle with it. And that's a hard thing for an institution to do.

At which Karen Schmidt, a new admissions officer who was sitting next to me in the audience, whispered in my ear, "Ugh! I wish the [topic] could just move on from this issue. It's all so negative. Everything she is saying is sounding so *negative!*"

Officers understood that at this stage in the choice process, students and their families were making fine distinctions. They understood that by mid-April, students' own coarse sorts had weeded out all but a few remaining options. Officers knew that at this point on the calendar, little things could matter a lot for the outcome of final decisions, which perhaps explained why, during the 2002 open house, Val Marin was displeased about the lewd jokes and gestures that one of the College's student music groups had included in its public performance the previous evening. The concert had been attended by many visiting students and their families. Word on the street was that young people in the audience had thought the show was great but that at least a few of the parents had not. "A minister whose daughter was accepted Early Decision met with Liam personally about it this morning," Val said. Her comment prompted my memory of a question from a parent during a separate event that morning: "What is the sexual climate on campus here, especially for women?" On such occasions especially, officers chose their words with care.

The most coveted admits and their parents got a lot of individualized attention during yield season. In April 2001, Val told me how she had spoken with the father of one kid "for forty-five minutes on the phone just this morning." His son had been offered one of the College's most generous merit scholarships. The awards, one of the College's strategies in the student aid game, were intended to lure top students away from the nation's most selective schools. Apparently the kid had narrowed his choice down to the College and an Ivy League school. As Val explained:

> [The dad] called me, he said, 'My son went to bed last night saying he's going to the College, and I've been thinking about it since then, and I need you to hold my hand,' he said. 'I need to know,' he said . . . 'what my son is giving up by going to the College in terms of future prospects.' And I talked with him, and I said of course [the Ivy League institution] is a fine school, with lots of opportunities, but your son will have similar opportunities at the College. Of course he

will. And I could say that with confidence. And apparently this father had called the business school at [the other school], his kid is interested in business, finance, and thankfully the business school speaks highly of us, thankfully, and they said good things about us, so that made him happy. And at the end of this long conversation the dad said thank you to me. He said 'Thank you, you did a good job of holding my hand.' And that's what it takes. To get these kids.

I learned firsthand that the effort officers invested to get kids during yield season could be exhausting. The fieldnotes I wrote of my experience during the 2001 open house include the following:

> A couple notes from the accepted-student open house. . . . First, I found out that I was exhausted at the end. On paper I hadn't been doing much—three sessions to describe the curriculum on Tuesday, then Susan called Tues night and asked if I could take over [another job] Weds AM. Additionally there was greeting families on Tuesday morning, suggesting classes, giving directions to buildings, etc. Also there was a brief appearance at a cocktail hour for parents on Tuesday afternoon. None of this was taxing work, really . . . [but] I do find myself very tired out—this is a realization: I've been doing emotion work. I've been managing my own emotions, making sure to be consistently positive and enthusiastic about the school without being fake, and I've been doing that for one and half days straight. Part of the work . . . involves feeling out where particular parents are at . . . e.g., . . . the parent . . . whose daughter is now considering us [and several other excellent schools]; the parent who has lots of questions about . . . Middle Eastern studies and Arabic, areas in which we offer very little; the parents at the cocktail hour, from Virginia, who seem very pleased by the school . . . but who are a bit of a challenge to talk to because they come from a very different background than me. . . . So, the point is that you're constantly taking stock of who you are talking to and trying to manage impressions accordingly.

Despite their best efforts, officers lost many of their top admits to other schools. It could be very frustrating. One day in April, I confessed to Susan Latterly my disappointment about an e-mail I had just received from a stellar admit I myself had interviewed for admission. The e-mail sang my praises to the mountains, then explained that its author would be enrolling somewhere else.

"Yep, that's just how it goes," Susan responded knowingly. "People will tell us, 'Oh, you guys were the best in Admissions, your publications are great, the people were so nice, loved the campus, and I'm going somewhere else.' It's like whatever we do, kids will still choose to go to the most highly rated school they can get into."

Still, there were always those few stellar admits whom officers were thrilled to woo away from other good schools, kids who had perhaps really hit it off with the soccer coach, or whose visits to campus had occurred on especially lovely spring days, or whose parents' hands had been held firmly enough that they could make a choice previously not imagined. Officers, of course, could not control the weather, but they worked hard to engineer whatever other good impressions they could. Though I do not know for sure, I suspect that admissions officers at the schools who got the kids the College lost during yield season were working just as hard as we were.

Virtually all of what social scientists have learned about the dynamics of student decision making in elite higher education concerns the objective distribution of students' final choices. Scholarship generally supports Susan Latterly's claim that "whatever we do, kids will still choose to go to the most highly rated school they can get into." Even though neither Susan nor the social scientists are incorrect, their insights alone do not fully account for the process through which young people and their families arrive at their final decisions.

My research suggests that, in its final stages, student decision making is partly an emotional choice.[6] Faced with deciding between schools that are objectively similar, families resort to the work of fine distinction, making final decisions on the basis of their feelings about places as well as by more ostensibly objective criteria such as financial aid and institutional rank. We would do well to better attend to such feelings. Aggregate patterns of student choices can indeed be modeled quantitatively, but my work suggests that the individual decisions composing those patterns require at least a satisfactory alignment of calculation and emotion. Bringing numbers and feelings into harmony is not always easy, which is why yield season could be stressful for parents, kids, and admissions officers alike.

chapter eight

THE ARISTOCRACY OF MERIT

A few of the faculty made mock protest against it, but in fact the arrival of students each fall was a happy occasion. The College was virtually useless without them, it seemed unplugged when they were away, a beautiful machine deprived of the electricity it had been so carefully designed to channel.

Engineers warmed up the system with incremental infusions of fresh life. First came the resident assistants (RAs), the student employees who serve as frontline administrators and social control agents in exchange for room and board. Next came the entering freshmen, for whom a full week of orientation was carefully arranged. Parents were sent home almost as soon as they had deposited their cargo of future alumni, leaving the fresh arrivals free to commence the business of assembling the next stage of their lives.

Freshman orientation is officially a beginning, but it also is the end of many years of preparation. Any sustained focus on the terms of selective college admission, including this one, is a waste of time unless it is used to look backward, into childhood and family life. For it is in the years-long production of accomplished applicants that our system of selective admissions has had its most profound consequences on the organization of American society.

If you were to ask any one of the parents of the new freshman class, driving home to their emptier houses, they could tell you: the journey to that campus began long ago. Even before their children were born, some of those parents made decisions with an eye toward college. Knowing that selective admissions are predicated on measurably high academic achievement, they purchased homes in communities with strong public schools. Anxious about future tuition payments, they started special trusts and savings accounts; for the same reason, some of them made or avoided career changes that would have significantly altered their earning potential. Some parents made a point of securing slots for youngsters in the kindergartens that feed prestigious urban private schools. Some parents, almost all of them women, decided to stay at home full-time with their children; forgoing what may have been financially lucrative and personally rewarding jobs, they heeded frequently voiced wisdom about the developmental and educational benefits said to derive from full-time parenting. Many women, of course, went to work just to make ends meet. Still others stayed in the workforce so that their families could afford the extras that so often seemed like necessities: private school tuition, ballet and music lessons, math tutors, travel.

Of course, the ability to make these choices was itself a luxury of privilege, and many less-advantaged mothers and fathers were obliged to prepare their children for college on lesser means. Perhaps resigned to the modest comforts of their own lives, they invested every resource they could muster to make their children's futures better. They rented homes they could barely afford or lived with relatives in order to reside in neighborhoods with good public schools. They navigated the bureaucratic labyrinths of large urban school districts to secure seats for their kids at one of their system's few bright spots. They found special college-prep enrichment programs, like Upward Bound and the College's own Start-Up initiative, that provided the college guidance and academic peer support lacking at their neighborhood high schools. They may have homeschooled their children through a couple of rough years. They applied for every scholarship, followed every lead, knocked on every door.

Whether rich or poor, all of these parents understood that high academic accomplishment is a baseline criterion for admission to a selective college or university. The simple fact that getting into a top school now requires at least decent grades, a solid preparatory curriculum, and respectable test scores goes far in explaining why parents do so much to ensure the quality of their children's early educations. It goes far in explaining the inflated prices of homes in good public school districts, the intense competition for the seats at private day schools in cities like New York and Chicago and Los Angeles, the growing demand for special AP and honors courses at high schools everywhere, and the booming and profitable business of test preparation. The transformation of the U.S. education system into an academic hierarchy has been so complete and so little disputed that virtually all Americans, rich and poor, now take it for granted.

Admission to places like the College typically requires considerably more than academic accomplishment, and mothers and fathers with their eyes on top schools begin investing in the development of their children's extracurricular abilities many years before college begins. They spend a lot of time in cars, ferrying their children between practices and games and recitals. They shiver in chilly grandstands while cheering their offspring through late-season play-offs. They spend thousands of dollars on lessons and league fees and theme camps dedicated to nurturing their children's athletic and artistic skills. They take out home equity loans to purchase pianos and violins. At least part of their incentive for doing all of this is the hope that their incremental investments will sum to the "talented" athletes and musicians favored by admissions offices at the nation's most selective schools.

It is not too much to say that preparation for the rigors of admissions evaluation has led to a distinctive style of life. In her provocative study of contemporary American families, Annette Lareau describes the mode of parenting typical among upper-middle-class households as *concerted cultivation*—"child-rearing strategies that favor the individual development of each child, sometimes at the expense of family time and group needs."[1] A cornerstone of concerted cultivation is the thoughtful nurturing of children's particular athletic, academic, and artistic capacities. Dutiful development of these capacities is presumed to require the assistance of third-party experts—athletics coaches, music teachers, and academic tutors—and competitive milieux on a par with each child's developing capacities. The ever more pervasive desire to expose children to challenging professionals and competitions helps explain why affluent boys and girls spend an increasing proportion of their out-of-school time in structured activities, particularly athletics, and why affluent parents spend so much time escorting children through complicated schedules.

The rise of concerted cultivation has had significant consequences for the character of everyday life. "Today, the center of the middle-class home is the calendar," Lareau writes:

> Scheduled, paid, and organized activities for children are noted (sometimes in a colored pen) in the two-inch-square open spaces beneath each day of the month. Month after month, children are busy participating in sports, music, scouts, and play groups. And, before and after going to work, their parents are busy getting them to and from these activities. At times, middle-class houses seem to be little more than holding places for the occupants during the brief periods when they are between activities.[2]

While Lareau is agnostic about the origins of this increasingly pervasive style of parenting, it seems hardly coincidental that the rise of concerted cultivation has occurred in tandem with the formalization of evaluation criteria at the nation's selective colleges and with the growing difficulty of being admitted to top schools.

In his now classic history of the development of the selective college admissions system, Harold Wechsler argues that from 1870 to 1930, the nation's most ambitious academic leaders secured a central role for their institutions in the arbitration of social distinction in America. "From their former status as peripheral institutions, the colleges and universities [took] on great social importance as the training ground for entrance into the upper middle and upper classes," Wechsler writes of this period.[3] Higher education leaders won their authority as class arbiters by fundamentally reorganizing the academy. They secured the fealty, philanthropy, and sons of wealth by making college life more athletic, more masculine, and more fun. They enhanced the status of academic knowledge by expanding the university to encompass the sciences, medicine, law, and engineering in addition to the study of Greek and Latin and God. They worked hard to clarify and standardize admissions criteria over the years, making measurable academic and extracurricular accomplishment the primary currency of admission. True enough, they often stumbled toward the dream of meritocracy. Systematic exclusions of Jews, women, and people of color from the most luxurious academic opportunities rendered the progress of meritocratic admissions slow and intermittent at best. Even so, there can be no dispute that early twentieth-century academic leaders succeeded in setting the terms by which aspiring young people would be judged fit for admission to selective schools. Virtually all of us now take it for granted that evaluation based on traceable and usually quantifiable academic and extracurricular achievement is the benchmark of fair treatment in college admissions. Reasonable people might disagree about the morality of aberrations from this benchmark—categorical advantages for nonwhite U.S. citizens, for example, or children of alumni. Very few of us, however, question the morality of the meritocratic ideal. Our general acceptance of the idea of meritocracy may be the greatest accomplishment of higher education's greatest leaders.

The system that the elite colleges and universities developed to evaluate the best and the brightest is now the template for what counts as ideal child rearing in America. Perhaps no single college president or dean of admissions fully realized that the development of clear measures of youthful accomplishment—standardized test scores and high school GPAs, athletic team win records, counts of AP classes and titles and formal accolades of all sorts—would in time transform the organization and the culture of bourgeois childhood, would make it more competitive, more expensive, more structured around the production of demonstrated accomplishment, and, perhaps most consequential for the ideal of meritocracy, ever more difficult for families of modest means to emulate. Regardless of anyone's meritorious intentions, that is precisely what has happened. Each year's entering class is the product of an elaborate organizational machinery whose upper tiers have been quite conscientiously designed to send elite colleges just what they are looking for.[4]

In this book I have tried to show that the distinction between college and what comes before it is essentially ceremonial. For the affluent upper middle class, the transition from high school to college is a seamless web of interdependencies: between guidance counselors and admissions officers; between youthful athletic talent and athletic league standings; between high property taxes, large tuition checks, and excellent academics; between aesthetic expectations and architecturally spectacular schools. Colleges rely on affluent families to produce and deliver most of their raw materials, while families in turn rely on colleges to certify those our society calls its most accomplished. The interdependence of privileged families and elite colleges is precisely why the ceremony of selective admissions is so important. It defines college entrance as an almost sacred moment of evaluation, in which supposedly universal standards of merit are applied to each and every applicant regardless of social station. For the most privileged kids in each year's applicant pool the real question is not if they will be admitted to an elite college but which ones will offer them spots. Even so, the frenzy of the admissions process serves to bless favored candidates with marks of honor that, however deceptively, seem neutral to class.

Just why scholars of higher education have so long ignored the consequences of this ceremony for the organization of childhood and family life is a sobering question. Perhaps we have presumed that the years before college entrance are somebody else's research problem. Perhaps we too have believed in the dream of meritocratic universalism, in the idea that a system of educational stratification might be equitable if only we could get the terms of evaluation right. Perhaps the moral worth of our own biographies is so deeply implicated in the system that it is hard for us to appraise it with critical detachment. After all, the admissions ceremony celebrates things that academics characteristically value highly: intellectual facility, stubborn persistence, good grades, fancy degrees.[5] It may be that our faith in the transcendent value of our own workplaces has blinded us to some uncomfortable possibilities: that the terms of college admission have become class-biased standards by which we measure the fruits of parenting and the preponderant means of laundering privilege in contemporary American society.

Fear of Falling

The College staged commencement with care. Ideally it took place outdoors, but because the local winters melted into fickle springs, physical plant workers set up for the ceremony in two locations: under the tall trees of the main quadrangle, and under the glaring lights of the field house. A special sign was installed near the main entrance to the campus for announcing, at the last possible moment, the final determination of venue. People talked a lot about forecasts and hoped for the best.

Commencement took place a full two weeks after the spring semester classes had ended. It took time for the underclassmen to move out of the dorms, for the print shop to turn out bushels of programs, for gardeners to plant annuals in a design heralding the seniors ("2001"), for the food service to prepare a Sunday meal large enough to feed all of the graduates and their families at one sitting. It took time for the intending graduates, and for personnel in the academic and student-life divisions, to tie up loose ends. Incomplete or inadequate schoolwork had to be duly recompensed and recorded. Charges of misbehavior during the heady last weeks of college—the violations of alcohol policy, the petty vandalism, the thankfully only occasional instances of interpersonal violence and sexual assault—needed time to churn through the school's disciplinary machinery. Much as deans and faculty disliked it, the task of adjudicating such matters consumed many hours of administrative attention each spring.

But in general, commencement was a happy occasion, and the College hosted it lavishly. There was the president's reception, obligatory for faculty, at which parents could chat with their children's favorite professors. There was a smaller, little publicized, invitation-only reception, hosted by the College's chief fund-raiser, in a house with stunning views of the surrounding countryside. There was baccalaureate, the religious service, with its respectfully pluralist program of Christian, Jewish, and Muslim prayers. There was a commencement dance on Saturday night. Commencement itself was a grand affair, and a ritual of individualized consideration. Each and every graduate was called by name.

At commencements, students are appraised as equals. Graduation gowns represent the shared status of those receiving the same degree. Officially acknowledged differences among the graduates are academic ones. The College's commencement program specified those whose grades earned them the accolades of summa and magna cum laude. It recognized those who had received special recognition by academic departments. It recognized the valedictorian. But the other myriad differences among the graduates—their racial identities, the affluence and influence of their families, the varied biographical paths that had brought them to this day—were not part of the ceremony.

Those differences were not invisible. One did not have to be a sociologist to notice that the commencement audience and the students and the officials on the dais were overwhelmingly, but not entirely, white, and that most of the graduates and faculty who had added scarves of vibrant African kente cloth to their robes were people of color. One did not need to be an expert in cultural analysis to recognize that the cars, clothes, and cadences of speech among the crowds all betrayed a range of parental wealth. But the message of the commencement ceremony, its implicit promise, was that the diplomas the College conferred that day superseded those differences. Voices from the dais reminded the graduates that their academic accomplishment had rendered them part of "the College family" and, on that basis, members of a distinctively privileged class.

Commencements are occasions for taking stock—for thinking about the present and the future by looking back—and in that spirit I offer a few closing thoughts about how this journey through selective admissions can be critically informed by recent history.

Americans' faith in the ability of higher education to certify youthful accomplishment is enduring and nearly universal. As the iconic neoclassical chapel at the center of campus suggests, this faith is partly a result of an Enlightenment inheritance that offers learning as a primary vehicle of human progress. Indeed, the United States is hardly the only country to invest in higher education as a strategy for social improvement.[6] But the specific role of college in the achievement of the good life in contemporary American society also has nationally specific origins.

The parents in the 2001 commencement audience came of age during a very different era of U.S. higher education. The 1950s, '60s, and '70s were heady years for those who worked on college campuses. During those decades, U.S. state and federal governments invested billions of dollars in public and private higher education. Part of the rationale for this massive expenditure was cold-war competition with the Soviet Union in scientific and technological innovation.[7] There were additional reasons, however, that have been less widely appreciated.

In contrast with the Soviet Union and the European social democracies, in the United States the officially favored strategy for dispersing twentieth-century affluence was to stay out of the way of business while simultaneously seeding the expansion of the middle class. Americans had long been skeptical of government intervention in capitalist markets, and after World War II this skepticism took on a newly powerful ideological resonance. Only communists planned their economies. Capitalist democracies rightly left business free to grow and flourish on its own.[8]

While Americans remained wary of direct government intervention into the economy, they wholeheartedly embraced higher education as a means of social engineering. In the postwar era the federal government actively encouraged the expansion of postsecondary schooling. It did so not only to maintain a global edge in science but also to nurture a virtuous and materially comfortable middle class. In 1946 President Harry Truman appointed the President's Commission on Higher Education to consider how colleges and universities could be deployed to advance a distinctively American version of the good life. The Commission concluded that massive government investment in higher education could engender

> social welfare, better living standards, better health, and less crime. . . . It is an investment in a bulwark against garbled information, half truths, and untruths; against ignorance and intolerance. It is an investment in human talent, better human relationships, democracy and peace.[9]

In subsequent decades the United States chose to build a social welfare system that was, by European standards, quite modest; at the same time it built the largest higher education system in world history. The expansion of the nation's postsecondary capacity gave substance to an official government commitment to making higher education a wide pathway to the good life. The idea that college should be easily accessible to the general population, what sociologist James Rosenbaum has dubbed "college for all," was made manifest in a variety of ways: in funding for thousands of additional seats at existing institutions; in the dramatic expansion of the community college sector; in generous government underwriting of instructional costs at research universities; and in a range of government grant and loan programs that made college tuition a manageable expense for millions of families with modest incomes. It took little time for Americans to begin to take it for granted that college was a viable and appropriate path to social mobility.[10] The United States maintained a relatively modest welfare state for its poor, even while it developed a huge, government-funded higher education infrastructure to ensure the welfare of its middle class.[11]

During the 1960s the little school I studied literally doubled in size. Its expansion was propelled by the demographic tidal wave of the baby boom, of course, but it was funded in large measure by governmental largesse. For the first time, unabashedly modernist buildings were added to the classic New England–style campus, their construction funded in part by a state dormitory authority. Meanwhile the work of the school's financial aid officers grew more complicated, as students and officers alike figured out how to exploit a growing portfolio of tuition grant and loan programs to everyone's optimal benefit.

The huge government investment in higher education was part of a consequential, if often implicit, compact between government, workers, and business that many cultural analysts call "Fordism." The term references the industrial philosophy of automobile magnate Henry Ford, who famously argued that the bricks and mortar of a robust capitalism were workers with sufficient job security and wages that they could afford to buy the fruits of their own labor. According to the Fordist dream, industry benefited from taking good care of workers because secure and affluent employees were the basis of mass consumer markets. This dream came true for millions during the 1950s and 1960s, when the sustained expansion of the U.S. economy supported some of the most comfortable worker compensation packages in world history.[12]

The Fordist compact came in two versions, one for blue-collar skilled and semiskilled workers, the other for those aspiring to white-collar managerial and technical occupations. The blue-collar version was championed by labor unions, and in the decades of the postwar economic boom, unions garnered wage and benefit packages generous enough for many industrial workers to purchase homes and automobiles and to support households with a single breadwinner. The white-collar version worked differently. Employers expected professional and managerial workers to leverage their own interests by bringing high levels of educational attainment, and the high-level skills their educations were presumed to confer, to their jobs.[13] In the second half of the twentieth century, educational attainment rapidly became the gradient divide that separated white collar from blue, as a college degree increasingly became an entry criterion into the higher-status and better-compensated positions of the upper middle class.

This was the historical and economic context in which the United States embarked on the largest expansion of higher education the world had ever known. Because higher education was broadly understood as a path of access to the upper middle class, the idea of college for all was supported by taxpayers and at the polls. And because the boom economy of the mid-twentieth century made many businesses profitable enough to pay high wages and sustain many managerial workers, the promised relationship between college completion and comfortable employment often proved true.

By the mid-1970s, however, the Fordist compact was already unraveling. Technological developments as mundane and marvelous as affordable air conditioning, expanded commercial air travel, advanced telecommunications, and mass computerization made it possible for employers to disperse their production operations all over the country and around the globe, pursuing low wages and business-friendly labor laws wherever they could be found. The geographic dispersion of manufacturing meant that employers were less obliged to appease the demands of local workers, which in turn diminished the power of labor unions. Jobs moved. Many of the textile, aerospace, and electric equipment manufacturers that had long brought prosperity to the College's own geographic region moved their operations to sunnier climates, right-to-work states, and overseas. The entire inland Northeast, long proud of its industrial prosperity, suffered precipitous declines in wealth and population in the 1970s.

Despite the economic migration taking place all around them, the esteemed colleges and universities of the region remained in place. They were anchored to the landscape by the physically obdurate assets of their beautiful campuses. Their bucolic locations, easily accessible from once-great industrial cities like Buffalo and Cleveland and Philadelphia, became gradually less appealing as the entire Northeast region lost its economic primacy. Addresses that formerly were clear assets became partial liabilities to many northeastern schools with national ambitions. Thankfully, the geographic facts were not entirely bad news. These schools enjoyed the patina of age and tradition that citizens of a young country granted to institutions "back East." They also enjoyed sturdy associations with their fiercest athletic rivals. By the 1970s the sports leagues that had done so much to define status clubs among eastern schools were well established and nationally respected. Like the schools' stately old buildings and verdant quadrangles, the benefits of these league associations would have been difficult to replicate elsewhere.

The dramatic changes in economic geography that shifted wealth away from the U.S. Northeast might well have spelled crisis for the costly private schools of the region. Not only were the affluent local families who were these schools' traditional clients farther afield; by the 1970s virtually every U.S. citizen lived within a day's drive of at least one public research university. Little schools on rural hilltops in the rust belt were hardly the only available options. Yet remarkably, over the subsequent twenty years, through the infancy and early childhood and adolescence of the class of 2001, competition for admission to these schools grew ever more intense. Ambitious students from all over the country sought to enter places like the College in ever greater numbers. It was an impressive, if largely unheralded, example of successful institutional restructuring, and a paradox of economic geography in post-Fordist America. As the inland Northeast declined in economic prominence, the region's costly private schools retooled themselves. They became reproduction insurance companies for an ever more anxious and peripatetic upper middle class.

To mothers and fathers worried about their children's futures in a highly mobile and uncertain world, schools like the College now purvey the promise of extra protection. Surely at least a few parents of the class of 2001 lost jobs long thought secure in the surge of corporate restructuring that began in late 1970s and has continued in years since. Surely at least a few of them found their offices redefined and differently compensated in the wake of leveraged buyouts and hostile takeovers. Some were forced to change job titles, zip codes, or careers to maintain their household's standard of living. Some of them watched with dismay as the value of their pensions declined and their out-of-pocket healthcare costs soared. Many of them, in one way or another, were obliged to learn that there is now rarely such thing as a lifelong employer. Those who did not experience such setbacks themselves almost certainly knew a neighbor or relative or colleague who had. All of these parents understand that maintaining the comforts of an upper-middle-class life will be considerably more difficult for their children than it was for their own generation.[14]

In light of such hard realities, the higher cost of sending one's children to an elite private college instead of a public university may seem like a small price to pay for additional life security. True enough, degrees from highly selective private schools have proven to offer only modest net benefits in terms of earnings over the life course. But it also is true that elite private schools are exceptionally good at retaining and graduating the students they enroll. In this respect institutions like the College are the ultimate safety nets. It is very difficult for those who are admitted to fall through them. Low student/faculty ratios ensure that academic problems are detected early. Student-life personnel attend to the social and psychological challenges of college life. Study-abroad programs sate youthful wanderlust. Gently paternalistic campus cultures accommodate second chances.[15] If securing a college degree is now more important than ever, mere admission to an academically selective institution is an excellent way to hedge bets about degree completion. In the present era, the phenomenon sociologist William Goode once called "protection of the inept" might be better described as insurance for the accomplished: elite schools no longer buoy wealthy children who are academically incompetent so much as guarantee that those who are capable enough to advance through the selective admissions race will almost certainly receive their diplomas.[16]

Schools like the College confer other relative advantages, however hard they may be to measure precisely. For an increasingly mobile professional and managerial workforce, degrees earned at schools with national and even international reputations may serve as ever more important cues about worker capability and character. For those who can expect to change jobs and places of residence multiple times in their adult lives, a diploma with a recognized name may be a useful calling card during job interviews—all the more so if the person on the other side of the desk happens to be a fellow graduate of that alma mater, or one of its athletic rivals. Although social scientists have long recognized the place of elite colleges in the biographies of corporate, government, and philanthropic leaders,[17] they have devoted less attention than they should to specifying how comparable educational experiences enable upper-middle-class groups to coalesce. Even if people do not attend the same institutions at the same time, their mutual participation in the world of elite schooling gives them a lot to talk about. Conversation among the comparably educated inevitably turns to talk of college: mention of similar or rival schools, sports, and chatty exclamations about siblings and friends known in common. If, as many social critics have complained, Americans have a very limited vocabulary for talking about class differences, they maintain an extraordinarily elaborate discourse of academic distinction. That this college talk is such a ubiquitous feature of upper-middle-class culture suggests that it is not just idle banter.[18]

Nor is it just about getting jobs. Perhaps their enduring fascination with the relationship between schooling and labor markets explains sociologists' long neglect of the things that most occupy the attention of students themselves: playing sports, making friends, scouting for sex, falling in love. This is a significant oversight. Elite private schools like the College, with their residency requirements and freestanding campuses, are what Erving Goffman called *total institutions*—organizations that bring virtually every aspect of their inhabitants' lives under the purview of a single administrative authority.[19] Inmates inevitably develop social worlds of their own making, and much of what makes any one school a distinctive and ultimately inimitable place is the culture its own students create within it, over time. Students create their worlds under conditions made by others, however. Who is admitted, who gets to stay, and who graduates are determined by the adults in charge. I suspect that this is a nontrivial component of parents' sense that elite college tuitions are good investments. Parents can go to sleep at night knowing that their children's potential friends and lovers have been elaborately screened. They can rest assured that not only academic but also extracurricular activity will be carefully monitored, that bad apples will be identified and, when necessary, separated from the bushel. Much like the comfortable suburbs in which many of them reside, elite colleges enable parents to control the social environments in which their children arrive at social and sexual maturity.

Lest this attention to socializing and sex seem too prurient, we should keep in mind just how important school is in the marital selection process, a phenomenon demographers call "educational homogamy." Simply put, people tend to marry those with comparable levels of education, and they often meet their future spouses in school. Educational homogamy is especially important for upper-class families, who tend to have the most to lose if their children choose poorly heeled mates. Indeed, the desire to sequester children from others below their station was why the urban upper classes began to patronize rural schools like the College in the nineteenth century.[20] The residential college system has proven to be a remarkably effective and durable mechanism for shaping marital outcomes. One recent study finds that graduates of elite colleges tend to choose marital partners who attended institutions of comparable prestige.[21] The role of college in defining pools of potential partners may be even more important in an era of high divorce rates, when men and women face high odds of having to look for spouses several times in their adult lives. The fabled endurance of old school ties may help graduates tie the knot more than once.

All of the marginal advantages that accrue to attending an elite college are especially beneficial for young women. Among those who become parents, women are more likely than men to reorganize paid work around their children, leaving and entering the workforce as their household incomes and children's needs allow or require. The value of an elite college degree as a marker of general capacity may be particularly important for those with gaps in their résumés. Gender inequalities in pay may further encourage women to burnish their educational credentials as much as they can; if the workforce they are entering continues to stack the cards against them, obtaining the marginal benefit of a diploma from a top school may seem all the more appealing. Finally, it is no secret that the adverse consequences of divorce disproportionately fall on women, who tend to shoulder most of the costs of raising children, have less earning potential than their former husbands, and fare less well than men in mate selection as they age. One thing that no departing husband or divorce court or passing years can take away from a woman, however, is her prior educational attainment. Girls and their parents may see investment in elite schooling as a buffer against the chronic uncertainties that attend contemporary marriage. Herein, as sociologists Claudia Buchmann and Thomas DiPrete have recently argued, is an at least plausible explanation for the consistent lead women have over men in college entrance, grades, and completion.[22]

Beyond College for All

Highly selective schools like the College set the standard for what counts as an ideal education, and their admissions protocols have come to define the priorities for K–12 schools nationwide. In the wealthiest public school districts, honors and AP classes crowd high school course lists, residents embrace bond issues to pay for the construction of new academic and athletic facilities, and parents eagerly support special fund drives for costly extracurricular programs. For schools serving families at the other end of our society's wealth distribution, however, the relationship between college expectations and K–12 offerings has played out quite differently. During the same years that evaluation practices at the most selective colleges and universities have become more academically competitive, many school reformers and politicians have supported a "back to basics" movement in K–12 education, encouraging cash-strapped public schools to focus their ever-tighter budgets on core academic offerings. Districts facing the greatest financial pressures, often the same ones serving large numbers of urban minorities, have been encouraged to jettison the "extras" that are said to inflate expenses. Athletics, performing arts, and debate programs often are sacrificed, along with the applied arts and vocational programs that tend to require costly infrastructures to maintain. If districts are unable to pay for everything, this reform reasoning goes, they should shore up their academic offerings at the expense of "extra" curriculars.[23]

Reasonable as they may sound on first hearing, back-to-basics reforms have dramatically narrowed the range of educational opportunity in America. As New York University sociologist Richard Arum points out, back-to-basics reformers have systematically eliminated many aspects of schools that make them at all appealing to students who are not academically inclined. Academics-only curriculums are fine for those who perform well in English and science and history classes, but what happens to those for whom academic course work is a perennial struggle? What encourages these students to stay in school when the only classes available to them are those in which they do poorly?

Reformers' focus in the era of college-for-all often has been oriented toward academic preparation at the expense of programs that appeal to students with other proclivities. To better serve a wider variety of students, Arum suggests that "curriculum design should take into account the variety of motivations, inclinations, and interests that students bring with them into the classroom."

> This advice, long ago articulated by progressive educators such as John Dewey, receives too little attention in contemporary reforms. Rather than making education more relevant, recent policies have promoted a deliberate narrowing of the curriculum to focus almost exclusively on traditional academic coursework. This reflects the reformers' long-term goal of preparing all students for four-year college training, but the reality is that the vast majority of students in many schools do not have much of a chance of achieving such aspirations.[24]

It is sobering to consider that, as the college-for-all ideal has become more deeply embedded into the organization of K–12 schooling, extracurricular opportunities have become more exclusively reserved for the wealthy. My travels through even a handful of the nation's twenty-five thousand high schools made it clear that the ones that best reward a variety of youthful capacities—the schools with thriving sports and arts and music programs—are precisely the ones that send large proportions of their graduates directly on to four-year colleges. The kids who already are headed to college enjoy the richest extracurricular programs, partly because the most selective colleges and universities expect and reward extracurricular accomplishment. Meanwhile, high schools in rougher neighborhoods struggle to keep a handful of extracurricular programs afloat. Back-to-basics reforms in the nation's poorest school districts may be fine for those students who are academically ambitious. But what about the other kids: the aspiring athletes and artists, the potentially gifted technicians and mechanics and craftspeople, the ones who have a hard time sitting quietly and reading books? What does an exclusively academic curriculum offer them?

At this point in American educational history, raising the question of whether a college preparatory curriculum should be obligatory in every high school is a politically risky thing to do. The college-for-all idea resonates nicely with both conservative and liberal educational agendas. Conservatives tend to presume that the "hard" academic subjects are more important for everyone than the "soft" extracurricular ones, regardless of the wide variation in student proclivity. College-oriented academic curriculums also appeal to liberals who, for better or worse, have largely championed the idea that college entrance is a magic doorway to the good life.

Meanwhile, the nation's most privileged families have quietly shifted the preferred system of admission into the upper middle class. The rules are different now than they were a generation ago. Anyone naive to the new system might do well listen in on cocktail conversation in Westchester County, Coral Gables, or Palo Alto. They can learn a lot by tracking the stickers affixed to the rear windows of expensive cars. There they will find the names of schools good enough to be worth long drives, schools with beautiful campuses and beautiful students; whose graduates occupy positions of influence in business, government, philanthropy, and the arts; whose diplomas and career services help secure good first jobs. In contemporary America, college may perhaps be for all, but the preferred institutions are for only a few.

Who, among each generation, will be admitted to these schools? When affluent parents confront this question for their own children, they tend to deploy the many means at their disposal to make meritocracy more fun. They fold arts-and-crafts and PE and drama classes in with the standard academic coursework. They make sure that their children have charismatic teachers and attend schools in which the dominant peer culture defines academic failure as uncool. They scout out baseball and soccer leagues and other recreations that their children particularly enjoy. They reward excellent or even adequate academic performance with generous allowances, ski trips, sports camps, new clothes. When it is time for the college search, these parents turn the enterprise into a quest for schools that "fit" their children just so. Hopes for the Ivy League may be jettisoned quickly for the artist or athlete or fun-lover of the family, who will be presumed to find a more amenable spot at a place like the College, or perhaps at one of its purported peers a few notches down the selectivity pecking order. Regardless of which schools their children choose and which schools choose them, there always is a spot for a full-payer at an institution of at least modest prestige. Whatever that place may be, parents can be more or less assured of faculties fat with energetic professors and academic programs gilded with sexy internships and study-abroad programs. They can be confident that a small army of student-life personnel will be on hand to keep drifters on course. Indeed, elite colleges' own interest in maintaining high statistics for student retention will work in these parents' favor. During the college years elite schools and families are partners in mutually beneficial efforts to keep students, even the weakest and least enthusiastic ones, moving forward. Under such conditions it is more than likely that almost everyone who enters a school like the College will make it to graduation.

Such schools educate only a tiny fraction of the nation's young people, but they specify the terms by which American families raise those we call our best and brightest. This is how a handful of small institutions wield such profound cultural influence. My inquiry has made it clear that the terms of admission are now quite demanding, but they nevertheless remain quite broad. There is no doubt about it, applicants made it to the College in a variety of ways. Some of them tested and studied their way to freshman year, others tackled and scored and swam much of the distance. Some got in on account of who their friends or parents were. Others were connected to large donations. A few made it on the merits of PQs, others on sheer charisma. We might view this variety of paths to admission as academic injustice, as so many forms of institutionalized cheating, but in the end I believe it simply reflects our enduring uncertainty about just what the standards for admission into America's most privileged classes should be. The College is an academic institution, and a justly proud one, but it also is proud of its twenty-eight varsity sports teams, its budding artists and musicians, its community service projects, diverse student body, spectacular campus, and loyal alumni. It is a school full of rich kids where half of the students receive financial aid, a cosmopolitan community out in the middle of nowhere. We might wish that all of our children could get to that place, but the hard truth is that however we write the rules of admission, there will never be room for everyone.

NOTES
ACKNOWLEDGMENTS
INDEX

NOTES

Introduction

1. Nicola Beisel and Pamela Walters have done much to shape my conception of social reproduction. See, for example, Nicola Beisel, *Imperiled Innocents: Anthony Comstock and Family Reproduction in Victorian America* (Princeton: Princeton University Press, 1997); and Pamela Barnhouse Walters, "The Politics of Family Reproduction and the Persistence of Separate-and-Unequal Schooling in the U.S." (paper delivered at the annual meeting of the American Sociological Association, Montreal, August 2006).

2. I echo the work of John Meyer here. See John W. Meyer, "The Effects of Education as an Institution," *American Journal of Sociology* 83 (1977): 55–77; also Meyer, "Types of Explanation in the Sociology of Education," in John G. Richardson, ed., *Handbook of Theory and Research in the Sociology of Education* (Westport, Conn.: Greenwood Press, 1986), 341–359.

3. I am indebted to Doug Massey, in conversation, for this insight.

4. For consistency and readability, I have replaced the school's name

with the phrase "the College" in all quotations and fieldnote excerpts that appear in the following pages.

1. A School in a Garden

1. Americans' ambivalence about the relationship between urbanity and intellect is deep and enduring. See Morton G. White and Lucia White, *The Intellectual versus the City, from Thomas Jefferson to Frank Lloyd Wright* (Cambridge, Mass.: Harvard University Press, 1962).

2. Excellent histories of early higher education in the United States include: John R. Thelin, *A History of American Higher Education* (Baltimore: Johns Hopkins University Press, 2004); Christopher J. Lucas, *American Higher Education: A History* (New York: St. Martin's Press, 1994); Laurence R. Veysey, *The Emergence of the American University* (Chicago: University of Chicago Press, 1965); Frederick Rudolph, *The American College and University: A History* (Athens: University of Georgia Press, 1990 [1962]); and the collected papers in Roger L. Geiger, ed., *The American College in the Nineteenth Century* (Nashville, Tenn.: Vanderbilt University Press, 2000).

3. For recent critical commentary on the growing competitiveness of selective college admissions, see the essays in Lloyd Thacker, ed., *College Unranked: Ending the College Admissions Frenzy* (Cambridge, Mass.: Harvard University Press, 2005).

4. Journalistic and "insider" accounts of selective college admissions include Jacques Steinberg, *The Gatekeepers: Inside the Admissions Process of a Premier College* (New York: Viking, 2002); Rachel Toor, *Admissions Confidential: An Insider's Account of the Elite College Selection Process* (New York: St. Martin's Press, 2001); Jean H. Fetter, *Questions and Admissions: Reflections on 100,000 Admissions Decisions at Stanford* (Stanford: Stanford University Press, 1995); Michelle A. Hernandez, *A Is for Admission: The Insider's Guide to*

Getting into the Ivy League and Other Top Colleges (New York: Warner Books, 1997).

5. For cross-national analyses of the relationship between higher education and social stratification in modern societies, see Richard Breen and Jan O. Jonnson, "Inequality of Opportunity in Comparative Perspective: Recent Research on Educational Attainment and Social Mobility," *Annual Review of Sociology* 31 (2005): 223–243; also the essays in Yossi Shavit, Richard Arum, and Adam Gamoran, eds., *Expansion, Differentiation, and Inequality of Access in Higher Education: A Comparative Study* (Stanford: Stanford University Press, 2007).

6. The paradigmatic text on the reproduction approach to educational inequality in U.S. social science is Samuel Bowles and Herbert Gintis, *Schooling in Capitalist America: Educational Reform and the Contradictions of Economic Life* (New York: Basic Books, 1976). Bowles and Gintis reprise their argument in light of subsequent scholarship in Bowles and Gintis, "Schooling in Capitalist America Revisited," *Sociology of Education* 75 (2002): 1–18.

7. Max Weber, "The 'Rationalization' of Education and Training," in H. H. Gerth and C. Wright Mills, eds., *From Max Weber: Essays in Sociology* (New York: Oxford University Press, 1946), 240–244.

8. Classic works in this tradition include Peter Blau and Otis Dudley Duncan, *The American Occupational Structure* (New York: Wiley, 1967); Christopher Jencks, *Inequality* (New York: Basic Books, 1972); Robert D. Mare, "Change and Stability in Educational Stratification," *American Sociological Review* 46 (1981): 72–87. For recent reviews, see Breen and Jonnson, "Inequality of Opportunity"; Grace Kao and Jennifer S. Thompson, "Racial and Ethnic Stratification in Educational Achievement and Attainment," *Annual Review of Sociology* 29 (2003): 417–442.

9. Randall Collins, "Functional and Conflict Theories of Educational Stratification," *American Sociological Review* 36 (1971): 1002–1019; Randall Collins, *The Credential Society: An Histori-*

cal Sociology of Education and Stratification (New York: Academic Press, 1979). Also David K. Brown, *Degrees of Control: A Sociology of Educational Expansion and Occupational Credentialism* (New York: Teachers College Press, 1995). Years before Collins crystallized the notion, Christopher Jencks and David Riesman laid important groundwork for the credentialing idea in *The Academic Revolution* (Garden City, N.Y.: Doubleday, 1968). For an excellent critical review of scholarship in this tradition from Weber's early work onward, see David K. Brown, "The Social Sources of Educational Credentialism: Status Cultures, Labor Markets, and Organizations," in "Current of Thought: Sociology of Education at the Dawn of the 21st Century," special issue, *Sociology of Education* 74 (2001): 19–34.

10. See Thelin, *American Higher Education,* 260–316; Jencks and Riesman, *Academic Revolution;* Clark Kerr, *The Uses of the University* (Cambridge, Mass.: Harvard University Press, 2001 [1963]). On community colleges, see Kevin J. Dougherty, *The Contradictory College: The Conflicting Origins, Impacts, and Futures of the Community College* (Albany: State University of New York Press, 1994); also Steven Brint and Jerome Karabel, *The Diverted Dream: Community Colleges and the Promise of Educational Opportunity in America, 1900–1985* (New York: Oxford University Press, 1989).

11. Richard B. Freeman, *The Overeducated American* (New York: Academic Press, 1976). See also Randall Collins, "Credential Inflation and the Future of Universities," in Steven Brint, ed., *The Future of the City of Intellect: The Changing American University* (Stanford: Stanford University Press, 2002), 23–46.

12. For a critical summary of the effects of this expansion on social stratification in the United States, see Josipa Roksa, Eric Grodsky, Richard Arum, and Adam Gamoran, "United States: Changes in Higher Education and Social Stratification," in Shavit, Arum, and Gamoran, *Expansion, Differentiation, and Inequality,* 165–191.

13. See, for example, Christopher Avery, Andrew Fairbanks, and

Richard Zeckhauser, *The Early Admissions Game: Joining the Elite* (Cambridge, Mass.: Harvard University Press, 2003); and the collected essays in Caroline M. Hoxby, ed., *College Choices: The Economics of Where to Go, When to Go, and How to Pay for It* (Chicago: University of Chicago Press / National Bureau of Economic Research, 2004).

14. I here cite two exceptions. Roger L. Geiger clearly describes the current status system predicated on admissions selectivity in "The Competition for High-Ability Students: Universities in a Key Marketplace," in Brint, *Future of the City of Intellect*, 82–106. However, Geiger has no complete explanation for just why admissions selectivity became such a prominent index of prestige. Second, Arthur L. Stinchcombe, in his *Information and Organizations* (Berkeley: University of California Press, 1990), provides an elegant analysis of the relationship between the scholarly productivity of faculty and the relative prestige of the schools that employ them. Stinchcombe's arguments are not incompatible with my own.

15. See, for example, Pierre Bourdieu, "Cultural Reproduction and Social Reproduction," in Jerome Karabel and A. H. Halsey, eds., *Power and Ideology in Education* (New York: Oxford University Press, 1977), 487–511; Bourdieu, *Reproduction in Education, Society, Culture* (Beverly Hills, Calif.: Sage, 1977); Bourdieu, "The Forms of Capital," in John G. Richardson, ed., *Handbook of Theory and Research for the Sociology of Education* (New York: Greenwood Press, 1986), 241–258; Bourdieu, "Sport and Social Class," in Chandra Mukerji and Michael Schudson, eds., *Rethinking Popular Culture* (Berkeley: University of California Press, 1991), 357–373. For an influential study that uses college completion as a marker of cultural distinctions between the middle and upper-middle classes, see Michèle Lamont, *Money, Morals, and Manners: The Culture of the French and American Upper-Middle Class* (Chicago: University of Chicago Press, 1992). For examples of scholarly work applying Bourdieu's insights to a range of cultural dis-

tinction projects, see Michèle Lamont and Marcel Fournier, eds., *Cultivating Differences: Symbolic Boundaries and the Making of Inequality* (Chicago: University of Chicago Press, 1992). My thinking on these matters has been much shaped by two articles by Paul Dimaggio: "Cultural Entrepreneurship in Nineteenth-Century Boston: The Creation of an Organizational Base for High Culture in America," *Media, Culture and Society* 4 (1982): 33–50; and "Cultural Entrepreneurship in Nineteenth Century Boston, Part II: The Classification and Framing of American Art," *Media, Culture and Society* 4 (1982): 303–322. A recent critical review of Bourdieu's influence on the sociology of education in the United States is Annette Lareau and Elliot B. Weininger, "Cultural Capital in Educational Research: A Critical Assessment," *Theory and Society* 32 (2003): 567–606. On the inscription of identity onto physical landscapes and the ubiquity of the garden as metaphor and catalyst for this fascinating process, see Maria Kefalas, *Working-Class Heroes: Protecting Home, Community, and Nation in a Chicago Neighborhood* (Berkeley: University of Chicago Press, 2003); and Chandra Mukerji, *Territorial Ambitions and the Gardens of Versailles* (Cambridge, Mass.: Cambridge University Press, 1997).

16. On parental investment in children's academic and extracurricular capacities generally, see Annette Lareau, *Unequal Childhoods: Class, Race, and Family Life* (Berkeley: University of California Press, 2003). On patterned preferences for various categories of applicants, see, for example, Thomas J. Espenshade, Chang Y. Chung, and Joan L. Walling, "Admission Preferences for Minority Students, Athletes, and Legacies at Elite Universities," *Social Science Quarterly* 85 (2004): 1422–46. A recent journalistic account of admissions preferences for the children of wealthy and alumni parents is Daniel Golden, *The Price of Admission: How America's Ruling Class Buys Its Way into College—and Who Gets Left Outside the Gates* (New York: Crown, 2006).

17. The important exception here is David Karen's empirical observations in the admissions office at Harvard College in the 1980s. See his "Toward a Political-Organizational Model of Gatekeeping: The Case of Elite Colleges," *Sociology of Education* 63 (1990): 227–240; also David Karen, "'Achievement' and 'Ascription' in Admission to an Elite College: A Political-Organizational Analysis," *Sociological Forum* 6 (1991): 349–380. Karen's work confirms patterned preferences for athletes, legacies, and members of certain minority groups. However, it provides only schematic analysis of how admissions officers manage these preferences and make trade-offs among them.

18. The sociological literature on decision making in complex organizations is large and diffuse. My thinking has been informed most strongly by James G. March and Johan P. Olsen, *Ambiguity and Choice in Organizations* (Bergen, Norway: Universitetsforlaget, 1976); James G. March and Herbert A. Simon, *Organizations* (New York: Wiley, 1958); Walter W. Powell, *Getting into Print: The Decision Making Process in Scholarly Publishing* (Chicago: University of Chicago Press, 1985); and Stinchcombe, *Information and Organizations*.

19. This logic is derived from a paper by Damon J. Phillips and Ezra W. Zuckerman, "Middle-Status Conformity: Theoretical Restatements and Empirical Demonstration in Two Markets," *American Journal of Sociology* 107 (2001): 379–429.

20. It would be virtually impossible to identify the particular people and places I depict, solely on the basis of the information in these pages. I have slightly altered applicants' grade point averages, test scores, and favored extracurricular activities. I changed the names of high schools and placed them in unspecified cities. I did not mention any of the College's direct institutional peers by name. In general I tried to capture the analytically salient features of places and people in ways that were faithful to empirical reality in character, if not in precise detail. I wrote this way in honor of the trust

extended to me by parties all over the country throughout this research.

21. Selectivity here based on an analysis of the admissions statistics reported in recent years in the *U.S. News & World Report* rankings. Many people beyond the field of college admissions are surprised to learn that so few undergraduate institutions admit less than 50 percent of their applicants. The task of the vast majority of the profession is not to sort the best applicants from the pool but to get enough to students to apply and enroll—work of lower status that officers at the selective schools sometimes describe as "filling seats."

2. Numbers

1. This insight is hardly my own. See, for example, Paul Fussell, *Class: A Guide through the American Status System* (New York: Summit Books, 1983); also David Brooks, *Bobos in Paradise: The New Upper Class and How They Got There* (New York: Simon and Schuster, 2000).

2. Max Weber, "Class, Status, Party," in H. H. Gerth and C. Wright Mills, eds., *From Max Weber: Essays in Sociology* (New York: Oxford University Press, 1946), 180–195.

3. See Michael Sauder, "Third Parties and Status Position: How the Characteristics of Status Systems Matter," *Theory and Society* 35 (2006): 299–321; also Sauder, "Symbols and Contexts: An Interactionist Approach to the Study of Social Status," *Sociological Quarterly* 46 (2005): 279–298. An elegant treatise on the dynamics of inter-organizational status generally is Joel M. Podolny, *Status Signals: A Sociological Study of Market Competition* (Princeton: Princeton University Press, 2005).

4. Harold S. Wechsler, *The Qualified Student: A History of Selective College Admission in America* (New York: Wiley, 1977). My thinking here has also been much informed by E. Digby Baltzell,

The Protestant Establishment: Aristocracy and Caste in America (New Haven: Yale University Press, 1964); and James McLachlan, *American Boarding Schools: A Historical Study* (New York: Scribner's, 1970).

5. The intensity of this inter-organizational status competition is depicted vividly in Jerome Karabel, *The Chosen: The Hidden History of Admission and Exclusion at Harvard, Yale, and Princeton* (Boston: Houghton Mifflin, 2005).

6. For Philadelphia, see E. Digby Baltzell, *Philadelphia Gentlemen: The Making of a National Upper Class* (New Brunswick, N.J.: Transaction Books, 2002 [1971]); for New York, see Wechsler, *The Qualified Student;* for Boston and Harvard, see Ronald Story, *Harvard and the Boston Upper Class: The Forging of an Aristocracy, 1800–1870* (Middletown, Conn.: Wesleyan University Press, 1980). What geographers sometimes call inter-urban status competition was a vital incentive for local elites in Boston, New York City, and Philadelphia to outdo their counterparts in patronizing institutions. See Nicola Beisel, *Imperiled Innocents: Anthony Comstock and Family Reproduction in Victorian America* (Princeton: Princeton University Press, 1997).

7. It is no accident that solutions to the puzzle of intercollegiate status described here, admissions selectivity and sports, were worked out during the same years that higher education leaders developed the College Board and its flagship product, the test now known as the SAT. Excellent analyses of the development of the SAT include Nicolas Lemann, *The Big Test: The Secret History of the American Meritocracy* (New York: Farrar, Straus and Giroux, 1999); and Michael S. Schudson, "Organizing the 'Meritocracy': A History of the College Entrance Examination Board," *Harvard Educational Review* 42 (1972): 34–69. I believe that these analyses and my own are mutually complementary.

8. For a review of this intellectual tradition, see Wendy Nelson Espeland and Mitchell L. Stevens, "Commensuration as a Social

Process," *Annual Review of Sociology* 24 (1998): 313–343. See also Theodore M. Porter, *Trust in Numbers: The Pursuit of Objectivity in Science and Public Life* (Princeton: Princeton University Press, 1995); Bruce G. Carruthers and Arthur L. Stinchcombe, "The Social Structure of Liquidity: Flexibility, Markets, and States," *Theory and Society* 28 (1999): 353–382.

9. Wendy Nelson Espeland, *The Struggle for Water: Politics, Rationality, and Identity in the American Southwest* (Chicago: University of Chicago Press, 1998).

10. See, for example, Barrie Thorne, *Gender Play: Girls and Boys in School* (New Brunswick, N.J.: Rutgers University Press, 1993).

11. See Lynn Zinser, "Will Figures Add Up to Fairness?" *New York Times,* 10 February 2006; also Katarina Witt, "No Soul on Ice," *New York Times,* 22 February 2006.

12. This may be part of the reason why the University of Michigan was such an early and prominent player in the effort to standardize criteria for college entrance. See Wechsler, *The Qualified Student.* It almost certainly was why University of Chicago president William Harper invested heavily in the quality of the school's football team and actively courted East Coast gridiron rivals in the 1890s. See John Sayle Watterson, *College Football: History, Spectacle, Controversy* (Baltimore: Johns Hopkins University Press, 2000), 39–63.

13. On the rise and consequence of the *USN* rankings, see Wendy Nelson Espeland and Michael Sauder, "Rankings and Reactivity: How Public Measures Recreate Social Worlds," *American Journal of Sociology* (forthcoming).

14. Sixty schools defined as "regional universities" and forty described as "regional liberal arts colleges" also were ranked in their own categories in 1994.

15. For related insights about numerical representations of reality, see Bruce G. Carruthers, "Accounting, Ambiguity, and the New Institutionalism," *Accounting, Organizations and Society* 20 (1995): 313–328; also John W. Meyer, "Social Environments and Organiza-

tional Accounting," *Accounting, Organizations and Society* 11 (1986): 345–356.

16. On numbers as instruments of social control, see Wendy Nelson Espeland and Michael Sauder, "The Discipline of Rankings" (unpublished manuscript, Northwestern University, 2006).

3. Travel

1. An excellent history of changes in admissions practices at private liberal arts colleges in this period is Elizabeth Duffy and Idana Goldberg, *Crafting a Class: College Admissions and Financial Aid, 1955–94* (Princeton: Princeton University Press, 1998). Enduringly useful accounts of this period are Christopher Jencks and David Riesman, *The Academic Revolution* (Garden City, N.Y.: Doubleday, 1968), and Clark Kerr, *The Uses of the University* (Cambridge, Mass.: Harvard University Press, 2001 [1963]). A more recent historical account is John R. Thelin, *A History of American Higher Education* (Baltimore: Johns Hopkins University Press, 2004), 205–362.

2. See Duffy and Goldberg, *Crafting a Class*. Also Patricia J. Gumport, "Universities and Knowledge: Restructuring the City of Intellect," in Steven Brint, ed., *The Future of the City of Intellect: The Changing American University* (Stanford: Stanford University Press, 2002), 47–81.

3. Caroline M. Hoxby, "The Effects of Geographic Integration and Increasing Competition in the Market for College Education" (May 2000 Revision of National Bureau of Economic Research Working Paper No. 6323). See also Duffy and Goldberg, *Crafting a Class*, 8–75.

4. Invoking the work of Pierre Bourdieu, Patricia M. McDonough aptly analyzes class variation in knowledge about the selective college admissions process. Patricia M. McDonough, *Choosing Colleges: How Social Class and Schools Structure Opportunity* (Albany: State University of New York Press, 1997). Also, Patricia M.

McDonough, "Buying and Selling Higher Education: The Social Construction of the College Applicant," *Journal of Higher Education* 65 (July–August 1994): 427–446.

5. See Caroline Hodges Persell and Peter W. Cookson Jr., "Chartering and Bartering: Elite Education and Social Reproduction," *Social Problems* 33 (December 1985): 114–129; also McDonough, *Choosing Colleges.*

6. On the competitive dynamics of the college race at top high schools, see Paul Attewell, "The Winner-Take-All High School: Organizational Adaptations to Educational Stratification," *Sociology of Education* 74 (October 2001): 267–295; also Thomas J. Espenshade, Lauren E. Hale, and Chang Y. Chung, "The Frog Pond Revisited: High School Academic Context, Class Rank, and Elite College Admission," *Sociology of Education* 78 (2005): 269–293.

7. The theoretical scaffolding of my analysis here is rational choice theory. For a useful primer, see Robyn M. Dawes, *Rational Choice in an Uncertain World* (San Diego: Harcourt Brace Jovanovich, 1988).

8. See Carol A. Heimer, "Allocating Information Costs in a Negotiated Information Order: Inter-organizational Constraints on Decision Making in Norwegian Oil Insurance," *Administrative Science Quarterly* 30 (1985): 395–417. My novel contributions to this largely imported line of theorizing are the importance of variation in status across organizations doing the negotiating; and the importance of face-to-face interactions in creating inter-organizational cooperation.

9. The inter-organizational coordination between high schools and selective colleges that facilitates successful student transitions directly parallels the kind of coordination between high schools and workplaces that James Rosenbaum argues are crucial for successful moves from school to work. See James Rosenbaum, *Beyond College for All: Career Paths for the Forgotten Half* (New York: Russell Sage Foundation / American Sociological Association, 2001). The need

for such structural bridges is likely universal for all organizations that seek to share personnel.

10. This information problem is a generic one for both individuals and organizations facing decisions. On the sourcing and processing of information in complex organizations, see Arthur L. Stinchcombe, *Information and Organizations* (Berkeley: University of California Press, 1990). For comparisons between formal organizations and families in the sourcing and processing of information, see Carol A. Heimer and Lisa R. Staffen, *For the Sake of the Children: The Social Organization of Responsibility in the Hospital and the Home* (Chicago: University of Chicago Press, 1998); also Carol A. Heimer, "Cases and Biographies: An Essay on Routinization and the Nature of Comparison," *Annual Review of Sociology* 27 (2001): 47–76. For an analysis of how network relations reduce uncertainty in consequential exchanges, see Paul DiMaggio and Hugh Louch, "Socially Embedded Consumer Transactions: For What Kinds of Purchases Do People Most Often Use Networks?" *American Sociological Review* 63 (1998): 619–637.

11. I detail the place of interviews in evaluation in Chapter 6.

4. Sports

1. See, for example, William G. Bowen and Sarah A. Levin, *Reclaiming the Game: College Sports and Educational Values* (Princeton: Princeton University Press, 2003); James L. Shulman and William G. Bowen, *The Game of Life: College Sports and Educational Values* (Princeton: Princeton University Press, 2001); Murray A. Sperber, *Beer and Circus: How Big-Time College Sports Is Crippling Undergraduate Education* (New York: Henry Holt, 2000); and Andrew Zimbalist, *Unpaid Professionals: Commercialism and Conflict in Big-Time College Sports* (Princeton: Princeton University Press, 1999). For a sensitive portrayal of the lives of varsity athletes, see Patricia A. Adler and Peter Adler, *Backboards and*

Blackboards: College Athletics and Role Engulfment (New York: Columbia University Press, 1991).

2. See Bowen and Levin, *Reclaiming the Game;* and Shulman and Bowen, *The Game of Life.*

3. Vivyan C. Adair, "Branded with Infamy: Inscriptions of Poverty and Class in the United States," *Signs* 27 (Winter 2002): 451–471.

4. The history reported in this section is derived from a range of sources: Benjamin G. Rader, *American Sports: From the Age of Folk Games to the Age of Televised Sports* (Upper Saddle River, N.J.: Prentice Hall, 2003 [1983]); John R. Thelin, *A History of American Higher Education* (Baltimore: Johns Hopkins University Press, 2004); Bowen and Levin, *Reclaiming the Game;* Mark F. Bernstein, *Football: The Ivy League Origins of an American Obsession* (Philadelphia: University of Pennsylvania Press, 2001); Roger L. Geiger, ed., *The American College in the Nineteenth Century* (Nashville, Tenn.: Vanderbilt University Press, 2000); John Sayle Watterson, *College Football: History, Spectacle, Controversy* (Baltimore: Johns Hopkins University Press, 2000); Christopher J. Lucas, *American Higher Education: A History* (New York: St. Martin's Press, 1994); Frederick Rudolph, *The American College and University: A History* (Athens: University of Georgia Press, 1990 [1962]); Ronald A. Smith, *Sports and Freedom: The Rise of Big-Time College Athletics* (New York: Oxford University Press, 1988); Laurence R. Veysey, *The Emergence of the American University* (Chicago: University of Chicago Press, 1965); David Riesman and Reuel Denney, "Football in America: A Study in Culture Diffusion," *American Quarterly* 3 (Winter 1951): 309–325.

5. Rudolph, *The American College and University,* 375.

6. Ibid., 376.

7. See Harold S. Wechsler, *The Qualified Student: A History of Selective College Admission in America* (New York: John Wiley, 1977); Nicholas Lemann, *The Big Test: The Secret History of the American*

Meritocracy (New York: Farrar, Straus and Giroux 1999); Peter Dobkin Hall, *The Organization of American Culture, 1700–1900: Private Institutions, Elites, and the Origins of American Nationality* (New York: New York University Press, 1984); Michael S. Schudson, "Organizing the 'Meritocracy': A History of the College Entrance Examination Board," *Harvard Educational Review* 42 (1972): 34–69. The development of college-preparatory boarding schools for elite children occurred simultaneously with the rise of elite higher education. See James McLachlan, *American Boarding Schools: A Historical Study* (New York: Scribner, 1970); Steven B. Levine, "The Rise of American Boarding Schools and the Development of a National Upper Class," *Social Problems* 28 (1980): 63–94.

8. See Smith, *Sports and Freedom*, 83–98. For a broad account of cultural anxieties surrounding masculinity at this point in U.S. history, see Gail Bederman, *Manliness and Civilization: A Cultural History of Gender and Race in the United States, 1880–1917* (Chicago: University of Chicago Press, 1995); E. Anthony Rotundo, *American Manhood: Transformations in Masculinity from the Revolution to the Modern Era* (New York: Basic Books, 1993); Michael S. Kimmel, *Manhood in America: A Cultural History* (New York: Free Press, 1996); also Jeffrey P. Hantover, "The Boy Scouts and the Validation of Masculinity," *Journal of Social Issues* 34 (1978): 184–195. Thanks to Onno Oerlemans for scholarly assistance on this point in general and on the Adirondacks example in particular.

9. My understanding of early women's sports is derived largely from Susan K. Cahn, *Coming on Strong: Gender and Sexuality in Twentieth-Century Women's Sport* (New York: Free Press, 1994), and Rader, *American Sports,* 218–237, 330–343.

10. On the impact of Title IX on intercollegiate sports, see Welch Suggs, *A Place on the Team: The Triumph and Tragedy of Title IX* (Princeton: Princeton University Press, 2005).

11. See Shulman and Bowen, *The Game of Life;* Bowen and Levin, *Reclaiming the Game;* Zimbalist, *Unpaid Professionals;* Sperber, *Beer and Circus.*

12. My argument here builds on an early insight of Frederick Rudolph: that incentives to regulate football matches in the late nineteenth century created novel means whereby school leaders could both think collectively and cooperate across organizational divides. "[Football] became so widely adopted that for the first time since the founding of Harvard College in 1636 colleges began to recognize the existence of intercollegiate relations. Institutions that had never found it advisable to consult on matters of curriculum now sought means of regulating their athletic relations." Rudolph, *The American College and University,* 374. See also Rader, *American Sports,* for a synthetic history of the formalization of intercollegiate athletics; Smith, *Sports and Freedom,* for a detailed study of the early origins of intercollegiate athletics in the United States and its selective inheritance from the British Oxbridge tradition; and Bernstein, *Football,* for an account of the especially prominent role of football in coalescing institutional peer groups. Although the general relationship between sports and institutional status has been pointed out by these historians, to my knowledge it has not been explicated sociologically in the way I provide here. This is especially remarkable because the linkage between athletic prowess and institutional reputation is no secret. See, for example, J. Douglas Toma, *Football U: Spectator Sports in the Life of the American University* (Ann Arbor: University of Michigan Press, 2003).

13. The classic statement on status as a distinctive form of power is Max Weber, "Class, Status, and Party," in H. H. Gerth and C. Wright Mills, eds., *From Max Weber: Essays in Sociology* (New York: Oxford University Press, 1946), 180–195.

14. These youthful status orders only occasionally have received the sustained sociological attention they deserve. The classic sociological treatise on the subject is James S. Coleman, *The Adolescent*

Society (Glencoe, Ill.: Free Press, 1961). A revealing recent treatment is Murray Milner Jr., *Freaks, Geeks, and Cool Kids: American Teenagers, Schools, and the Culture of Consumption* (New York: Routledge, 2004). For a review of the sociological scholarship on children's peer cultures generally, see William A. Corsaro, *The Sociology of Childhood* (Thousand Oaks, Calif.: Pine Forge Press, 2005).

15. On the role of higher education in the organization of French society, see Pierre Bourdieu, *The State Nobility: Elite Schools in the Field of Power* (Cambridge: Polity Press, 1996).

16. On the origins of the UAA, see Bowen and Levin, *Reclaiming the Game,* 32–35.

17. See Bowen and Levin, *Reclaiming the Game,* for several examples of this phenomenon.

18. On the phenomenological pleasures of boundary crossing generally, see Jack Katz, *Seductions of Crime: Moral and Sensual Attractions in Doing Evil* (New York: Basic Books, 1988). For a recent analysis of carnival rituals, see Barbara Ehrenreich, *Dancing in the Streets: A History of Collective Joy* (New York: Metropolitan Books, 2007).

19. Lucas, *American Higher Education,* 178.

20. This probably is why Americans imported from the British the general association of sports with university life, but not the British commitment to amateurism. In the United States, institutional excellence is marked not only by playing but also by winning. See Smith, *Sports and Freedom.*

21. Schools tend to have outputs that are difficult to measure, as classic studies in organizational sociology have pointed out. See John W. Meyer and Brian Rowan, "The Structure of Educational Organizations," 78–109 in Marshall W. Meyer, ed., *Environments and Organizations* (San Francisco: Jossey-Bass, 1978). However, pressures on institutions to measure their outputs for various clients appear to be upping the ante on accountability throughout the higher education sector. See, for example, Patricia

Gumport, "Universities and Knowledge: Restructuring the City of Intellect," in Steven Brint, ed., *The Future of the City of Intellect: The Changing American University* (Stanford: Stanford University Press, 2002), 47–81; also Roger King, "The University and the Regulatory State," in Roger King, ed., *The University in the Global Age* (New York: Palgrave/Macmillan 2004), 67–95.

22. My archival research indicates that this proportion of varsity-level participation held fairly constant over the twenty-five years prior to the period of this ethnography, 2000–2001.

23. The definitive study here is Shulman and Bowen's *The Game of Life*.

24. This local wisdom is corroborated by careful quantitative analyses of the academic credentials of recruited athletes at highly selective colleges and universities. See Shulman and Bowen, *The Game of Life*.

25. See Daniel F. Chambliss, "The Mundanity of Excellence: An Ethnographic Report on Stratification and Olympic Swimmers," *Sociological Theory* 7 (Spring 1989): 70–86; and Chambliss, *Champions: The Making of Olympic Swimmers* (New York: Morrow, 1988). On the incremental development of youthful talent generally, see the collected essays in Benjamin S. Bloom, ed., *Developing Talent in Young People* (New York: Ballantine Books, 1985).

26. Annette Lareau, *Unequal Childhoods: Class, Race, and Family Life* (Berkeley: University of California Press, 2003).

27. On schools, see Annette Lareau, *Home Advantage: Social Class and Parental Intervention in Elementary Education* (Lanham, Md.: Rowman and Littlefield, 2000 [1989]). On hospitals, see Carol A. Heimer and Mitchell L. Stevens, "Caring for the Organization: Social Workers as Frontline Risk Managers in Neonatal Intensive Care Units," *Work & Occupations* 24 (1997): 133–163.

28. One example that has received media attention recently is affluent families' growing taste for lacrosse. Parents like the game because it provides rigorous exercise and is less physically dangerous than football. Parents also like lacrosse because it is supported at the

varsity level by highly selective colleges even while the national talent pool for the sport is much smaller than in soccer, football, and basketball; consequently, excellence in lacrosse is relatively more likely to be rewarded by admissions officers. See Abigail Sullivan Moore, "The LAX Track," *New York Times Education Life,* 6 November 2005, 26.

29. For illustrative recent scholarship on the phenomenon demographers call "educational homogamy," see Christine Schwartz and Robert D. Mare, "Trends in Educational Assortative Marriage from 1940–2003," *Demography* 42 (2005): 621–646; also Matthijs Kalmijn, "Intermarriage and Homogamy: Causes, Patterns, Trends," *Annual Review of Sociology* 24 (1998): 395–421. I return to the topic of educational homogamy in Chapter 8.

30. Physically attractive men and women have significantly higher earnings than the less attractive throughout the labor market. See Daniel S. Hamermesh and Jeff E. Biddle, "Beauty and the Labor Market," *American Economic Review* 84 (December 1994): 1174–94.

5. Race

1. On the proportional representation of students from different racial groups at selective schools, see Douglas S. Massey, Camille Z. Charles, Garvey F. Lundy, and Mary J. Fischer, *The Source of the River: The Social Origins of Freshmen at America's Selective Colleges and Universities* (Princeton: Princeton University Press, 2003). On the racial composition of student cohorts at all baccalaureate institutions since the civil rights era, see Alexander W. Astin, Leticia Oseguera, Linda J. Sax, and William S. Korn, *The American Freshman: Thirty-Five Year Trends* (Los Angeles: Higher Education Research Institute, UCLA, 2002).

2. National Association for College Admission Counseling, *Statement of Principles of Good Practice* (Alexandria, Va.: National Association for College Admission Counseling, 2005).

3. On national representation as a marker of institutional quality, see Harold S. Wechsler, *The Qualified Student: A History of Selective College Admission in America* (New York: John Wiley, 1977); also Peter Dobkin Hall, *The Organization of American Culture, 1700–1900: Private Institutions, Elites, and the Origins of American Nationality* (New York: New York University Press, 1984).

4. See, for example, James McLachlan, *American Boarding Schools: A Historical Study* (New York: Scribner's, 1970).

5. This color line is an important component of the history of higher education in the United States. See, for example, Henry N. Drewry and Humphrey Doermann, *Stand and Prosper: Private Black Colleges and Their Students* (Princeton: Princeton University Press, 2001); Christopher J. Lucas, *American Higher Education: A History* (New York: St. Martin's Press, 1994); Frederick Rudolph, *The American College and University: A History* (Athens: University of Georgia Press, 1990 [1962]).

6. Emphasis in original. This and all historical documents specific to the College presented in this book are drawn from the College's archives.

7. John D. Skrentny, *The Minority Rights Revolution* (Cambridge, Mass.: Harvard University Press / Belknap, 2002). The analysis in this chapter also is broadly informed by John Skrentny, *Ironies of Affirmative Action: Politics, Culture, and Justice in America* (Chicago: University of Chicago Press, 1996).

8. See Jerome Karabel, *The Chosen: The Hidden History of Admission and Exclusion at Harvard, Yale, and Princeton* (New York: Houghton Mifflin, 2005); Skrentny, *The Minority Rights Revolution*, 165–178; Wechsler, *The Qualified Student*, 259–292; Elizabeth A. Duffy and Idana Goldberg, *Crafting a Class: College Admissions and Financial Aid, 1955–1994* (Princeton: Princeton University Press, 1988), 137–165.

9. As Skrentny makes clear in *The Minority Rights Revolution,* the civil rights and feminist movements mutually informed how insti-

tutional elites thought about, and practically pursued, organizational integration during the 1960s and 1970s.

10. This paragraph relies on key insights of the new institutionalist school of organizational sociology. For an overview, see W. Richard Scott, *Institutions and Organizations* (Thousand Oaks, Calif.: Sage, 2001). On patterned variation in organizational responses to political and cultural change, see Nella Van Dyke, "Hotbeds of Activism: Locations of Student Protest," *Social Problems* 45 (1998): 205–220; also Pamela S. Tolbert and Lynne G. Zucker, "Institutional Sources of Change in the Formal Structure of Organizations: The Diffusion of Civil Service Reform, 1880–1935," *Administrative Science Quarterly* 28 (1983): 22–39.

11. On the collective nature of higher education leaders' responses to the civil rights movement, see Duffy and Goldberg, *Crafting a Class,* 137–165.

12. Skrentny, *The Minority Rights Revolution,* 172.

13. Brief for Columbia University, Harvard University, Stanford University, and the University of Pennsylvania as Amici Curiae at 3, *Regents of the University of California v. Bakke,* 438 U.S. 265 (1978) (No. 76–811).

14. Ibid., at 4.

15. Ibid., at 14. Comparable arguments appear in other amici briefs submitted on behalf of academic organizations. For a review, see the United States Commission on Civil Rights, *Toward Equal Educational Opportunity: Affirmative Admissions Programs at Law and Medical Schools,* USCCR Clearinghouse Publication 55 (Washington, D.C.: U.S. Commission on Civil Rights, June 1978).

16. Eric Grodsky makes a parallel argument in "Compensatory Sponsorship in Higher Education," *American Journal of Sociology* (forthcoming).

17. *Regents of the University of California v. Bakke,* 438 U.S. 265, 2759–2760 (1978). The first quotation in this excerpt is from *Sweezy v. New Hampshire,* 354 U.S. 234, 263 (1957). The second

quotation is from *Keyishan v. Board of Regents,* 385 U.S. 589, 603 (1967).

18. The history of this process is well documented and analyzed in Skrentny, *The Minority Rights Revolution,* 85–142.

19. My observation at the College is corroborated by student reports from other predominantly white college campuses. See Sarah Susannah Willie, *Acting Black: College, Identity, and the Performance of Race* (New York: Routledge, 2003); Joe R. Feagin, Hernan Vera, and Nikitah Imani, *The Agony of Education: Black Students at White Colleges and Universities* (New York: Routledge, 1996); Walter R. Allen, Edgar G. Epps, and Nesha Z. Haniff, eds., *College in Black and White: African American Students in Predominantly White and Historically Black Universities* (Albany: SUNY Press, 1991); Jacqueline Fleming, *Blacks in College: A Comparative Study of Students' Success in Black and White Institutions* (San Francisco: Jossey-Bass, 1984). The excellent autobiographical accounts of being a minority student on an elite, predominantly white campus include Lorene Cary, *Black Ice* (New York: Vintage, 1991).

20. For ethnographic portraits of how this marking process plays out on an elite college campus, see Bonnie Urciuoli, "Team Diversity: An Ethnography of Institutional Values," in Anne Menely and Donna J. Young, *Auto-Ethnographies: An Anthropology of Academic Practices* (Peterborough, Ontario: Broadview Press, 2005), 159–172; and Urciuoli, "Excellence, Leadership, Skills, Diversity: Marketing Liberal Arts Education," *Language and Communication* 23 (2003): 385–408.

21. The scholarly literature on this issue is voluminous, but see, for example, Lani Guinier, "Admissions Rituals as Political Acts: Guardians at the Gates of Our Democratic Ideals," *Harvard Law Review* 117 (November 2003): 114–224; Martha C. Nussbaum, *Cultivating Humanity: A Classical Defense of Reform in Liberal Education* (Cambridge, Mass.: Harvard University Press, 1997).

22. For individuals, the classic theoretical statement is Erving Goffman, *The Presentation of Self in Everyday Life* (Garden City, N.Y.:

Doubleday, 1959). Scholars of the new institutionalism in organizational sociology have deftly applied this Goffmanian insight to formal organizations. For a review, see Walter W. Powell and Paul J. DiMaggio, eds., *The New Institutionalism in Organizational Analysis* (Chicago: University of Chicago Press, 1991).

23. Clearly selective schools like the College are not immune to spin, but standards of what counts as truth in public communication may vary by sector. This might be a productive area for future research. For revealing accounts of public relations in American politics and corporate workplaces, see Stuart Ewen, *PR! A Social History of Spin* (New York: Basic Books, 1996); and Robert Jackall, *Moral Mazes: The World of Corporate Managers* (New York: Oxford University Press, 1988), 162–190.

24. My metaphor here embodies the same causal logic as sociology's status-attainment model of social mobility, in which variation in the background characteristics of individuals is shown to be statistically associated, often quite powerfully, with life outcomes. See my discussion in Chapter 1. This certainly is not the only way to imagine the relationship between education and social stratification, as I hope the whole of this book makes clear. For a sustained critique of the status-attainment model of inequality, see Charles Tilly, *Durable Inequality* (Berkeley: University of California Press, 1998).

25. This brief picture summarizes decades of sociological research on educational inequality. Empirical support for the picture I am drawing here includes Adam Gamoran, "American Schooling and Educational Opportunity: A Forecast for the 21st Century," in "Current of Thought: Sociology of Education at the Dawn of the 21st Century," special issue, *Sociology of Education* 74 (2001): 135–153; Michael Hout, Adrian E. Raftery, and Eleanor O. Bell, "Making the Grade: Educational Stratification in the United States, 1925–1989," in Yossi Shavit and Hans-Peter Blossfeld, eds., *Persistent Inequality: Changing Educational Attainment in Thirteen Countries* (Boulder, Colo.: Westview Press, 1993), 25–49. For an

ethnographic picture of class variation in family life, see Annette Lareau, *Unequal Childhoods: Class, Race, and Family Life* (Berkeley: University of California Press, 2003). On the role of educational tracking in exacerbating racial inequality, see Samuel R. Lucas and Mark Berends, "Sociodemographic Diversity, Correlated Achievement, and De Facto Tracking," *Sociology of Education* 75 (2002): 328–348; also Samuel R. Lucas, "Effectively Maintained Inequality: Education Transitions, Track Mobility, and Social Background Effects," *American Journal of Sociology* 106 (2001): 1642–90. On the relationship between race, class, and parental investments in education, see Camille Z. Charles, Vincent J. Roscigno, and Kimberly C. Torres, "Racial Inequality and College Attendance: The Mediating Role of Parental Investments," *Social Science Research* 36 (2007): 329–352. That most students at selective colleges and universities are from the upper-middle and upper classes is well documented in Massey et al., *Source of the River.*

26. This is true despite the fact that black and Latino post-secondary enrollments have climbed over the past forty years generally. See Massey et al., *Source of the River,* 1–19; also William G. Bowen and Derek Bok, *The Shape of the River: Long-Term Consequences of Considering Race in College and University Admissions* (Princeton: Princeton University Press, 1998), 1–52.

27. For a sobering analysis of the relationship between race, real property ownership, and socioeconomic inequality, see Dalton Conley, *Being Black, Living in the Red: Race, Wealth, and Social Policy in America* (Berkeley: University of California Press, 1999). On the relationship between racial residential segregation and socioeconomic inequality, see Douglas S. Massey and Nancy A. Denton, *American Apartheid: Segregation and the Making of the Underclass* (Cambridge, Mass.: Harvard University Press, 1993). Links between residential segregation and students' academic and social worlds are amply documented in Massey et al., *Source of the River.* For an ethnographic portrait, see Mary Patillo-McCoy, *Black Picket*

Fences: Privilege and Peril among the Black Middle Class (Chicago: University of Chicago Press, 1999). On the dynamics of early motherhood among poor women, see Kathryn Edin and Maria Kefalas, *Promises I Can Keep: Why Poor Women Put Motherhood before Marriage* (Berkeley: University of California Press, 2005).

28. One recent study found that more than 26 percent of black men and more than 12 percent of Latino men in the United States had spent time in prison by age forty. The comparable figure for white men was 3.5 percent. Bruce Western, "The Impact of Incarceration on Wage Mobility and Inequality," *American Sociological Review* 67 (August 2002): 526–546.

29. As reported in Massey et al., *Source of the River*, 15–19.

30. Just why scores on standardized tests vary so significantly by race is one of the most pressing puzzles in education research. For a review, see Christopher Jencks and Meredith Phillips, eds., *The Black-White Test Score Gap* (Washington, D.C.: Brookings Institution Press, 1998).

31. Scholarship on the effectiveness of these programs at getting students into four-year colleges is very limited, but see Christopher Avery and Thomas J. Kane, "Student Perceptions of College Opportunities: The Boston COACH Program," in Caroline M. Hoxby, ed., *College Choices: The Economics of Where to Go, When to Go, and How to Pay for It* (Chicago: University of Chicago Press, 2004), 355–394.

32. Doug Massey and his colleagues document the greatly disproportionate numbers of black and Latino students at selective schools who are female. See Massey et al., *Source of the River*.

33. For a related analysis, see Mitchell J. Chang, "Preservation or Transformation: Where's the Real Educational Discourse on Diversity?" *Review of Higher Education* 25 (2): 125–140.

34. For extensive documentation of these points, see Bok and Bowen, *The Shape of the River*.

35. Mario L. Small and Christopher Winship, "Black Students' Grad-

uation from Elite Colleges: Institutional Characteristics and Be-
tween-Institution Differences," *Social Science Research,* forthcoming.

36. See Willie, *Acting Black;* Feagin, Vera, and Imani, *The Agony of
Education;* Allen, Epps, and Haniff, *College in Black and White;*
Fleming, *Blacks in College.*

37. See Skrentny, *The Minority Rights Revolution.*

6. Decisions

1. *Grutter v. Bollinger,* 539 U.S. 306, 334 (2003). The case regarding
Michigan's undergraduate college is *Gratz v. Bollinger,* 539 U.S.
244 (2003).

2. In November 2006, Michigan voters passed a referendum ban-
ning affirmative action in public education, public employment,
and state contracts, effectively ending the University of Michigan's
ability to explicitly consider race as a factor in admissions decisions.

3. My analysis in this section relies heavily on the work of Carol A.
Heimer and Lisa R. Staffen, "Interdependence and Reintegrative
Social Control: Labeling and Reforming 'Inappropriate' Parents in
Neonatal Intensive Care Units," *American Sociological Review* 60
(1995): 635–654; also Carol A. Heimer, "Cases and Biographies:
An Essay on Routinization and the Nature of Comparison," *An-
nual Review of Sociology* 27 (2001): 47–76.

4. Edwin Hutchins, *Cognition in the Wild* (Cambridge, Mass: MIT
Press, 1995). Arthur L. Stinchcombe's *Information and Organizations* (Berkeley: University of California Press, 1990) also informs
my analysis here. A catalytic conversation with Michèle Lamont
on 18 April 2005 is gratefully acknowledged.

5. For examples of this distancing phenomenon in hospitals, see
Carol A. Heimer and Lisa R. Staffen, *For the Sake of the Children:
The Social Organization of Responsibility in the Hospital and the
Home* (Chicago: University of Chicago Press, 1998); also Daniel F.

Chambliss, *Beyond Caring: Hospitals, Nurses, and the Social Organization of Ethics* (Chicago: University of Chicago Press, 1996).

6. Journalistic and "insider" accounts of selective admissions elsewhere suggest that the organization of decision making at the College is broadly representative of practices elsewhere. See, for example, Jacques Steinberg, *The Gatekeepers: Inside the Admissions Process of a Premier College* (New York: Viking, 2002); and Rachel Toor, *Admissions Confidential: An Insider's Account of the Elite College Selection Process* (New York: St. Martin's Press, 2001).

7. The official irrelevance of physical appearance to evaluation protocols at selective schools is relatively new. Appearance was explicitly considered at elite schools throughout the first half of the twentieth century, especially when applicants had Jewish surnames. See Harold S. Wechsler, *The Qualified Student: A History of Selective College Admission in America* (New York: John Wiley, 1977); Marcia Graham Synnott, *The Half-Opened Door: Discrimination and Admissions at Harvard, Yale, and Princeton, 1900–1970* (Westport, Conn.: Greenwood Press, 1979); also Jerome Karabel, *The Chosen: The Hidden History of Admission and Exclusion at Harvard, Yale, and Princeton* (New York: Houghton Mifflin, 2005). As recently as the 1950s, the College's application form included a blank space on which applicants were asked to attach personal photographs.

8. On the use of Apgar scores, see Carol A. Heimer and Mitchell L. Stevens, "Caring for the Organization: Social Workers as Frontline Risk Managers in Neonatal Intensive Care Units," *Work and Occupations* 24 (1997): 133–163.

9. Joshua Guetzkow, Michèle Lamont, and Grégoire Mallard, "What Is Originality in the Humanities and the Social Sciences?" *American Sociological Review* 69 (2004): 190–212.

10. My thinking on this matter has recently been informed by Charles Tilly's essay, *Why?* (Princeton: Princeton University Press, 2006). I found that Tilly's four categories of reasons—conventions, stories, codes, and technical accounts—all were represented at differ-

ent points and in different syncretic combinations, throughout the College's evaluation process. Finding out if there is parallel syncretism in other settings might give new texture to our understanding of just how complex evaluation in formal organizations can be.

11. See, for example, Caroline Hodges Persell and Peter W. Cookson Jr., "Chartering and Bartering: Elite Education and Social Reproduction," *Social Problems* 33 (1985): 114–129; also Patricia M. McDonough, *Choosing Colleges: How Social Class and Schools Structure Opportunity* (Albany: SUNY Press, 1997).

12. Contrary to popular wisdom, it turns out that interviews are poor predictors of future performance. See, for example, Richard A. DeVaul, Faith Jervey, James A. Chappell, Patricia Caver, Barbara Short, and Stephen O'Keefe, "Medical School Performance of Initially Rejected Students," *Journal of the American Medical Association* 257 (2 January 1987): 47–51; also Robyn M. Dawes, *Everyday Irrationality: How Pseudoscientists, Lunatics, and the Rest of Us Systematically Fail to Think Rationally* (Boulder, Colo.: Westview Press, 2001). Nevertheless my fieldwork shows that, regardless of their predictive utility, interviews can be very important for making *legitimate* decisions.

13. This finding is strongly corroborated by quantitative studies of athletics preferences in admissions practices at elite schools. See William G. Bowen and Sarah A. Levin, *Reclaiming the Game: College Sports and Educational Values* (Princeton: Princeton University Press, 2003); also James L. Shulman and William G. Bowen, *The Game of Life: College Sports and Educational Values* (Princeton: Princeton University Press, 2001).

14. *Grutter v. Bollinger*, 539 U.S. 306, 337 (2003).

7. Yield

1. See, for example, the collected papers in the volume edited by Caroline M. Hoxby, *College Choices: The Economics of Where to*

Go, When to Go, and How to Pay for It (Chicago: University of Chicago Press, 2004); Christopher Avery, Andrew Fairbanks, and Richard Zeckhauser, *The Early Admissions Game: Joining the Elite* (Cambridge, Mass.: Harvard University Press, 2003). Influential financial aid policy analyses by economists include Thomas J. Kane, *The Price of Admission: Rethinking How Americans Pay for College* (Washington, D.C.: Brookings Institution Press, 1999); and Michael S. McPherson and Morton Owen Schapiro, *The Student Aid Game: Meeting Need and Rewarding Talent in American Higher Education* (Princeton, N.J.: Princeton University Press, 1997).

2. Arlie Russell Hochschild, *The Managed Heart: Commercialization of Human Feeling* (Berkeley: University of California Press, 1983).

3. My review included twelve viewbooks: ten housed in the College's archive (from 1917, 1923, 1937, 1964, 1973, 1978, 1981, 1987, 1994, 1996); one that was in use during the period of my field research; and one that was published subsequent to my leaving the field. These are the only College viewbooks I know of, but these twelve might not represent an exhaustive archive.

4. See Caroline M. Hoxby, "The Effects of Geographic Integration and Increasing Competition in the Market for College Education" (May 2000 Revision of National Bureau of Economic Research Working Paper No. 6323); also Elizabeth Duffy and Idana Goldberg, *Crafting a Class: College Admissions and Financial Aid, 1955–1994* (Princeton: Princeton University Press, 1998). See also my discussion of this period in Chapter 3.

5. McPherson and Schapiro, *The Student Aid Game*. See also Ronald G. Ehrenberg, *Tuition Rising: Why College Costs So Much* (Cambridge, Mass.: Harvard University Press, 2000); Charles T. Clotfelter, *Buying the Best: Cost Escalation in Elite Higher Education* (Princeton: Princeton University Press / National Bureau of Economic Research, 1996). For a history of financial aid in U.S. higher education, see Rupert Wilkinson, *Aiding Students, Buying*

Students: Financial Aid in America (Nashville, Tenn.: Vanderbilt University Press, 2005).

6. I can only suggest this point, since I did not directly investigate the student choice process; I only inferred it from the indirect evidence of my fieldwork.

8. The Aristocracy of Merit

1. Annette Lareau, *Unequal Childhoods: Class, Race, and Family Life* (Berkeley: University of California Press, 2003), 39.

2. Ibid., 63–64. However remarkably, social scientists have only begun to appreciate just how elaborate parental investment in youthful accomplishment can be. In addition to Lareau's work, see Patricia A. Adler and Peter Adler, "Social Reproduction and the Corporate Other: The Institutionalization of Afterschool Activities," *Sociological Quarterly* 35 (1994): 309–328; Claudia Buchmann, Vincent J. Roscigno, and Dennis Condron, "The Myth of Meritocracy? SAT Preparation, College Enrollment, Class and Race in the United States" (paper presented at the Annual Meeting of the American Sociological Association, Montreal, 14 August 2006). A thorough and revealing study of parental time use is Suzanne M. Bianchi, John P. Robinson, and Melissa A. Milke, *Changing Rhythms of American Family Life* (New York: Russell Sage Foundation, 2006).

3. Harold S. Wechsler, *The Qualified Student: A History of Selective College Admission in America* (New York: John Wiley, 1977), 237–238.

4. Jerome Karabel alludes to this phenomenon when he writes of "the dark side of meritocracy" in the final pages of *The Chosen: The Hidden History of Admission and Exclusion at Harvard, Yale, and Princeton* (New York: Houghton Mifflin, 2005).

5. Here, I think, is how the organizational boundary between high school and college is simultaneously a moral boundary. See Michèle

Lamont, *Money, Morals, and Manners: The Culture of the French and the American Upper-Middle Class* (Chicago: University of Chicago Press, 1992). On symbolic boundaries generally, see Michèle Lamont and Virág Molnár, "The Study of Boundaries in the Social Sciences," *Annual Review of Sociology* 28 (2002): 167–195.

6. See John W. Meyer and Evan Schofer, "The World-Wide Expansion of Higher Education in the Twentieth Century," *American Sociological Review* 70 (2005): 898–920; also Francisco O. Ramirez, "The Rationalization of Universities," 225–244 in Marie-Laure Djelic and Kerstin Shalin-Andersson, eds., *Transnational Governance: Institutional Dynamics of Regulation* (Cambridge: Cambridge University Press, 2006).

7. See, for example, Rebecca S. Lowen, *Creating the Cold War University: The Transformation of Stanford* (Berkeley: University of California Press, 1997).

8. My thinking here has been definitively informed by Lizabeth Cohen, *A Consumer's Republic: The Politics of Mass Consumption in Postwar America* (New York: Alfred A. Knopf, 2003).

9. Quoted in William G. Bowen, Martin A. Kurzweil, and Eugene M. Tobin, *Equity and Excellence in American Higher Education* (Charlottesville: University of Virginia Press, 2005), 35.

10. See James E. Rosenbaum, *Beyond College for All: Career Paths for the Forgotten Half* (New York: Russell Sage Foundation, 2001). On the rise of community colleges, see Kevin J. Dougherty, *The Contradictory College: The Conflicting Origins, Impacts, and Futures of the Community College* (Albany: SUNY Press, 2001); also Steven Brint and Jerome Karabel, *The Diverted Dream: Community Colleges and the Promise of Educational Opportunity in America, 1900–1985* (New York: Oxford University Press, 1989). On the post–World War II expansion of U.S. higher education generally, see John R. Thelin, *A History of American Higher Education* (Baltimore: Johns Hopkins University Press, 2004), 260–316; Christopher Jencks and David Riesman, *The Academic Revolution* (Gar-

den City, N.Y.: Doubleday, 1968); and Clark Kerr, *The Uses of the University* (Cambridge, Mass.: Harvard University Press, 2001 [1963]).

11. For the most part, social scientists have been reluctant to talk about education as a form of welfare, preferring instead to view schools and other welfare systems as separate state projects. One widely cited exception is Arnold J. Heidenheimer, "Education and Social Security Entitlements in Europe and America," 269–304 in Peter Flora and Arnold J. Heidenheimer, eds., *The Development of Welfare States in Europe and America* (New Brunswick, N.J.: Transaction, 2003 [1981]). Thanks to Chiqui Ramirez and Pam Walters for their encouragement of this line of thinking.

12. On Fordism generally, see Antonio Gramsci, "Americanism and Fordism," 277–318 in Quintin Hoare and Geoffrey Nowell Smith, eds., *Selections from the Prison Notebooks* (New York: International Publishers, 1971); Scott Lash and John Urry, *The End of Organized Capitalism* (Cambridge: Polity Press, 1987); Michael Piore and Charles Sabel, *The Second Industrial Divide* (New York: Basic Books, 1984). On the political and psychic consequences of the end of Fordism in the United States, see Jacob S. Hacker, *The Great Risk Shift* (New York: Oxford University Press, 2006); also Richard Sennett, *The Culture of the New Capitalism* (New Haven: Yale University Press, 2006).

13. The question of the extent to which college degrees represent real skills (what economists call "human capital") or primarily mark status has been hotly debated at least since Ivar Berg published *Education and Jobs: The Great Training Robbery* (New York: Praeger / Center for Urban Education, 1970).

14. On the consequences of postindustrial restructuring for middle-class families and U.S. culture generally, see Katherine S. Newman, *Declining Fortunes: The Withering of the American Dream* (New York: Basic Books, 1993); Katherine S. Newman, *Falling from Grace: Downward Mobility in the Age of Affluence* (Berkeley: University of California Press, 1988); Barbara Ehrenreich, *Fear of*

Falling: The Inner Life of the Middle Class (New York: Pantheon, 1989); Hacker, *The Great Risk Shift;* and Sennett, *Culture of the New Capitalism.*

15. For a thoughtful portrait, see P. F. Kluge, *Alma Mater: A College Homecoming* (Reading, Mass.: Addison-Wesley, 1993).

16. William J. Goode, "The Protection of the Inept," *American Sociological Review* 32 (1967): 5–19.

17. Classic sociological statements on this point include C. Wright Mills, *The Power Elite* (New York: Oxford University Press, 1956); and G. William Domhoff, *Who Rules America?* (Englewood Cliffs, N.J.: Prentice-Hall, 1967).

18. This argument echoes Francie Ostrower's analysis of the pivotal role of philanthropy in the constitution of the U.S. upper class. See Francie Ostrower, *Why the Wealthy Give: The Culture of Elite Philanthropy* (Princeton: Princeton University Press, 1995).

19. Erving Goffman, *Asylums: Essays on the Social Situation of Mental Patients and Other Inmates* (Garden City, N.Y.: Anchor Press / Doubleday, 1961).

20. See David B. Potts, *Wesleyan University, 1831–1910: Collegiate Enterprise in New England* (New Haven, Conn.: Yale University Press, 1992); also James McLachlan, *American Boarding Schools: A Historical Study* (New York: Scribner, 1970).

21. Richard Arum, Josipa Roksa, and Michelle J. Budig, "The Romance of College Attendance: Higher Education Stratification and Mate Selection" (unpublished manuscript, New York University, 2007). On educational homogamy generally, see Christine Schwartz and Robert D. Mare, "Trends in Educational Assortative Marriage from 1940–2003," *Demography* 42 (2005): 621–646; also Matthijs Kalmijn, "Intermarriage and Homogamy: Causes, Patterns, Trends," *Annual Review of Sociology* 24 (1998): 395–421. A classic analysis of the romantic selection process is Willard Waller, "The Rating and Dating Complex," *American Sociological Review* 2 (1937): 727–734.

22. See Thomas DiPrete and Claudia Buchmann, "Gender-Specific

Trends in the Value of Education and the Emerging Gender Gap in College Completion," *Demography* 43 (2006): 1–24; also Claudia Buchmann and Thomas DiPrete, "The Growing Female Advantage in College Completion: The Role of Family Background and Academic Achievement," *American Sociological Review* 71 (2006): 515–541. See also Jerry A. Jacobs, "Gender Inequality in Higher Education," *Annual Review of Sociology* 22 (1996): 153–185. Ideally this book's suggestions about the relationships between sports, bodies, sex, and marriage in elite higher education will be read as worthy extensions of Paul DiMaggio and John Mohr's now-classic work on cultural capital and marital selection. See DiMaggio and Mohr, "Cultural Capital, Educational Attainment, and Marital Selection," *American Journal of Sociology* 90 (1985): 1231–61.

23. There is a vast advocacy literature on back-to-basics reforms. See, for example, Abigail Thernstrom and Stephen Thernstrom, *No Excuses: Closing the Racial Gap in Learning* (New York: Simon and Schuster, 2003); Samuel Casey Carter, *No Excuses: Lessons from 21 High-Performing, High-Poverty Schools* (Washington, D.C.: Heritage Foundation, 2000); E. D. Hirsch Jr., *The Schools We Need: And Why We Don't Have Them* (New York: Anchor Books, 1999); Martin L. Gross, *The Conspiracy of Ignorance: The Failure of American Public Schools* (New York: HarperCollins, 2000); Charles J. Sykes, *Dumbing Down Our Kids: Why American Children Feel Good about Themselves but Can't Read, Write, or Add* (New York: St. Martin's Griffin, 1996).

24. Richard Arum, *Judging School Discipline: The Crisis of Moral Authority* (Cambridge, Mass.: Harvard University Press, 2003), 198–199.

ACKNOWLEDGMENTS

My first and greatest debt is to the people with whom I worked in the College's Office of Admissions and Financial Aid in 2000–01. Thinking about the trust they extended still moves me. It is not an overstatement to say that the year and a half I spent in that office changed my life. I hope this book gives back to those people a little bit of what they gave to me: an honest perspective on their daily work and a fresh appreciation of its place in the broader contours of contemporary American life.

Many others throughout the College—in the President's and Development offices, in the Athletics, Human Resources, and Student Life divisions, in the library, and on the faculty—lent assistance in interviews and countless informal conversations. Beyond the College, admissions officers and guidance counselors and private consultants from all over the country were kind enough to talk with me about their work. I would have a small story to tell were it not for them.

I would not have had the time to talk with all of these people without the support of the National Academy of Education / Spencer Foundation Postdoctoral Fellowship program. The year of professional leave funded by the fellowship literally made the whole project possible. It also connected me to an ecumenical group of scholars and educators who nurtured my entry into what was, in 2000, a new field of study for me. I owe particular thanks to Sarah Barnes, Kerith Gardner, Elizabeth Watkins, and Jon Zimmerman in this regard.

My interest in college admissions began in a still-flowing stream of conversation with my former teacher and now colleague, Wendy Espeland, about the role of quantification in educational decision making. Years ago, Wendy infected me with her interest in the sociological consequences of numbers. Her encouragement and intellectual largesse have been invaluable ever since.

Other mentors cast long shadows through these pages. Howard Becker, Nicki Beisel, Elisabeth Clemens, Carol Heimer, Art Stinchcombe, and Pamela Walters have deeply influenced my thinking about families, schools, and the organizational circuitry connecting them. Michèle Lamont has been a ghost in my head for some time now, assuring me that a little ethnography might have something large to say while challenging its author to ever clearer specification of the relationships between colleges, culture, and the mechanics of evaluation.

It has been my great good fortune to write this book at New York University's Steinhardt School, as I can imagine no better setting in which to think through the past and present of American higher education than at this decidedly forward-looking institution. There are few academic traditions that NYU has failed to buck, rewrite, or simply ignore, and the inevitable inconveniences that come with such swagger have been a small price to pay for the sheer thrill of being part of the place. Educators everywhere, hear this: the future belongs to NYU. Steinhardt's Department of Humanities and Social Sciences in the Professions was my professional and often personal haven during the years in which this book was written. I wish every scholar could have a department as humane and intelligent as mine.

A few parties across the University have been especially generous to this project. A good measure of social-science talent was assembled regularly at the NYU Education Workshop, whose participants were subjected to more iterations of my arguments than even I can count. The lessons conveyed in that forum have made me a much shrewder analyst. Floyd Hammack's steady stream of clippings and advice meant a lot to me. Dalton Conley, Kathleen Gerson, Ruth Horowitz, Eric Klinenberg, Harvey Molotch, Ann Morning, and Larry Wu took this project seriously from the moment I arrived at NYU and have paid it that compliment ever since. Caroline Persell was an early and constant source of encouragement. Amy Schwartz and Leanna Stiefel assured me that I was capable of figuring out educational economics, and helped me do it, too. During a particularly difficult couple of years, Richard Arum and Jon Zimmerman demonstrated more faith in me than I thought was deserved. It would be hard to thank them enough for that. Ann Marcus provided lively and intelligent counterpoint to my musings about higher education's big picture, and showed by example that one person really can make a difference. As Director of the Steinhardt Institute for Higher Education Policy, Ann supported a conference on the sociology of higher education in the spring of 2006, an event that proved to be a watershed in my thinking about colleges and class at this point in U.S. history. The sheer magnitude of talent and generosity at that conference gave me the courage to finish this book. Lucy Frazier, Tamika Bota, and Kamilah Briscoe expertly solved the myriad administrative puzzles I confronted in the course of getting it done.

Elizabeth Armstrong, Joshua Aronson, Richard Arum, Amy Binder, Kamilah Briscoe, Lani Guinier, Arik Lifschitz, Cynthia Miller-Idriss, Doug Massey, Ann Morning, Jim Rosenbaum, John Skrentny, Art Stinchcombe, and Diana Turk read particular portions of the book and helped me hone points of fact, logic, and theory. Annette Lareau did much to inspire the connection I make between college admissions and family life. I am grateful to her for the many conversations we shared during her sabbatical year at NYU's Center for Advanced Social Science Research. Mike Sauder, Dan Shaw, Harold Wechsler, and Anna Zimdars all read the entire manuscript and provided detailed, often line-by-line, notes—huge acts of friendship and collegiality.

Neil Gross, Jason Owen-Smith, Josipa Roksa, Evan Schofer, John Skrentny, Bonnie Urciuoli, and Marc Ventresca were kindred spirits throughout the many years it took to bring this effort to fruition—my invisible college. Jorge Balan, Steve Brint, Dan Chambliss, Charlie Clotfelter, Tom Espenshade, David Karen, Doug Massey, Chiqui Ramirez, Jim Rosenbaum, Mario Small, Gene Tobin, Chris Winship, and Caitlin Zaloom all offered valuable advice. Audiences at Harvard, Princeton, Rutgers, UC–San Diego, and NYU provided critical feedback on earlier versions of my arguments.

I am not sure if it was foresight or folly that led Elizabeth Knoll, my editor at Harvard University Press, to extend a contract for this book before a single word of it had been written. Elizabeth's early commitment probably brought her more trouble than she had imagined it would. Somehow she put up with it, and I am grateful. Elizabeth's keen intelligence is reflected in the title *Creating a Class,* which began on her side of the desk and dangled before me, a carrot on a stick, for months before I grasped it fully. Elizabeth also secured the attentions of two anonymous reviewers for the first draft of the book manuscript whose comments markedly improved the work presented here.

I am grateful to the Press for commissioning Wendy Nelson as the project copyeditor. Wendy's careful corrections and suggestions greatly enhanced the accuracy and readability of the text. Here at NYU, Dana Grayson completed last-minute library research and fact-checking with aplomb; Annmarie Zell provided generous assistance with legal citations.

Edward Wheatley and Mary Mackay were great friends throughout the many years it took to bring this project to completion. They offered their humor and hospitality a hundred times at least, making both work and life more worthwhile. They also introduced me to Anthony McClaran, who was kind enough to host me for a visit to the offices of Britain's Universities and Colleges Admissions Service in Cheltenham, England. Anthony and his colleagues vividly reiterated the most basic sociological lesson, that the order of things taken for granted in one society can be assembled quite differently in another. That took me a long way.

My family encouraged this effort patiently. Their willingness to include me in the college search for my eldest niece, Kendal, gave me a window into the emotional and practical difficulties of the process that I otherwise would not have fully appreciated. Kirk Pillow shaped my heart and my head to a degree that would be impossible to specify here, but I will say this: he taught me that aesthetic, emotional, and rational responses to the world are inseparable. It will take some time for sociologists to catch up with him here. One who might catch up first is Elizabeth Armstrong, who showed me that talking candidly about bodies and sex "is overwhelmingly important" for a full understanding of social inequality. Amy Binder—well, what to say? She is the sort of colleague who makes you wonder how you could have made it through the last ten years without, the sort of friend who always answers the phone and whittles down your mess of impressions into something potentially interesting, who makes you a better thinker and a better person over time.

I reserve final thanks for Arik Lifschitz. Here, Arik, is one of the more exotic things we crazy Americans have done with modernity. Puzzling it through this far is what has kept me at my desk for the past three years. Thank you for your patience, love, keen intellect, and wry wit.

Errors and shortcomings of this book are entirely my own.

INDEX

Aesthetics: of the College, 1, 5–6, 17–18, 25–27, 95; and social class, 17–19; of human bodies, 19, 137–139; 293n7; and decision making, 54, 88–90, 208–209; of high schools, 59–85

Affirmative action: history of, 144–155, 184–185, 292n2; and organizational status, 179–183; and admissions decision making, 203, 217–219, 221–222

Arum, Richard, 260–261

Athletics: and organizational status, 16–17, 100–112, 255; and campus aesthetics, 95–96; history of in higher education, 100–105; and gender, 101–105, 126–130; coaches, 112–119; recruitment, 114–130; and socioeconomic inequality, 130–137; parental involvement in, 130–139; and human bodies, 137–139

Blau, Peter, 12

Bourdieu, Pierre, 18–19

Buchmann, Claudia, 259–260

Civil Rights Act of 1964, 154

Collins, Randall, 12–13

Credential inflation, 13–14

Credentialing, 12–13

DiPrete, Thomas, 259–260

Distributed cognition, 189–190, 217–222

Duncan, Otis Dudley, 12

Early Decision, 66, 70, 84, 168, 185, 203, 229, 270n13

Emotion work: and impression management, 29–30, 86–87; in the evaluation of applications, 190–191, 213, 223–225; and college choice, 229–233; 235–241; defined, 230

Espeland, Wendy, 36

Faculty, 29–30, 113

Financial aid, 26, 56, 191–225, 233–235

Football, 100–103, 110–112, 126–130, 203, 222. See also Athletics

Fordism, 253–255

Goffman, Erving, 258

Gratz v. Bollinger (2003), 184, 188–189

Grutter v. Bollinger (2003), 184–185, 188–189, 225–227

Hochschild, Arlie, 230
Homogamy, educational, 138–139, 258–260, 285n29
Hoxby, Caroline, 58
Hutchins, Edwin, 189

Impression management, 85–90, 155–161, 235–241
Individualism: and universalism, 8–10, 250; in evaluation, 20, 186, 197–217; organizational production of, 53–55, 65, 68–69, 72–76, 83–85, 197–217; as a mechanism of inequality, 186, 197–217, 225–227
Interviews, 53, 92–94, 208–209, 294n12

Jencks, Christopher, 12

Lamont, Michèle, 199
Lareau, Annette, 132, 245
Liberal arts colleges, history of, 6–7; organizational distinctiveness of, 9–10; as a racially coded organizational form, 171–172
Lucas, Christopher, 112

Marx, Karl, 11, 32
Methods and data, 3–4, 7–8, 22–25, 267n4, 273n20, 295n3

President's Commission on Higher Education (1946), 251–252

Recruitment: strategies of, 52–94; history of, 55–59; and athletics, 114–130; of racial minorities, 161–179, 140–144. *See also* Athletics; Affirmative action

Regents of the University of California v. Bakke (1978), 150–153, 184
Rosenbaum, James, 252

Sauder, Michael, 33
Skrentny, John, 146, 150
Small, Mario, 179
Social class: theories of education and, 10–16, 289n24; and elite schooling, 14–16, 258–259, 261–263; and parenting practices, 14–16, 130–139, 242–248; and variation in college guidance, 63–85, 191–222, 277n4, 278n5; and variation in college preparation, 161–173
Social reproduction: defined, 2; and social class theory, 11; and athletics, 130–137; of human bodies, 137–139; and organizational self-interest, 173–179; and college choice, 229–230; and college preparation, 242–248, 296n2; parental anxiety about, 255–260. *See also* Homogamy, educational
Sports. *See* Athletics
Status, organizational: and admissions selectivity, 16, 30–51; and intercollegiate athletics, 16–17, 100–112, 282n11; theories of, 32–33; in U.S. higher education history, 33–35; quantification of, 30–51; minority enrollment as an index of, 179–183

Title IX (Education Amendments of 1972), 104–105

U.S. News & World Report rankings, 44–45, 90, 122, 219, 233, 274n21

Weber, Max, 11, 32–33
Wechsler, Harold, 34, 246
Winship, Christopher, 179